7TH EDITION

the
travel writer's
handbook

*How to Write — and Sell — Your Own Travel
Experiences*

JACQUELINE HARMON BUTLER AND
LOUISE PURWIN ZOBEL

SURREY
BOOKS

AN AGATE IMPRINT

CHICAGO

Printed in the United States.

Library of Congress Cataloging-in-Publication Data

Zobel, Louise Purwin, 1922-
  The travel writer's handbook : how to write--and sell--your own travel experiences / Jacqueline Harmon Butler, Louise Purwin Zobel. -- 7th ed.
      p. cm.
  Includes bibliographical references and indexes.
  Summary: "A guide to conceiving, writing, and selling travel writing"--Provided by publisher.
  ISBN-13: 978-1-57284-131-4 (pbk.)
  ISBN-10: 1-57284-131-1 (pbk.)
  ISBN-13: 978-1-57284-700-2 (ebook)
  ISBN-10: 1-57284-700-X (ebook)
  1. Travel writing--Handbooks, manuals, etc. I. Butler, Jacqueline Harmon. II. Title.
  G151.Z62 2012
  808.06'691--dc23
                                  2012000475

12 13 14 15   10 9 8 7 6 5 4 3 2 1

Surrey Books is an imprint of Agate Publishing, Inc. For prices on bulk quantity purchases, contact Agate via agatepublishing.com.

To our wonderful families and all the budding travel writers who will be inspired and enabled through this book.

ACKNOWLEDGMENTS

I was happy to be asked to update the 6th edition of *The Travel Writer's Handbook* with Louise. We are now on the 7th edition and I'm on my own. Louise passed away in June 2008 at the age of eighty-six. However, so much of Louise's content from past editions is still very relevant today, and some of it is included in this book. Her style and sense of humor really came through in her writing. I like to think she is organizing trips (and writing about them) in heaven.

There have been so many changes in the travel writer's world since Louise published the first edition back in March 1980. Electronic gadgets and computers have become a very important part of our lives and were in their infancy back then. I've done my best to give you information on the digital age. As we all know, things change fast in the cyber world.

Thanks to everyone who assisted in bringing the 7th edition of *The Travel Writer's Handbook* up to date, especially my agents Michael Larsen and Elizabeth Pomada and my editor Doug Seibold.

Special thanks to Cathleen Miller, Georgia Hesse, Lee Foster, and fellow members of the Bay Area Travel Writers: especially to Richard Jordan, Laurie King, Diane LeBow, and Mark Longwood. Also thanks to Spud Hilton, Serena Bartlett, and David Cartwright. And to all the students I have taught and who have taught me a thing or two about travel writing.

I'm grateful to my children, Laura and Timothy, and the rest of my family for encouraging me to follow my dream and become a travel writer.

Jacqueline Harmon Butler
Summer 2011

CONTENTS

INTRODUCTION

While some publications—both print and online—have quietly shut down operations, that neither forecasts the end of travel nor the end of the written word. Even when the popularity of some destinations changes as a result of world events, travel itself remains a constant. The desire to see and experience what others have enjoyed remains a desire of the reader. Yes, there is a need for travel writers today and beyond.

Some of you reading this book may already be travel writers, hoping to discover useful tips and shortcuts. You will discover them. Some of you are probably successful writers in other fields, yearning to move in a different direction, trying to find the tools that will help you. You will find them. Doubtless some of you are writing-relatives—English teachers, advertising copywriters, newsletter editors, and others who feel they can become successful travel writers by learning how to move in the right direction. You will learn how. Certainly some of you are travel writers, writers of exciting letters, tellers of inviting tales. You want to professionalize your product. You can do it. And some of you, with no background at all in writing or traveling, are reading this book because you think it sounds like fun to be a travel writer. It is.

This book is for each of you. If you've ever had anyone say, "You write such wonderful letters—you ought to publish them," or "When you tell about that trip, it sounds simply fantastic—why don't you write it all down?" or "We loved looking at your pictures and your videos—you made it all so interesting"—this is the book you need.

While not a book on basic writing techniques (it assumes you already know how to write grammatical English sentences, and that what you don't know about punctuation, you'll look up), it does offer helpful avenues to organizing and writing travel articles, both print and electronic. It explains the importance of market research and subject research before, during, and after you travel. It suggests successful approaches to editors and online content managers. It tells you how to write the most popular types of travel articles and gives you an in-depth look at the business of being a travel writer, including such diverse subjects as how to use the query as a sales tool, where to obtain illustrations, and what to take off your income tax.

While not exactly a book on travel either (it assumes a basic familiarity with traveling, whether around the corner or around the world), the advice you will find here on preparing for a trip, as well as profiting from it, should be welcome to any traveler. It's important to remember, too, that the travel-oriented article may just as well be about your own neighborhood—an exciting, faraway destination to others.

Louise and Jacqueline have taught travel writing to college and university students of all ages, as well as to cruise ship passengers of many nationalities, and to online participants around the world. They both have served on the faculty of many writers' conferences and published in many kinds of media. Much of their travel has been by plane, train, bus, taxicab, streetcar, cogwheel rail, cable car, automobile, ship, subway, gondola, launch, rowboat, mule, and safari bus, but much more of it has been by shoe leather. We have enjoyed sharing our travels with our readers, and we hope you will enjoy sharing your travels with your readers. That is what this book is about—writing good travel stories that other people will want to read.

Though writing of itself should please and satisfy the writer, and may even have some therapeutic value, here we are talking about writing as a public profession—writing about your travel experiences for the enjoyment and the edification of your readers. Professionalism leads to pleasure *and* profit for the travel writer. The trip is more enjoyable when you know you'll be writing about it. And it is possible to make your vacation pay for itself.

The ideas expressed in *The Travel Writer's Handbook* have, in our experience, proved helpful, and we hope they will prove helpful to you. But, of course, there is no assurance that all the pieces of the puzzle will always fit together advantageously. In the end, each of us must find our own way to satisfaction.

As a travel writer you will feel a great responsibility—the writer's responsibility to the reader. Later travelers see what you have seen, not only in the setting of your words but also within the framework of the emotional responses you transfer. The need for truth and accuracy in both hard facts and intangibles can never be emphasized enough.

While successful travel writers never forget the importance of accurate detail, they also know that equally important is how the writer—and the reader—feel about that detail. For no matter how literal your piece may be—counting the miles to every turnoff and the dollars for every dinner—in travel writing, as in most kinds of writing, it is the people and the emotions that matter. How did you *feel* about the experience? Without the *feeling*, your reader might as well look up "Paris" in the encyclopedia.

Emotions are awakened by the travel itself; and the desire to write is stimulated by new faces and new places. Travel and writing complement each other, and the travel writer finds that thinking about the reader and trying to increase the reader's enjoyment enhances his own excitement in the adventure.

The travel writer's success is determined by how precisely he defines his audience. All good writers know that the reader is not only a partner in the writing but is the ultimate boss. The travel writer has to *care* about the reader enough to break though the barrier of ink to the magic of shared feeling.

PART ONE

CHAPTER 1

Joining Substance to Style

It was a cold, damp January morning in San Francisco, and fog made it seem even colder as Jacqueline made her way from the car park to the international terminal of the airport. After checking in, she hurried into a café, seeking a big cup of hot coffee.

"Please hurry. I'm catching a plane," she told the waitress.

"Where to?" she asked.

"Barbados."

"Where in the world is that?"

"It's in the British Virgin Islands, near Bermuda."

"Barbados!" She fairly breathed the word. "Lucky *you*!"

"Well, I'm a travel writer … that's my job."

"*Job!*" the waitress gulped. "A job that takes you to Barbados in January—geez, I'd love to have a job like that."

Being a travel writer is one of the most desired jobs, right up there with being an actor or rock star.

Being a travel writer can take you to Hawaii in February, to New Orleans in August, to India in time for the monsoon. If you like to write and you like to travel, if you're the kind of person who's continually captivated by new places, new ideas, new faces, you may find that this job sometimes seems less like work than play. But it's always more work than it seems.

Depending on how you look at it, the travel writer never takes a vacation—or lives in the vacuum of perpetual vacation. The hours are flexible, so you end up working most of them. To us, Saturday is a working day. So is Sunday. So is every day, 365 days a year. The travel writer's job is ongoing and demanding. It's also intriguing and rewarding.

What Makes You a Travel Writer?

Being a travel writer sounds so easy and glamorous. All you have to do is write about the beautiful, exciting places you visit. You write about the people you meet, the landscape, the weather, the flora and fauna, and the wonderful food and wine you taste. You might even throw in something about history, politics, culture, and folklore.

But a travel writer needs instinct, insight, imagination, and enthusiasm. As a travel writer, you not only see and hear, you investigate and interpret and try to understand. You meet people of different cultures and different backgrounds. You learn new customs, embrace new thoughts, and absorb new knowledge.

Your main purpose is to share your travel experiences. But this is not your only purpose. Your purpose is also to write a travel article that entertains and informs your readers. As well, you want to be able to transport the reader to the destination you have visited. Your purpose might also be to convince your readers to take a trip to the destination you are writing about. Your purpose will, in part, depend on the type of travel article you are writing.

Not satisfied only to ask *what*, the travel writer wants to know *who* and *how* and, more important, *why*. He or she recreates the travel experience, lending it relevance and perspective. In his desire to enhance his reader's enjoyment, he draws on his own spirit of adventure, rousing senses that tend to lie dormant and discovering that, as Herman Hesse says, "The true profession of man is finding his way to himself."

New places and new faces stimulate perception, encouraging you to delve more deeply, observe more carefully, and focus more clearly. As a travel writer, you will never be lonely, never be bored, as you share with your readers the people and places, adventures and activities of your trips.

You'll find yourself behind the scenes in search of stories, and you'll come across areas and information to which the average person has no access. Tell people you're a travel writer, and nothing's too much trouble for them to show you or take you to. Again and again, you'll be led to a front seat instead of a back one; picked up and chauffeured by someone assigned to show you around; or provided with a meal, a briefing, and a ticket to an event you didn't even know existed. It's always more fun to be on the inside looking out.

While travel writing, of itself, is not a notably lucrative field—not in the same ballpark as, say, electrical contracting or dentistry—its fringe benefits are irresistible. As we'll see later in this book, the travel writer can sometimes accept exotic hospitality, sometimes deduct expenses from his income tax, and often arrange lecture engagements and other related professional activities. You'll know the gratification of seeing your name in print, and your **byline** may lead to professional advancement in other fields. You'll appreciate comments of friends and colleagues; enjoy **email** and phone calls from strangers.

For many of us, a special advantage of being a travel writer is the feeling of doing meaningful work, even on vacation. Raised in the Puritan ethic of "keep busy," we sometimes feel uncomfortable in a state of complete relaxation for more than a few days. It seems as though we *should* be learning, absorbing, taking notes, and becoming experts. Being a travel writer gives you a legitimate motive for listening, taking notes, and learning. You know that later you'll use this information in some meaningful manner.

One prolific writer replied to a question about how long it took him to write a particular article with, "How long did it take me? All my life." He went on to explain, "Everything I've ever been or done or thought or known or experienced somehow went into the writing of this particular piece. I couldn't have written it exactly this way a year ago, and if I were to write it a year from now, it would be still different." The most successful travel writers use every place they've ever been and everything they've ever done and thought, known and experienced, as their jumping-off point.

Travel Writers Come in All Sizes and Shapes

The term "travel writer" is all-inclusive. It encompasses newspaper and magazine travel editors, staff writers, columnists, and **freelancers** as well as public relations and advertising practitioners, writers of radio and television scripts, art reviewers, compilers of cookbooks, publishers of travel newsletters, and producers of armchair travel books, audiovisual materials, and travel videos. It includes those who deliver content to travel **Websites** or software, write for **e-zines** or **blogs**, and contribute to their own Websites or those of others.

Travel writers also include guidebook writers, whether nuts-and-bolts or literary and imaginative, and writers who need a place as background for other work—anything from juvenile stories and whodunits to historical novels and musical comedies.

This book will speak to all types of travel writers but will focus on the freelancer who provides travel material for newspapers and magazines in print and **online**.

For some of you, travel writing will be a full-time profession, for others a part-time occupation. Some of you part-timers may also write other types of material, and much of the information in this book applies, of course, to other types of writing as well.

Because readers vary—in their needs and desires, age and financial position, level of education and travel experience, temperament and lifestyle—a diverse group of people will succeed at travel writing. It's hard to draw a profile of the successful travel writer, but there are certain qualities every travel writer needs.

In addition to instinct, that spontaneous impulse that moves you to the right place at the right time, and insight, that quality of discernment that apprehends the inner nature of things, the travel writer also needs imagination, or the creative ability to visualize something not currently present. Add to these great quantities of enthusiasm, the force that propels the writer forward and carries the reader along.

A travel writer should also cultivate the characteristic of curiosity (and a bit of nosiness), the readiness to observe, to eavesdrop, to look (figuratively) through the keyhole, always wondering what's waiting around the bend in the road. You have to be active, eager to see new places, and alert to simple pleasures. You might want to use Agatha Christie's Miss Marple or Hercule Poirot as examples for finding clues to a potential story. Sometimes a simple detail will lead to a discovery that will turn into an interesting story or article.

You need to be energetic and willing to work hard. You need to be healthy, as well as a good sport, ready to accept inconvenience. You should be a good listener, sensitive and perceptive, good at drawing people out, and interested in and knowledgeable about a variety of matters.

If you know another language, that's great. But even if you don't, you should learn a few basic words of your target area. There are foreign language apps that you can use on your smartphone or other **mobile device** (more about that in Chapter 16). You have to be good at understanding unfamiliar accents and prepared to make conversation through pantomime, crudely drawn pictures, and fingers pointing to words in the dictionary.

To be a travel writer you need faith in yourself and in your opinions.

Trust Yourself

The travel writer is not the passive tourist who always eats at the name restaurant because "everybody goes there." You'll seek out your own adventures and feel confident that what you have to say about them will prove valuable to others.

If *you* think something is attractive, you don't need anyone else there to admire it. If *you* think it's worth writing about, it's worth writing about. You must be observant, conscious of small details, accurate in recording them, and prepared to undertake any amount of work to verify existing particulars or to uncover new ones.

Because both traveling and writing are things everybody wishes to do "if I ever found the time," the travel writer must *make* the time. If you want to be successful, you must learn to use your "thinking time" to best advantage so that your writing time may be used for writing. Thinking about what you'll write while you're standing in line, stopped at the signal, or waiting in the departure lounge means your time at the keyboard will be spent writing. You need self-discipline and the conviction that waiting for ideal working conditions will never put a word on paper.

You also need to be an aggressive salesperson, knowledgeable about markets, confident of your own abilities, and aware that a manuscript in the desk drawer has no chance of selling.

You Need "Plus Value" for Success

To make your work salable in today's competitive world, the most important characteristic you need is "plus value," that special something that makes your piece better than the next person's. It exists, but it's hard to define. Yet all successful manuscripts have it.

Plus value, that patina of excellence that triggers a positive response in the editor and, later, the reader, may result from any of several advantages: a universality that communicates clearly; a strong connection with a topic of current interest; a personal background that lends depth to the experience; a theme so true we can't fail to recognize it; a conviction so firm it's only logical to listen; research so extensive it's impossible to discredit; information so relevant we can't ignore it; or writing so polished that reading is effortless.

Of all the characteristics today's successful travel writer should have, the most essential is the ability to produce stories of higher quality than the editor specifies or the reader anticipates. You need plus value.

When we speak of "success," we're equating it with publication, preferably publication with pay. While you never want to be caught in the trap of writing *only* for the money, money *is* the yardstick of professionalism. When somebody's willing to pay for what you write, you have, in a sense, succeeded.

On the other hand, the principles of effective travel writing applied to the standard trip postcard or Christmas newsletter can only improve them. What the traditional "Having a wonderful time—wish you were here" is really saying is, "*I'm* having a wonderful time. Don't *you* wish you were here? I'll bet you're jealous. I sure hope so." Whether it's a postcard or a bestseller, the writer's concern for the reader is the difference between failure and success. When you write on your postcard:

> I thought of you when the outboard refused to catch this morning—how many balky outboards have we coped with? I can hardly wait for you to see this place—you'll love the sandy beach and the gentle waves and the fishing—well, I'll tell you all about it when I get home.

your reader's jealousy is mitigated by the fact that you wrote to *him*, specifically and concernedly.

This creative relationship with the reader, this feeling of kinship, should always predominate in the travel writer's mind. With so many people traveling on wheels, waves, and wings these days, could there possibly be enough stay-at-homes to provide a reading audience for all the travel material being published? There most definitely is an audience, and one of the goals of every travel writer should be to encourage the never-before-traveled folks to get out there and get going.

Do You Know Your Reader?

Do you know your reader and what interests her? You should.

There is no such thing as writing "generally." Good travel writing is always addressed to a specific reader, and it's essential to visualize that reader. Market research tells us who our reader is; the travel writer tries to anticipate and answer her questions. For some articles and some destinations the questions may be: What is it like to take that trip? Where are the best places to stay, eat, and shop? What sights should I see? What time of year is best? What shall I wear? How much will it cost? Under other circumstances, the questions may be: What kind of people live there? What are they like? How can I meet them? What and where are the flora and fauna? How can I see it? For still other pieces, the reader's questions might include: How can I get there? What special training do I need? How long should I stay? And some readers may be saying: Why should I stay away from there? Or if I go, what precautions must I take?

Whether your reader is an active or an armchair traveler, whether he's planning a similar trip or reminiscing about one he's taken or simply enjoying a vicarious view of the world, it's up to you, the writer, to give him the kind of story he wants. You bring to life reminiscences and breathe possibility into planning. You pave the way for later travelers by telling them what it's like so they see it in the setting of your words and within the framework of the emotional responses you have developed.

This saddles the writer with tremendous responsibility. Your opinion has great influence on others. A bad word from you, and a restaurant will lose customers. Recommend a delightful, out-of-the-way Paris hotel full of charming French customers, and a year later it's so full of American tourists there's no room for the French.

Be careful with negative reviews of restaurants, hotels, people, cities, and even countries. Focus more on the positive aspects of your experiences. Your job is to encourage travel and not gripe about the negative things you might encounter.

Whether you're going around the world or around the corner, you must take this responsibility seriously. You must know what you're saying and be sure you're telling it exactly as it is. You may be surprised at how much this book emphasizes research. But don't let it frighten you. Many activities you've never thought of as research are continually adding to your store of knowledge.

Research, remember, is an exchange of ideas. Often it's done on the ski slopes or at the theater or at a sidewalk café. *Research!* Of course! So sit down and order some refreshment. Look around you. Listen. Ask questions. Take notes. Record how it feels, tastes, and smells. If you've already gone on the trip you plan to write about, and you didn't take all the pre-travel steps this book advises, don't despair. You can still write a travel article. But it will be harder to develop the plus value without the preliminaries.

Your Reader Has Great Expectations

Today's readers expect a lot of plus value in a travel story because they're sophisticated. They've probably traveled a good deal themselves, and, with the rise of the **Internet** and mobile devices, they're as close to an opera at the Baths of Caracalla as they are to a song in the shower. Travel is one of the most important facts of modern life. And today it's big business.

Travel is now one of the largest industries in the United States, and seers predict that it will continue to grow. Asia and Eastern European countries are also experiencing a huge growth in travel.

Travel has a long history. Remains of caravansaries and entertainment centers that catered to visitors have been discovered at the most ancient archaeological sites. Over two thousand years ago the goddess Artemis/Diana lured pilgrims to her new temple at Ephesus, one of the ancient world's Seven Wonders. The goddess had a very efficient public relations organization, with branches on three continents. They used every inducement to encourage tourists to visit Ephesus, sign up for the temple sightseeing tour, and take home a silver souvenir. (Some scholars think they probably offered charter rates on the express galleys, but so far no advertisements for this have been uncovered!)

Are people today interested in travel? A national magazine offering a free brochure about an upcoming festival received five thousand requests in the first twenty-four hours. When Ethiopia was mentioned in a travel talk, officials had to close the Ethiopian tourist office for three days to get caught up with the backlog of visa applications for travelers headed there. One of Louise's students, Owen Johnson, authored a brief article in the *Los Angeles Times* Travel section about a tiny town in Germany. Within a week, the town's chamber of commerce had fielded sixty phone calls from people in

California requesting information about how to get there. Each travel article published finds new readers, thus building an ever-increasing audience for future travel articles, by that author or by others.

You don't have to travel to exotic places to be a travel writer. That which is "down home" to you may be glamorously distant to others. It may not seem like *travel writing* when you tell about the haunted house that's a big attraction in your neighborhood, the new lodge at a nearby ski slope, or the local farmer's market. But that's what travel writing *is*—telling readers about something interesting beyond *their* own backyards.

If it's in *your* backyard, celebrate. If your own milieu is a backwater, you can be the first to tout its attractions. And even well-traveled areas can provide new angles of interpretation. How about inspiration from the homes of all the writers who've lived on Long Island? Backyard barbecues in Las Vegas? Touring California's wine country with a teetotaling relative? Palm Springs in summer?

Wherever you live, wherever you travel, there's a story in it that somebody wants to read. Whether you go around the world or around the corner, when you discover the plus values of that particular travel experience, you'll be ready to share your pleasure with your readers.

Some people, of course, travel around the world but never leave home. They follow Michelin's advice for weeks but don't find anything as good as Sally's Creamery at First and Main. The Black Forest isn't as pretty as Turner Woods back home, Arlington Cemetery is only a larger version of their own church graveyard, and Saks Fifth Avenue doesn't have a thing better than their own Emporium at Second and Elm.

The travel writer *celebrates* the differences in manners and customs. While she is interested in seeing temples and museums, she's more interested in learning lifestyles.

Travel should have an important purpose. It should result in meaningful experience. As Thoreau says, "It's not worthwhile to go around the world to count the cats in Zanzibar." The travel writer needs to be excited about her trips, so plan destinations and activities that intrigue you. Expand your horizons. Cultivate the urge to see, know, and enjoy so you can inform, entertain, and motivate your reader.

As a travel writer, you'll find that your own attitude is intrinsic to the value of the trip. In the words of Emerson, "Though we travel the world over to find the beautiful, we must carry it with us or we find it not." Travel writing encourages deeper insights and a gratifying sense of belonging. While we welcome the travel experience, we realize that we have to take something to the experience as well as bring something away from it.

If you're already a vital, sparkling, positive person, travel writing becomes you. Spin the globe and let your travel dreams take flight.

CHAPTER 2

Putting Yourself on Stage

In the digital age, it's more important than ever to build a reputation. In person, of course, you should keep commitments and be on time. Be someone people can count on to do what you agree to do. Let people know you are reliable, meet deadlines and keep appointments. Make sure that you write truthfully and your stories are well researched. These days, most writers also have Websites or blogs to showcase their work. If you don't already have one or both, it's a good idea to get them if you want to compete with other writers for the online portion of the worldwide audience.

The Internet offers special opportunities to compete on an even footing with all other providers, large and small. Using email; social networks such as **Facebook**, **Twitter**, and **LinkedIn**; or other media sharing Websites like YouTube can easily give you an opportunity to form your own network of followers. Niches can and should be developed. For example, if a particular place in the world is what you know best, take advantage of that information by displaying examples of your writing about it.

Social networking is the grouping of individuals into specific groups based on interests or relationships, like small rural communities or a neighborhood subdivision. The friends that you can make are just some of the many benefits to social networking online. Another one of those benefits includes diversity, because the Internet gives individuals from all around the world access to social networking sites. This means that although you are in the United States, you could develop an online following in Denmark or India.

No matter which of the social networks you use, be sure to complete your profile completely wherever appropriate. List all your qualifications, specialties, areas of expertise, publications, and awards, including a recent head-only photo of yourself. Many people will find you by conducting a keyword search on the social network site or using Google, so make sure you've seeded your profile with all the relevant details.

Websites

There are many variations of Websites, and you can create one yourself by using one of the many templates available online. Develop a modern-looking site and optimize it for search engines. You will gain much more from your Website if you maintain it yourself.

Your Website should look clean and professional. Keep it uncluttered with flashy graphics, voices, or music that plays automatically. They make your site slow and irritating.

Your Website should contain your biography, a recent head-only photo of yourself, a few samples of your work, press releases, and details on how to contact you. You can add or change pages as you develop your portfolio of material.

The Title of Your Website and Blog

Acquiring the rights to your domain name is important even if you don't put up your Website or blog right away. Jacqueline can't stress enough the importance of acquiring the rights to your chosen domain name. One of her fellow travel writers tried to buy her own name, only to find it had already been taken by someone else with the same name. Jacqueline had trouble with her blog name, FoodFlirt.com, already being in use. She decided to call it FoodFlirtOnline.com and secured the name. There are many domain hosts to choose from, including GoDaddy.com and NetworkSolutions.com.

The .com, .net, etc. labels are called the Top Level Domains (TLD) and are "suggested" ways of differentiating the type of Website you are running:

- .com is commercial
- .net is an Internet service provider
- .edu is an educational organization
- .org is a not-for-profit organization

People don't always follow these rules. For example, no one checks up on you to make sure you're a not-for-profit if you use the .org in your Website URL. Other domain names differentiate countries (.ca is Canada, .sk is Sweden, etc.), and you have to follow some rules in registering these.

Blogs

Blogs can lead to amazing results. Think of the success of Julie Powell, who blogged about teaching herself to cook. She vowed to cook each and every one of the 524 recipes in Julia Child's *Mastering the Art of French Cooking* within a year. By the end of the year she had publishers knocking on her door with book contracts, and ultimately received a movie contract.

All that from a daily blog about cooking!

Blogs are gaining in popularity because they are more immediate than other types of communication. You can add to your blog whenever and from wherever you want. However, it's a good idea to blog at least once a week, with bits of information, photos, thoughts, and ideas. Try to keep your content on target with the niche you are developing as a travel writer. Be it restaurants in Paris, a bike ride along the West Coast of the U.S.A., or sightseeing in Morocco, you can build up a following by encouraging your readers to comment on content.

Some writers feel that a blog is easier to maintain than a traditional Website. The short, serialized content of blogs encourages regular readership and repeated exposure to your writing style.

You can choose from several free blog hosts such as WordPress.com or Blogspot.com. Take some time to cruise through their Websites to see if they are appealing to you. There are a variety of templates to choose from for the look of your blog, and you can add your own photos and text at will.

To become a blogger it's important to read other blogs. This will give you insight into what works and what doesn't and help you develop the style you want for your own blog. A good place to begin research for your blog is to browse blogs about travel. You can find these types of blogs by searching on Websites like technorati.com/blogs/directory/ or blogsearch.google.com.

Blog posts should be short and to the point. Nearly any tidbit relevant to your readers can be material for a blog post:

- Information, such as destination reviews.
- Events, festivals, and celebrations.
- Food and recipes from nearby and far away.
- Question and answer. Ask your readers where they are going or have been.
- Interviews. Chat with someone about his or her experience in traveling to a specific destination.
- New gadgets that would appeal to travelers.

Following several other tips can increase traffic to your blog and make it more attractive to readers:

- Comment on other blogs in your niche. This will attract fellow bloggers and their readers who follow the link in your comment back to your blog.

- Add photos. Add a sprinkling of photos to illustrate the subject matter of your blog.
- Always write in the first person.
- Write catchy headlines to draw in your readers.
- Hook your readers in the first sentence.
- Don't be boring and don't rant. This will drive readers away from your blog.

Spud Hilton, travel editor for the *San Francisco Chronicle*, gave us the example of the wide-eyed, clueless tourist raving about these amazing places—*called cafés!*—that you can find all over Paris, and cautioned us not to be that person. Spud also warned against the danger of losing your authentic voice, instructing us not to write something we'd never say in real life (such as telling a friend about the "luxuriously appointed" hotel we stayed at).

As you can see, you could blog about almost anything. However, since you are building your travel writer's platform, it's a good idea to keep your posts relevant to travel.

Open connections on your blog to Facebook, Twitter, LinkedIn, YouTube, and other social networking Websites. It's important to get your name connected and these networks can help do that for you. Using social networks can be time-consuming, so limit your activity and always reference your own blog or Website in your comments or additions.

Business cards are a must. You can purchase business card kits at most office supply or stationery stores, and you can easily design and print them on your computer/printer yourself. There are also inexpensive online printers, or you can have them made up at your local copy shop. Whatever you choose, proofread carefully before printing. Include your name, address, phone numbers, email, blog address, and Website URL. Be sure the design is attractive and represents you as a professional. Carry your business cards with you at all times and pass them out freely.

Travel Writers' Organizations

Joining a group of professional travel writers is extremely beneficial. Not only will you have a built-in network of like-minded writers, but you can list the membership on your business cards, Website, blog, and social networks, and you will get the all-important press pass. A press pass will often get you into events, museums, and exhibits free, and without waiting in line.

Look into the qualifications of various travel writers' organizations. Below is a list of only a few. You can easily Google "travel writers' organizations" to find more. Read the individual qualifications carefully before applying for membership. Many of the organizations have different levels of membership.

- NATJA (North American Travel Journalists Association), the premier professional association of writers, photographers, editors, and tourism professionals, is dedicated to redefining professional development for the travel industry.
- SATW (Society of American Travel Writers), now in its fiftieth year, promotes responsible journalism, supports and develops members, and encourages conservation and preservation of travel resources worldwide. Writers must have a substantial portfolio in order to join SATW.
- IFWTWA (International Food, Wine & Travel Writers Association) is a global network of people involved in the hospitality and lifestyle fields and the people who promote them by informing others about them. It has been a non-profit organization, run by and for the benefit of its members, since it was founded in Paris in 1954.
- BATW (Bay Area Travel Writers, Inc.), based in San Francisco, California, is a not-for-profit professional association of writers and photographers with outstanding achievements in travel journalism. These professionals share their unique stories in newspapers, magazines, books, Internet publications, and travel industry publications.

Writers' Groups

Jacqueline recommends joining a writers' group. They can be very beneficial in finding your writer's "voice." She connected with several women at a travel writers conference at Book Passage in Corte Madera, California, and they formed a group, calling themselves the Wild Writing Women. Taking writing classes often leads to forming small writers' groups. If you Google "travel writers' groups," you will find many choices. Some meet in person, some online. Spend a little time researching, and you will surely find a group that will work for you.

Having someone else critique your work is extremely important. It's so easy to fall in love with a story you've written and have a blind eye to grammar mistakes as well as the flow of the story.

CHAPTER 3

Research Is the Answer.
What's the Question?

While it might seem as though the trip itself is the story and pre-trip research is unnecessary, "being there" is never enough. To write successfully about travel, we need to begin at the beginning and learn all we can before we leave home.

Research helps you decide where to travel in the first place. You may be wondering about that—how the travel writer decides on a destination. People often ask which comes first, the assignment or the desire to visit a particular place. Does an editor ever suggest you go to Blanketyville and do a story? The answer is, sometimes. Or do you indulge a lifelong dream of seeing Blanketyville—and then decide to write about it later? Again, the answer is, sometimes. Most often, though, the impetus for exploring a particular place begins with the research that makes that place seem attractive to write about. And the research usually starts with an informal encounter or casual reading—things we'll be talking about in this chapter.

Research not only helps you decide where to go, it tells you how to get there, where to stay, where to eat, what to see, what to do, what to buy, and what's likely to prove valuable to the travel writer. Pre-trip research saves you time because you'll be sure to see the things that most interest you, and you'll know what you're seeing when you arrive at your destination. You'll be familiar with the lifestyle you'll find; you'll be able to add to your store of knowledge without beginning at the beginning. You've probably already discovered some of the aspects you want to write about, and you're already thinking about a fresh approach to some of the places of interest. Your theme and your angle are defined. With pre-trip research you're in a good position to ask the right questions, and you're more likely to find yourself behind the scenes, where you want to be.

Travel research is a subtle skill. You may consciously say to yourself, "Today I'm going to the library to read up on Yellowstone," or "I'm going to call the Tollivers and ask about their trip to Yellowstone." But more likely, you'll research Yellowstone when you run into the Tollivers socially, or come across a "Yellowstone" link when you're looking for something else online. The Internet is now the main source of gathering information, and you can copy and paste information relevant to your story angle easily into a saved folder you title "Yellowstone Park." Contacting the Tollivers for their personal experiences can give your research a more personal angle.

Using the Internet to research places, topics, etc. is very easy. Just Google the name or item you are looking for and a list of related items will come up on your computer screen. It's amazing the amount of information one can find through the Internet.

However, be sure to check the dates the Internet posts were made and make sure the places recommended or written about are still there.

"Carry Knowledge with You"

Samuel Johnson quotes an old Spanish proverb that says, "He who would bring home the wealth of the Indies must carry the wealth of the Indies with him." So it is with travel, says Johnson: "A man must carry knowledge with him if he would bring knowledge home." The travel writer with pre-researched knowledge will bring home stories with plus value.

The successful travel writer subscribes to the iceberg theory—know ten times as much as you're telling. The part that's unseen beneath the surface gives you the voice of authority that makes your readers sit up and take notice. An information overload enables you to choose which materials to use, rather than simply using whatever you happen to have; and doing lots of research helps you to assimilate, understand, and enhance the parts you do use. When you produce a well-researched travel article, editors respect you.

Also, as we'll discover later, the travel writer has to do enough preliminary research to write compelling **query letters** to prospective editors. Research always becomes easier the more you do it. Some push-button mechanism in the brain starts sending out signals: "Yes, this goes with and enriches something I'm now beginning to understand," or "No, I already know all about that—I won't bother with this piece of research."

Research: Live and Library, Offline and Online

We used to divide subject research into *live* and *library*, but in this computerized world we need to consider additional resources. However, we still find the various research opportunities so intertwined that we need them all.

Your friend Jim tells you Pennsylvania is the most fascinating place he's ever seen. He shows you the pictures he took on his last vacation at the National Recreation Area in the Poconos. You ask questions, and he answers them. That's live research. If he also brings over a book on Pennsylvania he wants you to read, and you read it, that's library research. If you query your Internet search engine about Pennsylvania, and the computer comes up with usable results, that's research too.

You then scan your own bookshelves and go to your public library to find materials to guide you in deciding which parts of Pennsylvania to see, how to get to your gateway city, and what kind of transportation you'll use from there. Perhaps you'll go to a travel Website that gives you a quick fix on Pennsylvania prices, or you'll check out the official Pennsylvania state home page. You may spend some time researching information on the Internet Public Library (www.ipl.org).

Next you contact the Philadelphia Convention and Visitors Bureau, the National Park Service, the Gettysburg Travel Council, and the Pennsylvania Dutch Visitors Bureau. You check out the Visit PA Website. Then you call Cousin Susie, who honeymooned in the Poconos and lives in Pittsburgh.

By now you've decided which facets of Pennsylvania are likely to have the most plus value for articles you will write. Back to the Internet you go for specific information on Valley Forge, the Amish Farm Home, the U.S.S. *Olympia* at Penn's Landing, and the Philadelphia Zoo.

You can see how pre-trip research is a combination of writer and written word, writer and visual description, and writer and other human beings. Live research includes observation and interviews, both of which we'll discuss in Chapter 13. Less formal than interviews are encounters. The encounter is less structured than the interview, and often it's just the kind of casual give-and-take the travel writer needs. You absorb easily what the other person has to offer, using the information to fill in the chinks in your own knowledge. Somehow this comes through in your finished story, making you sound less didactic because it isn't only *you* speaking to the reader—it's you along with your reference sources.

As soon as you've done enough preliminary research to ask sensible questions, talk to everybody you think can help you—airline representatives, steamship company representatives, government officials, other travel writers and editors, college students from far away, friends and friends of friends, and anybody else who has already been where you plan to go. Rent, borrow, or buy appropriate CDs, videos, and audio tapes. Attend community college courses and illustrated lectures, as well as films about the area you plan to visit. Browse or download electronic information sources including podcasts. And don't hesitate to ask questions.

Prepare yourself in advance, for instance, for visiting a town in a developing country. What will you look for? Does that country claim it offers free, compulsory education? But will you see school-age children playing in the street during school hours? Do the houses have electricity? Plumbing? Privacy? What are the residents like? Do they have radios, books, mirrors, ice, and newspapers? If you've done your homework, you'll know what you're looking at and what it means.

If you'll be visiting a ruin, do enough homework to people it with those who once lived there, worked and played, made love, made war. Picture them relaxing in their atriums, fountains playing, on a warm summer evening, or poring over their clay tablets as they discuss the inflationary spiral of household expenses. If you get to know the *people*, a ruin is more than a pile of old stones.

It's almost impossible to conduct formal live research until you've laid a foundation of library or online research. You have to know the right questions to ask—you have to already be familiar with the subject before composing a questionnaire or conducting an interview or even taking advantage of an encounter. So let's consider, in addition to informal live research, some of the less formal research you can conduct in your home library.

Again, some of your best resources will be those you really don't think of as research tools. You probably subscribe to a Sunday newspaper, and maybe one writing-oriented periodical, such as *Writer's Digest*. Your home bookshelves should already contain an up-to-date dictionary, a thesaurus of some sort, and possibly a style manual such as Strunk and White's *The Elements of Style*, as well as a recent edition of *Writer's Market* or some other marketing manual.

What else does the travel writer need at home? That depends partly on your computer skills and equipment and how much information you can access online. It depends also on how close you live to a public library, how good the library is, how often you go there, and how much it means to you to *own* the book or magazine and to be able to mark it up, cut parts out, put it aside to read next week, or take it along. And don't forget to begin your *futures* file early—stockpiling information you may need at some future time. When you *do* get ready to visit the places described in your files, you'll find the saved information invaluable.

The Travel Writer's Home Library

A quick sampling of our own overstuffed travel shelves reveals a diversity of books, ranging from *A Traveller's Guide to Caribbean History* to the *Insight Guide to the Waterways of Europe, Adventures in Japan,* and *Let's Go Turkey*. Lonely Planet has travel advice ranging from *Travel with Children* to *Europe on a Shoestring* to their in-depth guidebooks on every country on this planet.

There are all kinds of books on "how to get there"—from motorcycles to tramp steamers—and a myriad of information on places to stay, places to eat, places to shop, learning opportunities, and sightseeing of all types. There are classics like Paul Theroux's *The Pillars of Hercules* and books of travel tales by ancient travelers from Herodotus to Marco Polo. *A Book of Traveller's Tales*, compiled by Eric Newby, a literary travel writer of no small stature, gives the reader a taste of the past—from Anthony Trollope to John Charles Fremont. Several volumes of *Literary Trips* transport readers from Franz Kafka's Prague to John Steinbeck's Cannery Row. The *Chronicles Abroad* series covers great cities, according to Somerset Maugham, Thomas Mann, Jean-Paul Sartre, Orson Welles, Benjamin Disraeli, Leo Tolstoy, Lawrence of Arabia, and other travelers inclined toward literary reporting.

This book, in its original first edition, was the first book ever directed specifically to the would-be travel writer, and it has been judged the definitive book on the subject. But in addition to *The Travel Writer's Handbook* in this new, updated version, there are many excellent books that provide insights into nonfiction writing in general.

Books on Writing

Rudolf Flesch, Henry Fowler, Jacques Barzun, and Theodore Bernstein stand ready to advise on the niceties of the writing process itself. Such books as *Bartlett's Familiar Quotations*, *The Home Book of Quotations*, or *The Oxford Dictionary of Quotations* belong on the travel writer's bookshelves or on easy electronic access. The *Oxford English Dictionary* (OED) contains nearly half a million words and two million quotations. The *Dictionary of American Slang* helps keep your language up to date.

Bartleby.com has an excellent Website for answering questions about English usage (bartleby.com/usage), and it even has the full text of Strunk's *Elements of Style*. Many other language aids reside online, including Merriam-Webster (Merriam-Webster.com), with its dictionary, and Thesaurus.com, with synonyms and antonyms as well as a daily crossword puzzle.

Searching for special tips, shortcuts, and hints from the pros? Look for *The ASJA Guide to Freelance Writing*, written by members of the American Society of Journalists and Authors. Although not brand new, it's still helpful when some of the most experienced writers in the world tell how they handle their computers, their phone lines, their financial arrangements, and what books they refer to for their special needs. They reveal how to treat reluctant interviewees, how to promote a book on television, how to get help with research, and how to find envelopes at bargain prices.

Books on Photography

Since awareness of photographic techniques, sources, prices, and markets is part of the travel writer's essential knowledge, you'll want to read several books on photography.

Photographer's Market, published annually, not only gives advice on setting up a business, preparing a portfolio, and submitting your work both digitally and by traditional mail, but also provides a comprehensive, up-to-date list of photography buyers. Buyers range from advertising agencies to audiovisual firms and include consumer magazines, trade journals, and company publications. The listings tell you the name of the buyer, what each publication needs in the way of photographs, and what it will pay for them.

Additional books about the digital world, as well as magazines and advice, can help you over the rough spots. (More on photography in Chapter 14.)

Books on Using Computers

Dummies books have inundated the market with simplified information on everything from *Internet for Dummies* to *Starting an eBay Business for Dummies*. If you're past the "Dummies" stage, try a title in the *Bibles* series.

Probably the most current hard-copy information on computing is available in magazines, and there are dozens—maybe hundreds—available at newsstands and bookstores, as well as everywhere computer equipment is sold. Magazines such as *MacLife*, *PC World*, and *Wired* cater to the knowledgeable users. Some publications are pitched to owners of specific hardware or specific software, users in certain geographic areas—from San Diego to Vancouver—or people who use computers for particular purposes, such as archaeology or genealogy.

Guidebooks

You'll surely want to read at least one guidebook on where you think you might like to go—or several guidebooks while you're deciding what your destination will be. But consider the different types of guides so you can make a sensible selection. You can often purchase guidebooks for less than half of their marked price at bookstores' end-of-year sales. You can buy used guidebooks for a few cents from Friends of the Library sales, rummage sales, or thrift shops.

If you're using a previous year's guide, be sure to update it from the public library's current copy. Restaurant and hotel information becomes obsolete quickly. And while sightseeing information on Old Faithful or Pike's Peak doesn't change much with the years, still, we all know that Niagara Falls was turned off for a while, Yellowstone had a devastating fire, and currently you can't always enter the Parthenon or the stone circle at Stonehenge.

When buying guidebooks for your home library, select those most appropriate for your own writing. Just as *you* have in mind *your* reader as you research and write, so do guidebook writers visualize *their* readers. Ask yourself what kind of traveler your guidebook is written for—the shaggy teenager in blue jeans or the little old lady with blue hair.

Baedeker, the doyen of guidebooks, devotes twenty-five pages of its London guide to the British Museum, while covering hotels and restaurants in a page or two. But many long-out-of-date Baedekers are superior resources for finding out how things once were, and libraries keep them around for that purpose.

There's a guidebook series directed to just about any type of traveler. The Sierra Club Adventure Travel Guides are, logically, devoted to adventuring as well as to ecological concerns. Lonely Planet publishes a wide variety of travel and destination guides, including specialty books for budget and adventure travel as well as a City Guides series. Insight Guides are well-illustrated cultural experiences that give you an excellent background for the country but not too much on everyday arrangements.

Rick Steves offers a collection of excellent travel books on Western Europe. His original book, *Rick Steves' Europe Through the Back Door*, is an excellent resource for out-of-the-way places and has been updated often since the first edition. However, since this book is very popular, some of Rick's discoveries are becoming increasingly visited. Sometimes the quaint hotel or small town he recommends is now overwhelmed with American tourists.

So far, most of the guides we've spoken of are continuously updated. Others are revised at random intervals, as author, publisher, or readership demands. You have to look at the copyright date to tell when the book was published. Many dated guides do come out annually; but because of research and writing time and traditional publication schedules, much of their material is two years old by the time we're ready to use it. So update guidebook information yourself whenever you can.

Apps for mobile devices are becoming increasingly popular. They offer an amazing amount of specific destination information, offering everything from maps to information on restaurants, hotels, and assorted points of interest such as monuments and street fairs.

Online Guides

All guidebooks have an online presence. Their sites offer a wide array of travel information, including excerpts from their publications and news features, as well as links to reserve flights, hotels, and rental cars.

What else can the travel writer find online? You are only limited by your imagination and your favorite search engine. Forums and chat rooms accessed through various travel and writing Websites can be invaluable resources for the travel writer. A variety of Websites, as well as online writers' newsletters and magazines, such as *Bookwire, WritersOnLine, Writers Write, Poets and Writers*, and others, provide information about writing and marketing, as well as answers to copyright questions, conferences, and contests. *ShawGuides* has switched from print to Internet editions of guides to writers conferences and workshops; photography, film, and new media workshops and schools; language vacations; and other gatherings.

Special-Interest Guidebooks

Many guidebooks, while seemingly of interest only to specific groups of travelers, contain material of widespread value. Globe Pequot Press's *Europe by Eurail*, while addressed primarily to the train traveler, and overflowing with authoritative worldwide railroad information, also discusses jet lag, hotel reservations, and what to do if you lose your passport. Its country-by-country section includes maps and sightseeing material, as well as plans for one-day train excursions and scenic rail trips.

Guidebooks such as *Freedom Without Borders: How to Invest, Expatriate and Retire Overseas* usually appeal to those with more time than money but occasionally offer a good universal idea. As the number of traveling retirees grows, and as we writers become increasingly aware of senior citizens as a potential audience for travel material, more and more guidebooks will be addressed to them. Do we need to be reminded that the baby boomers are fiftyish and sixtyish now and looking for AARP travel experiences?

Let's Go Europe, on the other hand, is intended for the young and adventurous. Although some will be traveling by car, this book assumes many will be biking, walking, or hitchhiking. It gives the rundown on student accommodations, food, and sightseeing. Its advice for England: "The drinking age is eighteen, but this isn't strictly enforced." Other longtime favorites are *Thomas Cook European Rail Timetable* for the railroad buff. There are also guides to religious shrines of various denominations, advice for the would-be healthy traveler, and insights into faraway spas for the fitness seeker. Bed and breakfast books also proliferate.

Today's guidebooks often advise on particular activities—biking, hiking, camping, fishing, sailing, etc. Even guides to shopping and finding outlet stores tell their readers how to do it. Family adventures and travel activities to share with children attract a very important audience. Background guides for environmental tourism, a major interest of many readers, abound. Not only do a number of guidebooks concentrate on weddings and honeymoons, but Globe Pequot Press publishes a series of "Romantic Days and Nights" in some of America's largest cities.

Omnigraphics publishes oversized, expensive but excellent books such as *Parks Directory of the United States* and *Holidays, Festivals, and Celebrations of the World Dictionary*.

Motoring Guidebooks

The Michelin Guides are intended for the knowledgeable and sophisticated motorist. Their red and black symbols of quality have long been a report card the traveler can trust. Michelin has plenty of maps and city plans and includes "plain but adequate" hotels and "good food at moderate prices," as well as more deluxe suggestions.

Within the United States, AAA's individual state or regional tour books are geared to the driving traveler accompanied by children. AAA's books are set up with a brief "What to See" in each city in the state, arranged alphabetically, and then a chart and information on the recreational possibilities. About three-fourths of each book deals with specific accommodations and restaurants, again in alphabetical order by city. These digest-size books are distributed free to AAA members, as are maps, camping books, and special tour guides. They are also available to non-members at a small fee.

This barely scratches the surface of available guidebooks. Whether you're a youth hosteler, a garden lover, a tombstone viewer, or a bird watcher, you'll find a travel guide to help you do your thing. If it's not completely current, you can usually update it on the Internet. But before you invest too much time in too many general guides, be sure they're the ones whose approach and orientation will really help you and the audience for which you write.

Reference Works

Two indispensable books are *Merriam-Webster's Geographical Dictionary* and *Merriam-Webster's Biographical Dictionary*, both published by Merriam, both thumb-indexed and packed with valuable information. *The Columbia Webster Gazetteer of the World* is good, too. The *Toll-Free Phone Book* or one of the other directories of 800 numbers, as well as a ZIP code directory, are essential tools and are available.

Librarians say nearly 90 percent of reference questions can be answered from an almanac. The *World Almanac and Book of Facts, Information Please Almanac,* and others are all produced annually and all arranged slightly differently, with different emphases. You might want to own more than one—or search for the one that suits you best. Outside the United States, the

Canadian Almanac and Directory and *Whitaker's Almanac* (for Britain) serve the same function.

You can't be a travel writer without an atlas, either print or electronic. True, boundaries and political entities change so fast you need to update your maps almost monthly, but a good basic atlas or two is essential for general geographical information. There's nothing like an atlas to help you decide where to go. Whether your travel writing specialty is literature, genealogy, history, or Biblical scholarship, you'll find an atlas designed especially for your needs. Are you a treasure hunter? The *Atlas of Treasure Maps* shows three hundred locations of buried treasure in the Western Hemisphere, but there is no guarantee of a *find*.

Finding map information on the Internet can sometimes be almost a lifesaver. Sometimes, though, the directions can take "the long way." Some new cars have a GPS (Global Positioning System) built into the dashboard, which can be extremely useful in a strange city. Many mobile devices also have a GPS. Check with your phone carrier to find out how to access a GPS for foreign places.

Jacqueline usually turns to the Internet for research projects. She likes the ease of gathering data from a wide variety of online sources and by using the copy-and-paste system on her computer, she can save snippets of information to relevant files for later reference.

Specialty Publications

Depending on the kind of travel writing you're doing, you'll want to have the most helpful reference materials within arm's reach. A writer who concentrates on the historical aspects of travel needs a historical atlas. This would be supplemented by a book on mythology, handbooks on art and architecture, and several standard volumes of world history. Other travel writers might find it more helpful to invest in or download guides to sports, airplanes, antiques, wild animals, music, stamps, botany, or the *New York Times International Cookbook*. As we focus more sharply on special facets of traveling, we need more and more background material to digest.

Much of this information is available on the Internet. Just be sure to copy relevant data and file it in specific research folders.

Classics and Sources

Have you longed to see Alexandria after reading Lawrence Durrell? Or promised yourself a trip to Spain with a copy of *Don Quixote* on your lap? Are you considering a visit to Colleen McCullough's Thorn Bird country or Nathaniel Hawthorne's New England or James Michener's Hawaii? Some of the world's best travel guides are Charles Dickens and Mark Twain, Ernest Hemingway and Joseph Conrad, Robert Louis Stevenson and Pearl Buck,

Somerset Maugham, Charles Darwin, Rudyard Kipling, Jack London, Herman Melville, and John Steinbeck.

Travel bookstores are springing up in every city and hamlet. If you need a guide to the next town or a language lesson for the next continent, you are very likely to find it. As the travel industry becomes the second largest in the United States, it spawns more and more shops devoted to *everything* the traveler needs—including reference books. So you're in a good position to take advantage of the pre-trip learning period.

Handy Brochures

Touring maps of all kinds are the travel writer's tools. As the free ones become ever harder to come by, hoard what you have.

For your travels by car, both AAA and the National Automobile Club provide custom-made trip kits and strip maps for their members.

CD-ROMs are strong on maps and travel information, and, of course, a vast amount of material can be downloaded from the Internet. Using a search engine like Google or Ask.com, just key in your destination. An amazing amount of information is available this way.

Specific city or country apps are becoming more and more available and are easily downloaded to your mobile device. Check with your carrier for details.

For more information about apps, please go to Chapter 16.

Touring materials also include museum guidebooks, which should be ordered before a trip. Many of the guidebooks are available online but sometimes having a "hard" copy with maps and tidbits of information about the collections is very handy.

If you plan a foreign trip in the fall, the English-language tours may be finished, and the government tourist offices have probably run out of travel literature. Experienced travel writers suggest emailing or writing in the spring to tourist offices of the places you expect to visit, asking them to send you all their English-language information as soon as they have it. Again, much of the travel brochures and information will be available.

Periodicals

You'll surely want easy access to the newspapers and magazines you expect to write for. You'll doubtless subscribe to or send for samples of many travel-oriented publications, not only the big ones but everything from *Family Motor Coaching* to *Endless Vacation* to *Transitions Abroad*. Again, depending on your own specialized interests, you may turn to *Bon Appétit* or to *Lakeland Boating* and *Yachting*.

Don't forget to subscribe, if only briefly, or at least look up at the library or online, a newspaper in the area you're planning to visit. The *Philadelphia*

Inquirer, for example, gives you the *feel* of the city, an overview of what it's like, and alerts you to the colorful New Year's Day Mummers Parade, the Little League World Series, or the June celebration when the colonially costumed people of Elfreth's Alley, the oldest continually occupied residential street in the United States, hold their annual fete.

Other local papers tell you about special activities, so you can plan your vacation or weekend jaunt around the Oyster Shucking Championships in Leonardtown, Maryland; the World Championship Inner Tube Race in Yuma, Arizona; or the Fishworm Judging Contest in Sterling, Colorado.

Try to buy the magazine(s) of the area you'll be visiting. This is the kind of background information you need to pursue the live research you'll do on the trip itself, and there's always the possibility that this periodical will become a market for *your* story.

Don't be timid about requesting photocopies of newspaper and magazine articles published long ago when you hear of something that might provide just the research pivot you need. We've found periodicals remarkably generous in filling requests for copies of special stories. Another writer once asked, without much hope, for a copy of a magazine article on camels written 116 years ago. Within an amazingly short time, this treasure appeared in her mailbox. Usually this service is free; if not, the cost is only a few cents.

As the tide of printed material threatens to engulf us, it becomes increasingly important to know what information is where. Bless the magazines that provide annual or semi-annual indexes. Some still provide printed ones, but most magazine indexes are online.

U.S. Government Publications

The U.S. government is one of the world's biggest publishers. Take advantage of it. The government even puts out several publications to help you discover what is available:

- *Consumers Guide to Federal Publications* gives 300-odd subject lists from architecture and automobile insurance to surveying and mapping, and Spanish publications.
- *Selected List of U.S. Government Publications* gives 130–150 publications with wide appeal. Issued biweekly—ask to be placed on the mailing list.
- *List of Government Bookstores* lists periodicals by various government agencies.

There are a number of other aids to finding your way around in the maze of federal publications. Either visit the U.S. Government Online Bookstore (bookstore.gpo.gov), write to the U.S. Government Printing Office, or contact the U.S. Government Bookstore nearest you to order. Material is free or modestly priced.

Several other lists and compendiums are especially valuable to the travel writer. *Maps (United States and Foreign)* not only includes weather maps and distribution of various segments of the population but also lists general reference maps of foreign countries. The lists of miscellaneous and special purpose navigational charts, sheets, and tables are helpful, too.

"Background Notes" are short, factual pamphlets (usually eight pages) written by State Department officers for about 160 countries. The pamphlets, which are invaluable for taking along on your trip, cover the country's land, people, history, government, political conditions, economy, and foreign relations. They also include a profile, brief travel notes, a map, a list of government officials, and an excellent reading list.

Much more detailed, the Defense Department's Area Handbooks for 100-plus countries, from Afghanistan to Zambia, are just about the best guidebooks you can buy.

The government also publishes a directory of 1,500 industrial plants and federal installations, including copper mines, breweries, and newspapers, all of which offer free tours.

If you're traveling near a president's boyhood home, the *Guide to Genealogical Records in the National Archives* might be helpful. *Key Officers of Foreign Service Posts* is a good buy or download if you think you'll get overseas and need to know the name of your ambassador. The Civil Aeronautics Board will send the free *Fly-Rights: A Guide to Air Travel in the U.S.*, and the U.S. Customs Service will send, also free, booklets on customs hints and on the generalized system of preferences for 101 nations and thirty-six dependent territories where you're likely to buy certain items. Customs will also help the writer with material on smuggling, tariff laws, and what people try to get away with.

The Bureau of Consular Affairs of the Department of State produces *Your Trip Abroad*, a good roundup for the beginning traveler. If your readers will be interested in camping in national parks, travel accommodations for the handicapped, international relations, backpacking, or outdoor sports, send for the government booklet that gives you all the details.

If you like to vacation away from crowds, request information on lesser used national parks from:

National Park Service		U.S. Forest Service
Department of the Interior	or	Department of Agriculture
Washington, DC 20240		Washington, DC 20250
www.nps.gov		www.fs.fed.us

The National Park Service publishes reams of helpful information and also presents the visitor with special leaflets at most of the attractions it administers, such as Valley Forge National Historical Park and San

Francisco's Fort Point. The Park Service's *Guide to the Historic Places of the American Revolution* is a gem.

Next time you're in Washington, DC, visit the Library of Congress— it's fascinating. If you're visiting Washington, be sure to write or call your congressman for help in securing tickets to special attractions. Allow plenty of time. Ask your congressman, too, for assistance in finding information about anything connected with the federal government.

The Library of Congress Reference and Bibliographic Service will help those outside the Washington area find material for a small fee. You can obtain a copy of anything there unless it's restricted or needs copyright clearance. One writer, doing a roundup of Civil War battlefields, asked for—and received—the Reports of the Secretary of War to the 33rd and 34th Congresses in the 1850s. For this kind of help, get in touch with:

Chief, General Reference and Bibliography Division
Library of Congress
Washington, DC 20540

Local Government Publications

Various agencies of state governments also print free or low-cost material valuable for the travel writer, from a beautifully complete, 879-page *California Historical Landmarks* to a leaflet on *Three Lincoln Shrines in Illinois*. South Dakota booklets tell all about the Black Hills and the Badlands, Delaware emphasizes its coastal vacationland, and Oregon has all sorts of literature on forests and trees, while the quarterly leaflets, *New York in Summer, New York in Winter*, etc., concentrate on the Big Apple itself. Philadelphia also publishes seasonal booklets, as well as *Philadelphia: A City for All Seasons!* Unsurprisingly, California's Department of Transportation issues a *Safety Roadside Rest Area Report*. North Carolina's *One Day at a Time* details eleven different tours for visitors.

You can also write to individual areas for information. Denver publishes *Mile-Highlights*, Fort Lauderdale recommends the Everglades, and the El Paso Convention and Visitors Bureau publishes *El Paso*. Islands, from Martha's Vineyard to Guam, call themselves to your attention.

Worldwide, 600-plus areas are affiliated with Destination Marketing Association International, many of which issue seasonal calendars listing special events. Look up the events online or send a postcard requesting the calendar to:

Destination Marketing Association International
2025 M Street, NW, Suite 500
Washington, DC 20036
www.destinationmarkcting.org

Don't forget historical societies as a source of pre-trip research material. The Mount Vernon Ladies' Association of the Union will inform you about Mount Vernon, and the Preservation Society of Newport County, Rhode Island, has information on the mansions located there. San Francisco's Chinese Culture Foundation has information on the Chinese Heritage Walk and the Chinese Culinary Walk, and the Nevada County Historical Society will bring you up to date on Gold Country restorations.

Sometimes several political entities join together to promote their joint travel-recreation area. They publish huge amounts of material. Pennsylvania Dutch Country (www.padutchcountry.com), Cape Cod and the Shenandoah Valley all do their best to lure visitors. So do the Caribbean Travel Association, the Organization of American States, and the Pacific Asia Travel Association.

Literature from Other Areas

Early in your subject research, write to the travel promotion bureaus of the countries you'll be visiting. Every country wants to present—aggressively— its most attractive features. Tourist office publications do a fantastic job of telling the rest of the world what they have to offer. Read the literature carefully. A single line reference may produce an idea that will spark a story idea. A. R. Roalman, for instance, contemplating a trip to Japan, found in the tourist-office literature a single sentence about the oldest wooden building in the world. Queries to *Popular Mechanics* and *American Forest* netted pre-trip assignments, and on-scene research developed additional noncompetitive stories.

If you read the travel brochures—either government or commercial—it's hard to believe there is anything but sandy beaches with girls in bikinis and majestic, snow-covered slopes. Everybody seems to live in picturesque thatch-roofed cottages and picnic in sylvan settings.

To get a more realistic picture and to plan intelligently, first cross out all the adjectives in the promotional brochure. Then read the last page for the straight facts. The relationship of one day to another, one country to another, within the tour framework, gives you an idea of what the tour people consider important about the area. Look for the words "We stop at" or "We visit."

One of the travel writer's most important skills is learning to read *between* the lines. A European tour that offers half a day in Florence and during its day and a half in Paris provides half a day of city sightseeing and a trip to Versailles plus "an afternoon free for relaxing or perhaps a visit to the famous Louvre Museum" is *not* a tour for art lovers. If you're writing an art-oriented article, don't bother reading *that* tour brochure.

Miscellaneous Freebies

Online forums can provide all kinds of useful knowledge to the travel writer, and there are many other areas of free information. Don't spurn public relations handouts. As a matter of fact, when you're beginning your research, *ask* for handouts. In addition to writing to tourist offices, a good technique is to place free ads in newsletters that go to hundreds of PR people. These weekly or biweekly newsletters are sent to PR specialists who buy subscriptions for the privilege of sending materials to writers like you. Replies to you from these PR specialists often result in useful information, great ideas, and welcome hospitality.

Sometimes you can even inquire in a book section, such as that in the *New York Times*, or on an online bulletin board for the information you need. You'll soon be inundated with news about anything remotely related to the subject you've asked for.

Inflight magazines, those publications you find in the seat pocket in front of you as you struggle into your seatbelt, and in-room magazines, which you find on your desk in many hotels, are valuable sources of information for pre-trip subject research. When you make your plane and hotel reservations, ask for copies to be sent to you in advance.

Booklets put out by the American Society of Travel Agents (ASTA) remind you that your homeowner's insurance may not cover your cameras and mobile devices and offer a number of other good, basic suggestions. The Institute of Certified Travel Agents offers resources that explain everything from ITX (an inclusive tour excursion airfare) to open jaw travel (where the round trip has different points of origin and return).

Ecology Is Here to Stay

The travel writer needs to be aware of upcoming and ongoing trends. While the reader may still be interested in rooting around for his ancestors or receiving advice on how to dress for a successful national convention, a couple of major trends today are adventure travel and "green" travel. Even sedentary grandparents are taking up ballooning, scuba diving, snowmobiling, windsurfing, and white-water rafting. The more adventurous go dog-sledding on the arctic wastes, kayak exploring in Thailand, paragliding into dormant volcanoes, and tracking the Bengal tiger in India.

If you feel that adventure travel will lead you to a story you can't bear not to tell, there are many books to help you with before-trip research. *Ultimate Adventure: National Geographic Ultimate Adventure Sourcebook* is one of the best. *The Green Travel Sourcebook*, which Daniel and Sally Grotta have subtitled "A Guide for the Physically Active, the Intellectually Curious, or the Socially Aware," speaks to a slightly different audience. They think of the green traveler as one who welcomes the physically challenging adventure, as well as one who explores the natural environment and the entire ecosystem. They also include the green traveler who delves deeply into the learning experience, the one who travels to underdeveloped countries to help the people in some way, and the one who volunteers to dig at an archaeological site or take underwater photographs to document marine activity. With the goal of preserving the environment, of "taking nothing but photographs and leaving nothing but footprints," green travelers are also concerned with humanitarian matters and cultural interchange.

The Sierra Club, of course, publishes many books that enhance the pleasure of the wilderness experience, always keeping in mind the importance of preserving and improving the natural state. The pocket-sized Totebooks the club publishes range from *Starr's Guide to the John Muir Trail and the High Sierra Region* to *Hiking the Grand Canyon*, and all are wonderfully detailed guides.

Outward Bound challenges, expedition cruises, special ecotours, greater interaction with native populations, and other occasions to experience new adventures and a stronger relationship with the worldwide environment are becoming an ever-more important facet of travel. Opportunities for joining such organizations as Earthwatch, where volunteers observe and record facts about the earth's natural state, are increasingly popular. Much pre-trip research material is available to the traveler who plans to write about adventure and ecology. The Galapagos Islands, for instance, have become such a popular destination that the visitor goes well prepared with information. And upon returning, that same visitor can become a sought-after supplier of interesting material for an entire galaxy of environmentally oriented magazines, e-zines, CD-ROMs, and other outlets. As more and more readers realize the effects of tourism on the environment, the travel writer should show awareness of plans to protect and enrich our planet, in ways both large and small.

Use Discretion

Although travel writing resources proliferate, they aren't all necessarily helpful and accurate. The travel writer has to approach pre-trip research with discretion. Some of what you read is good—some of it is garbage. For instance, Louise read a book for women cruise travelers that advised those with children to try to engage the children's counselors as babysitters in the evening. If this is not possible, suggested the author, perhaps you could persuade your room steward or the purser to sit with your children. *The purser!* She knew instantly that author had never been on a cruise and immediately lost faith in everything else the book said.

However, the more involved you become with travel writing, the more convinced you will be that you can never do *too much* research. As you learn to use what you glean from both formal and informal sources, you'll realize that the information overload makes destination decisions easy and constitutes unmistakable plus value.

Keeping track of your collected data is important. Create computer files by destination and then add folders by category: hotels, sights, transportation, etc. This is also advised for hard-copy materials. Designate a special place in either a file cabinet or file boxes and create files, again by destination and sub-categories. If the data is more generic, for example, transportation in Europe, make a specific file. That way you won't be duplicating the same information for various European cities. Remember it is easier to file and find information in computer files than physically having to root through cumbersome paper files.

As we consider what to do before your trip, while traveling, and after your return, we'll look into other forms of research, such as online information, telephone interviews, face-to-face encounters, questionnaires, and on-the-scene observation. But in the next chapter let's consider some of the valuable aids the travel writer can find on library shelves or in cyberspace.

So, what is it I tell prospective travel writers? The rules are simple enough: get your facts straight and tell us a story.—Tim Cahill

CHAPTER 4

Tapping Your Natural Resources

"Library research!" My friend threw up her hands in amazement. "What do you mean—*library research*! You're *going there*, aren't you? Isn't that enough?"

Going there is seldom enough for the travel writer. Nobody but another writer seems to realize that travel articles require subject and market research before you go, while you're traveling, and after you return home. Subject research is the glue that holds your story together. It's the credibility you achieve by presenting someone else's opinion along with your own. It's the way to understand what you're seeing before you see it, while you're seeing it, and after you've seen it. Subject research is the keystone of the writer's craft; it's a big part of the plus value.

The danger is that the research will become an end in itself. The writer becomes so enamored of the research materials that he or she keeps postponing the actual sitting down at that keyboard. It isn't enough to *do* the research—you have to *plan* the research. First, decide in a general way at least what you hope to achieve by the research you are doing. Then, decide how much time you have to get it all together. Spend your time researching in the most likely places for the most important information. When you are looking for the "most likely," ask yourself, "Who would know?" and "Who would care enough to pursue it?"

Are you beginning to think the travel writer spends a lot of time on research? You're right. Does it all sound formidable? Really it's not. A lot of the topics we'll cover you've probably known about for a long time—you just never thought of them as research. This chapter introduces you to conducting the research that provides a firm framework for other library, Internet, or face-to-face quests for information.

Entire books are devoted to the description and use of research resources, but this is only a quick guide to finding what the travel writer needs.

Ask Your Friendly Librarian

Our most valuable resource is still the reference librarian. Librarians exist to provide information. They are delighted to provide that information. We have researched in many libraries—public, university, and special, in the United States and abroad—and we've always found librarians helpful and eager to supply whatever we requested. First introduce yourself to the librarian. Explain that you are a writer. You'll find that nothing is too good for you. You're important to the library—you create library material. Often a phone call to the reference desk will answer a simple question. Be sure your question is specific. *Not* "Tell me about Thailand" or "Tell me about polygamy," but "Does the present king of Thailand have more than one wife?"

Ask your librarian to acquaint you with the library's vertical file or electronic catalog, which will surely contain maps, guidebooks, menus, museum catalogs, photographs, theater programs, and hundreds of nonbook items that will help in your pre-trip research. You probably know that most libraries file their materials according to either the Dewey Decimal system or the Library of Congress system.

Sometimes you have to be a super-sleuth to find what you seek. If the electronic or card-based catalog doesn't show what you're looking for, turn to the multi-volume *Books in Print*, print or electronic, to see if the book exists. You may have difficulty finding the heading the library cataloger used for the subject you're trying to find. Will it be under "archaeology" or "history" or "ancient history" or "European history"? Ideally, it will be under all of them, each with a "see also" reference.

But sometimes you have to work hard to come up with a classification that you and the cataloger agree is what you're looking for. Consulting Library of Congress subject headings may send you off in the right direction, but even so, it's confusing. Do you need something on the Peace Corps, for instance? Don't give up too easily. Try "United States—Peace Corps." Sometimes there'll be a cross-reference card telling you to see a different or additional subject heading. Persistence pays off.

If the book is not held by your local library, check with your librarian to discover what an inter-library loan can do for you. Louise once found a book in Sydney, Australia's main library that she later wanted to refer to at home. Her local library queried regional libraries, the California State Library in Sacramento, and the Library of Congress. Nobody had the book. But the local library finally found it and borrowed it from a special library in Toronto.

When the author Hayes Jacobs wrote in the 1960s, "If a writer lives near a good library, he is especially blessed, if he lives near a poor one, he ought to think about moving," he did not, of course, visualize today's Internet.

Computers Speed Research

Although some libraries still retain their traditional card catalogs, the list of those that have completely computerized their collections grows longer every day. What replaces the banks of alphabetized index cards, filed by subject, title, and author? Comfortable chairs in front of computer screens, with directions for getting connected. You can look up the library's holdings by author, exact title, subject, series, or call number. Or you can browse among subjects and titles by inserting a key word. It's like browsing among the stacks, as your electronic servant brings related topics to the screen. Not only will your screen tell you which branch and location contains your selection, but it will also indicate whether or not your selection has been checked out, and if it has been, when it's due back. In many libraries you can even request a book that might not be in their stacks but can be transferred from another library.

You don't even have to go to the library to obtain this information. If you have a computer and an Internet connection, a few keystrokes and a password will put you through to the library's catalog. This service is free. Additionally, hundreds of database vendors of thousands of databases await your subscription. Some of these databases will give you titles, some will give you abstracts, some will give you full text—or all three. Ideally, you will select a few from all the titles available and ask for abstracts; then select a very few abstracts and ask for full text. You can have the text printed out and mailed or faxed to you, have it appear on your computer screen, or listen to it over a telephone line.

Information Abounds

Newspapers, magazines, books, encyclopedias, official records—practically anything is available somewhere. Do you want to scan all the Yellow Pages directories in America for an all-inclusive picture of travel services? Do you want to compare winter weather in Miami and Cancun or to compile the geographical distribution of Starbucks Coffee locations? Just ask. For instance, Sacramento writer Michele McCormick was preparing a speech she was scheduled to give at a lawyer's conference, so she looked for some lawyer jokes.

By using newsgroups, listservs, and message boards, you can put all kinds of questions to perfect strangers. "Has anybody traveled across the Atlantic on a Russian ship? How was it?" "How would you spend a free day in Paris?" "What's the rock-bottom price to rent a car for a month in Tahiti?"

Travel agents, of course, use several programs that search, book, and confirm airline reservations, hotels, and other services. You, too, can access these programs, and sometimes your careful perusal will spot a bargain.

If, however, you feel unable to cope with "Enter," "Ctrl," "Alt," and "Esc," you can have somebody else do the search for you. Some libraries will do it free, depending on the question. If this service is not available from your library, look in your phone book under "Information Retrieval Services & Research." Costs of subscribing to an information service may be monthly or by the amount of use or a combination of both. An information broker charges for out-of-pocket expenses plus a search sum.

Whichever way you conduct your search—either personally, with an individual computer maven, or through an information broker—give considerable thought to framing your search questions. Will you ask for background material on the Japanese drink *sake*? Or will you just type, "sake"—and come up with screens full of information that include all instances of people exclaiming, "For heaven's *sake*!" Do you want a census of all the English-speaking countries of the world—or just the ones where English is the *first* language? Use the thesaurus on your computer to select the perfect search words. Keep your search question brief and simple, using as few capital letters and punctuation marks as possible, and be sure to seek the kernel that counts.

Almost Everything Is Indexed

Whether hard copy or microfiche, one of the travel writer's most valuable tools is the *New York Times Index*. This multi-volume, frequently indexed series gives you the exact date, page, and column for articles on your subject in the *New York Times*. It also gives a synopsis of the article that may answer your question, so you don't have to look up the newspaper itself. Louise didn't have to look through months of newspapers to find out, for instance, exactly when the pope visited Ephesus—information she needed for half a sentence of a major travel article.

If you need a national or international story from your unindexed local newspaper, you can assume the story appeared approximately the same day it appeared in the *New York Times*. So once you have the date, you can find the paper in the file at your library or local newspaper office or from a service. The *Wall Street Journal* and other periodicals also publish helpful indexes, so whether it's online or on the shelf, voluminous amounts of data are available.

Large library newspaper rooms keep back issues of the world's leading papers, either physical copies, microfilm or microfiche, or collections, for many years. That's how Louise found out about the *Frank H. Buck*. Her research on the tanker *Lyman K. Stewart*, which collided with the freighter

Walter A. Luckenbach and sank in San Francisco Bay in 1922, turned up information about the *Stewart's* sister ship, the *Frank H. Buck*. After some digging she discovered that the *Buck*, also, met her end on a foggy Saturday afternoon in San Francisco Bay. The *Buck* collided with the luxury liner *President Coolidge* at nearly the exact spot where the *Stewart* had met the *Luckenbach* fifteen years earlier. Both ships spilled oil all over the bay as they were buffeted against the Land's End rocks, where their remains rust today. She did most of the research in newspapers published at the time, and the story turned out to be bigger than expected.

City directories, both old and new, in addition to telephone books, help you track down the exact fact you're missing. They not only give information about each household but also often include listings by addresses and by telephone numbers, supplemented by maps and general facts about the area. William Rivers tells of a researcher trying to retrace the steps of Mark Twain in Hawaii:

> In one of his "Letters from the Sandwich Islands". . . . Twain mentions a wonderful party at "Sam Brannon's bungalow." The problem: Where was Brannon's bungalow? A hundred years had passed, Honolulu had changed, and everyone living in Brannon's time was dead . . . If he (the researcher) had been looking for a living resident of Honolulu, he would have needed only a City Directory and a city map. He needed no more to fix the location of Sam Brannon's bungalow. The City Directory of Honolulu for 1865 lists Brannon and his address, and a map shows the precise location.

Google or one of the other online search engines can help you find names and addresses for practically anything.

Facts on File: Weekly World News Digest with Cumulative Index (www. factsonfile.com), a classified loose-leaf digest of news arranged under broad subject headings, is an index Louise always consults when she begins an article on a country she hasn't researched for some time, just to be sure she has kept up with what's been going on in that country.

Facts on File has another advantage—it's more accurate than the daily newspaper, put together at top deadline pressure, can hope to be. We all know that newspapers give us many clues but are usually not scholarly authorities. Books, on the other hand, present a problem to the library in many fast-changing fields. They're obsolete almost as soon as they're printed. For this reason, libraries tend to spend greater and greater proportions of their budgets for periodicals, where the time lag is not so great. Books on some subjects, however, provide valuable information even when their copyright dates aren't current. The rule of thumb for accuracy is: if three people say it's true, it's likely so to be.

There's a Reference Book for Every Subject

Some books, of course, are definitive, regardless of their age. Need to know anything about food? *Larousse Gastronomique* should give you the word, and they say if you need to ask what it is, you aren't ready to use it. Helen Gardner's *Art Through the Ages* is an old standby.

Want to know something about specific people? Perhaps the address of someone still alive? Try the British *Who's Who* or *Who's Who in Canada*. *Who's Who in America* is supplemented by *Who's Who in the West, East, Midwest,* etc., and *Who's Who in American Law, Government, Religion,* etc., as well as the *Directory of Medical Specialists* and *Who's Who of American Women* and other biographical directories. All this information can be easily accessed through a search engine such as Yahoo, Ask, or Google. While not as useful when it comes to contacting research sources, there are several directories of notable Americans, Britons, and Canadians of the past. *Who Was When? A Dictionary of Contemporaries* places subjects in historical perspective. It may come in handy to know that Abraham Lincoln lived at the same time as Emperor Maximilian of Mexico.

Some libraries are full or partial depositories for federal or state publications, and these materials may be cataloged and shelved like other library books or may be classified as government publications and arranged alphabetically or numerically in a separate place.

Of course you're not going to read *all* of this literature for any one article or even any one subject. Yet, here at the library, the "memory of the human race," you're bound to find, among the morass of superfluous and useless information, the kernel of a fresh idea, the perfect quote, the reference to the authority you didn't know existed, the very special something that provides the plus value for your story.

Quickly finding exactly what you need either at the library or online is an art that comes with practice. Soon you'll learn how to flip through an index and see if there's anything you want, look over an entire section of books and scan down an online search list and pull out only the single most authoritative ones. You learn, too, to skip over material that's unwanted *now*, while making a mental note (perhaps also a physical one of the URLs) about where to find it in case that's the very thing you need next month or next year.

Obviously the travel writer's reference materials mentioned here are merely a sample of what's available either in your library or online.

Encyclopedias Are Specialized, Too

Encyclopedias we all know about—or at least we think we do. An online search of encyclopedias reveals an amazing choice, from *Encyclopedia Britannica Online* to Wikipedia. Many writers find researching at home in their pajamas in the middle of the night is more to their liking than having to get dressed and go out to their local library.

However, with CD-ROMs, an entire encyclopedia, along with an index of every word, can be contained on a single disk. As the software proliferates, the travel writer will be acquiring new tools, both at home and at the library.

Most libraries have both the *Encyclopedia Britannica* and the *Encyclopedia Americana*. The *Britannica*, especially, has changed greatly in its newer editions, with the facility for quick answers to quick questions in the twelve-volume Micropaedia, and more complete answers in the seventeen-volume Macropaedia. These are general encyclopedias, as are the single-volume *Columbia Encyclopedia* and the multi-volume *Collier's, Chambers, Academic American,* and *World Book* encyclopedias.

Special Libraries for Special Research

Did you know there are entire libraries devoted to sailing ships or Shakespeare, American Indians or American wine, insects or international trade? These special libraries are maintained by professional organizations, charitable foundations, trade associations, consulates, labor unions, and sometimes by the estates of private individuals. From the Folger Shakespeare Library in Washington to the Joseph Conrad Library at the Seamen's Church Institute in New York, special libraries are a windfall for the travel writer. If you live near one, it's usually not too hard to secure permission to inspect its treasures. There are many small town historical libraries that can provide lots of story ideas for the travel writer, often without even having to go very far from home. Jacqueline lives near the Petaluma History Museum in Sonoma County, California, where chickens ruled the roost back in 1911.

Sometimes, too, you can obtain special privileges at a nearby university library, or perhaps at the morgue of your local newspaper. In any of those circumstances, be sure to express your appreciation for the opportunity and try to be as little trouble as possible.

How to Organize Your Research

Once you begin your own library research you have to decide how to arrange the information you're accumulating. If it's a borrowed book, you're not going to mark it up, of course; but develop the habit of reading with pen in hand. Insert paper bookmarks with directions to yourself to send for or look up additional information, or to photocopy the page or make a special note for a special article. Try to include all pertinent information—dates, call numbers, authors' names—to make re-finding the material as painless as possible.

Be sure to indicate whether the gem of information you're jotting down is a direct quote from someone else or has been paraphrased into your own words. Even paraphrased, you may need to give credit if what you're using is a proprietary fact—something which that particular author dug out for himself, something nobody else knew about, as opposed to a common fact, which can be found in many places and is known to many people.

Whether you outline your story first, then key in the various fragments of research material, or collect the fragments in separate file folders, or color code with a rainbow of pens, or make a separate file card for each fact, or devise some more acceptable system of your own, getting your research together is a hard job. A number of travel writers admit, "I do a lot of filing on the floor while I'm working on a project!"

You'll find extensive cross-indexing worthwhile if you want to find all the information you've squirreled away. Never be tempted to file anything under "miscellaneous." If it's worth noting, it's worth labeling.

None of the travel writers interviewed for this chapter seemed thoroughly satisfied with their present methods of accumulating and arranging information. Each one said, "If you find a good way, please let me know!"

Using your computer to store files is a bit easier to control because you don't have all those little clips, articles, notes, and brochures to deal with. Jacqueline recommends you open a computer file and give it the title of the story and/or place/country you are working on. Then, within that file, you can have many sub-files with various titles such as: hotels, restaurants, people, places, interesting facts, etc.

Magazine Articles Are a Great Resource

Do you now feel as though you know everything you need to know about researching your subject? Wait! Don't leave the library yet! Not until we discuss the value of the *Readers' Guide to Periodical Literature* in print or online, which tells you where to find magazine articles on your subject. The *Readers' Guide* does three things for you: it tells you what else has been published on your subject and where and when; it tells you whether or not your target market has published anything on your subject recently (which we'll discuss with market research in Chapter 5); and it provides additional research resources by showing you where to find articles that may teach you something about your subject. As a footnote to the advantages of magazine articles as research sources, let's not forget that the authors are often available to provide additional information or fresh quotations.

In looking for magazine articles you'll have to define your subject in the same terms the cataloger uses, but there are hints in the *Guide's* cross-references. If you find nothing in the *Readers' Guide,* even after you've considered several synonyms for your subject, you may need a different guide. Is your subject very scholarly? The *Social Sciences and Humanities Index* covers the scholarly journals. If your subject is more likely to be found in specialized periodicals, try the indexes that list articles about science, art, music, business, psychology, or engineering. Another indexing service covers such popular publications as *Woman's Day* and *Weight Watchers Magazine*.

There's no doubt that the quantity and quality of the market research and the subject research differentiate the amateur, who says, "Some day I must get around to writing up the story of my wonderful trip to Paris and send it to one of the big magazines—I'm sure they'll buy it," from the professional, who says, "I want to be sure I have all my facts straight on the Paris sewer trip—what time it leaves, how much it costs, and the other details. Then I'll search the Internet to see who's published what about the Paris sewers lately."

The professional's reasoning might contemplate a negative market list—don't try *XYZ Magazine* because they just ran a Paris sewer story— but it might also uncover an "Underground Barcelona" article published recently. Wouldn't they like a companion piece? An online search is bound to yield some historical background for a Paris sewer story, and it might provide clues about people to contact for anecdotes or quotes to sandwich between the bare facts.

CHAPTER 5

To Market, to Market

"Amateurs talk about writing; professionals talk about marketing" is a cliché well known to writers—well known because it's true.

Again and again we've heard one professional writer respond to another's description of a project with, "Good idea. Where are you going to send it *first?*" And again and again we've heard one pro respond to another pro's tale of rejection with, "Too bad. Where are you going to send it *next?*"

Ask an amateur whom he's writing the article for, and he's likely to reply, "Oh, nobody special. I'm just writing it kind of generally." *There is no such thing as writing generally.* Successful writing is always for somebody. It's for a particular publication, a particular reader. Successful writing is aimed and slanted, facts astutely selected to appeal to a well-defined segment of the reading public.

We need to be aware, too, that practically any publication will be receptive to travel material if the material is geared to its *specific* audience. In a minute we'll take a typical travel experience and consider where it might sell. But first—how do you go about finding that audience? You begin with marketing manuals. Study them at the library before deciding which is most convenient and complete for your needs.

Major Marketing Guides

Writer's Market is the marketing manual most familiar to freelancers. *The Writer's Handbook* is also popular, though it will cease publication after its 2011 edition. *Writer's Market* contains listings for more than four thousand periodicals, publishers, and organizations that are potential buyers of freelance material. Travel material can be packaged and presented in a multitude of forms, but the most familiar is the newspaper or magazine feature. Potential travel article buyers appear in *Writer's Market* every year under the basic headings of consumer publications and trade, technical, and professional journals. The market lists are updated via the monthly magazine *Writer's Digest*. Each listing gives the publication's address, the name of at least one editor (sometimes several in charge of different types of material), the publication's emphasis, and its readership. The listing also mentions the number of freelance manuscripts used, the kind of material the publication will consider buying, rights purchased, normal reporting time, connection, if any, with an electronic publication, and how the freelancer should get in touch. The book also tells about agents, syndicates, scripts, contests, and other outlets for writing.

Writer's Market Online has all the resources of the print edition combined with a yearlong subscription to their online database. It has excellent search capacity, enabling you to search for publications in a particular genre, subject category, or location; those with particular pay rates; those that buy reprints, pay on acceptance, and don't demand all rights.

Merely browsing through market manuals will give you many ideas for articles, as well as introduce you to hundreds of publications of which you're unaware. You'll find many pleasant surprises as you thumb through them. They will give you a springboard, a jumping-off place, marketing ideas of your own, as well as ideas for shaping and writing the piece itself. If one of these publications should not happen to work well for you, still it catalyzes the recognition of another that may turn out to work better.

Other Guides to the Freelance Market

The annual *Literary Market Place*, published in two volumes, gives all sorts of information about book publishing, literary agents, and related topics but not much on periodical publication. It does, however, include a section on electronic publishing that answers such questions as, "Where can I find someone to convert a manuscript into machine-readable form by optical scanning?" or "How can I take an image from a video camera and reproduce it as an illustration?"

The *International Literary Market Place* is arranged alphabetically by country, with information on each about public holidays, mailing requirements, literary agents, major libraries, translation agencies, and a vast amount of material.

Both *Ulrich's International Periodicals Directory* and the *Standard Periodical Directory* list their sixty thousand-odd entries under about 250 "field of interest" classifications. Browse through them next time you're at the library. Look over the *Gale Directory of Publications and Broadcast Media*, the *Directory of Publishing Opportunities*, and the *Editor & Publisher International*

Year Book too. Each approaches its periodical listings from a different direction and includes different information.

Be Sure to Study Your Target Magazines

With thousands of periodicals publishing all sorts of material, whatever kind of travel story you write, there's a market for it *somewhere*. As you pore over the various marketing aids, jot down the names (and page references) of the likeliest prospects for the subject(s) you have in mind. Then read copies of the publications themselves.

The multi-volume *Working Press of the Nation* is designed for publicists, but it can be extremely helpful to freelancers. It covers newspapers, magazines, newsletters, and internal publications, as well as TV and radio.

It's the unexpected sales that really spell success for the writer. If you're trying to sell an editor an article similar to those he's already using, STOP! Do something else! Sell him a piece he doesn't even know he wants.

Markets Here, There, Everywhere

Travel + Leisure covers exotic destinations and exciting activities, right? Yet Max Gunther published "Foil Your Local Burglar: How to Protect Your Home While You're Away," obviously a subject of great interest to *Travel + Leisure* readers. *Better Homes and Gardens* published an article on "Station Wagon Camping," a likely subject, when you stop to think about it, for home-loving readers. *Sea*, a magazine of recreational boating, warned its seagoing readers about sunburn in an issue at the beginning of boating season.

There are over 100 large-circulation magazines that use some travel content. You can Google the "250 top magazines by circulation."

There are also smaller regional magazines that pay less but can provide appealing layouts of your work and allow you to become a favored provider. Most newspapers are no longer a viable market because the travel sections have shrunk to only a couple of pages.

There is simply no substitute for studying at least three or four recent issues of each of your target markets, either in print or online. This not only tells you whether or not this publication is a likely buyer for your idea, but actually helps you shape the idea. Read each issue from cover to cover, including the ads. The ads, often designed by professional readership analysts, provide strong clues. Are these readers more interested in saving money or in having the best? Are they in need of more tax shelters or more ways to fix a hamburger? Are they tennis players or wheelchair users? Scrutinizing the advertisements and editorial material is the best way of judging what each market is likely to want.

The *Wooden Horse Publishing* Website (www.woodenhorsepub.com) is a wonderful online resource that keeps track of who wants what in print and electronic publications; it also lists current and new magazines with contacts, editorial calendars, demographics, and writers guidelines. They have a monthly online newsletter with updates.

Some of the online media delineate their readership very frankly in their e-zines or on their Websites, and they expect the writer to pay attention. *The Robb Report*, which describes itself as the "Bible of Luxury," indicates that most of its readers can afford to buy anything they want, and nothing but the best of travel circumstances will do for them.

Away.com talks about "planning an active vacation" and wants articles on paragliding, horseback riding, fly-fishing, and other strenuous activities. An article on finding adventure in Japan provided a myriad of details about climbing Mount Fuji.

Many of these magazines are available at the library. Others can be purchased at the newsstand. Still others appear on the Internet. But how can you obtain copies of the more obscure publications?

There are a number of ways. One is by studying the *Writer's Market* listings that say, "Free sample copy on request." Underline those as you go through the book, then check to see if they have a Website that could be used to request a free sample copy. If not, address postcards to magazines you want, pressing onto the other side of the postcard a label with the message, "Please send a sample copy and information on your requirements as suggested in *Writer's Market*. Thank you." Then sign them. For publications that charge for sample copies, write a letter with a similar message, adding "$1.50 check is enclosed," or whatever. If a magazine doesn't say anything in its listing about sample copies, send a form letter requesting them, which usually results in their arrival.

What are some of the other ways to find obscure magazines not generally available at the library or the newsstand?

Look for Other Opportunities

Always search for hidden markets. You'll build up an "old boy/old girl" network as you move along in freelancing, but meanwhile take advantage of whatever you can find—from chat rooms and message boards to the local newspaper. When the editor of *Guest Informant*—which you often find in your hotel room—told Louise how desperately she needed writers in a couple of cities, she was able to give her the name of a colleague in one of them, which was the beginning of a mutually satisfactory literary relationship. There are markets, and there are ways to find them.

Market research not only helps you find the obvious and hidden markets and shows you what else has been written on your subject, it helps you know *how* you should write for your target markets. Your final target will determine your *exact* focus and slant, but you'll be doing your general planning well in advance. Will your piece be in first person, in third person, in a combination "I-you," or in a hidden viewpoint that takes the reader right on scene without revealing who is giving the information? Will your language be formal or informal? Your tone serious, helpful, nostalgic, humorous? Will you use quotes, anecdotes, fictional techniques? Do the markets you have in mind require more research than you will be able to complete? Is the approach you intend to take appropriate for the age, sex, political inclination, financial condition, and educational level of the audience you seek?

When you try to sell stories on camping, national parks, or Greek Island cruises to a travel magazine; anti-burglary advice to a home and garden publication; or sunburn warnings to a health journal, your competition is keen. The secret of successful marketing is to analyze the reading audience and to try to give those readers what they don't yet know they want.

Again and again we see travel articles in magazines that we wouldn't normally think of as travel markets For instance, somebody found an angle for an article entitled "Greek Island Odyssey" to appeal to the readers of *Cosmopolitan*, not a huge purchaser of travel material. The author explains the rationale:

> I sailed on the *Viking of Kos.* . . . There were 25 in my group—most of us young and unattached, about half men, half women. Many were in interesting transition—between love affairs, jobs, marriages, countries— and eager to talk about their personal situations as well as their common goal of immersing themselves in Greece.

Would you believe it—the Lands' End catalog frequently prints travel articles sandwiched between the pages of ads for warm jackets and chino pants. They pay pretty substantially for them, too.

You might think regional magazines and Sunday supplements would stick to their own areas, yet we often find articles about Hawaii in New England publications and ski stories in Florida.

Home economists and food writers continually find good markets in boating, bicycling, outdoor, and camping publications—everybody wants to know what to take along on a picnic lunch or a dinner cooked on a portable barbecue.

"A Caretaker for All Seasons," an article exploring the profession of house sitting from both sides of the "sit," is a likely enough story for an inflight magazine, but "The Tugs," about tugboat travel, at first seems a strange inflight choice. Think about it, though—air travelers are interested in sea travel, too, and it's an innocuous, time-passing kind of story, the kind the inflights want.

An article about Kyoto in an Alaska Airlines inflight magazine alerted Louise to markets she hadn't thought of. It's assumed that articles you send to an inflight will be about that airline's destinations. She wondered if Alaska was beginning flights to Japan. But at the bottom of the story was the answer in the **sidebar** "Getting There": "Kyoto is accessible via Alaska Airlines Mileage Plan partner, Northwest Airlines/KLM." So destinations of the mileage partners are welcome, too.

Plan Your Article Itinerary

Analyze the stories in your sample publications and begin preparing an itinerary for your manuscript. Where will you send it *first?* Then where will you send it *next?*

Psychologically, an itinerary for each story you're contemplating is one of the travel writer's most valuable supports. When you have all possible markets listed on your itinerary sheet, if your query or your story gets a "Sorry, no thanks," you already know where you're going to send it *next*.

After arranging your preliminary itinerary, return to your magazine indexes. How recently have your target markets covered your subject? Is it too soon to suggest that subject again? If there have been a great many stories, you may feel the marketplace has been saturated, unless you have some new, absolutely irresistible angle. If you find *nothing* on your subject, you may wonder whether for some reason that subject is too taboo among major media or whether you've looked it up incorrectly and should search for a synonym for the heading you're looking under. Or this may be a lucky accident for you: to be first with the story.

Sometimes it's harder to research your subject's recent publication history on Websites or in e-zines, but it's helpful if you can do it. Then you can plan a firmer itinerary.

There are several ways of devising an itinerary. If money is your primary goal, the first publication you would try for would be *Reader's Digest* or *Playboy* or *Woman's Day*. Your descending order would list lower-paying markets, on down through the cent-a-word possibilities. However, there's another factor to consider: does the magazine pay on acceptance or on publication? *On acceptance* means you'll get your check a couple of weeks after you get the "Yes, we want it." *On publication* means you'll get paid when and if your piece appears in print. Some editors are very fair about this and only accept material they know they'll be using in the near future. Others are tempted by the opportunity to build up a free inventory, and your story may sit "in inventory" for months or years.

In general, an editor is more likely to publish promptly something he's already paid for. Sometimes a periodical will pay immediately for the article but will hold all the photographs you've sent until the staff is actually laying out the issue. Then they'll return the unused photos and send a check for those they use. That seems reasonable, doesn't it? But if you're the kind of writer who doesn't really believe it's *sold* until it's *paid for*, beware of pay on-publication involvements.

If you want to sell a piece quickly, you might begin your itinerary with the publication that seems to you the most likely market for this particular story. After you've done your market research, read several copies of your selected targets, and eliminated those that have recently used your subject, you should be in a position to judge which publication would most want what you have to offer, and which market would be the next most probable, on down to the long shots and the lucky accidents. Your individual itinerary will show some combination of these.

Consider the Hundreds of Markets Before You Go

Let's take a mythical trip and see what we can do about finding candidates for a marketing itinerary. In thumbing through *Writer's Market*, don't merely turn to one section and stop there. *Every* section lists publications likely to buy travel material. From *Babytalk* to *AARP The Magazine*, hundreds of periodicals are potential markets for your work. So study *Writer's Market* carefully and creatively. Study the print possibilities and search out the online mentions, as well as their information in *Writer's Market Online*, *Writers Net*, and similar references. Begin to identify all the possible audiences for your trip story as soon as you know you will be traveling.

Say you're scheduled to take a trip on the *Mississippi Queen*—fourteen days on the Ohio and Mississippi Rivers, from Cincinnati, Ohio, to Minneapolis/St. Paul, Minnesota. Traveling with you and your spouse will be your three children: Mike, a high school football player; Melanie, an inquisitive nine-year-old; and Brucie, a toddler in diapers. Your eighty-four-year-old mother-in-law and your recently divorced thirty-two-year-old sister Sue, a bank executive in training, will also accompany you. Butterball, your Siamese cat, whom you've left in a cat hotel, and the tank of tropical fish a neighbor boy is supposed to feed, will not accompany you.

When doubts arose about the departure of any Mississippi River boats, you decided to take the trip anyway—by road.

Both you and your spouse get three weeks' vacation, so you'll travel a thousand miles to Cincinnati in your RV, taking six days to see the sights along the way. After the trip, some members of your party will fly home on a commercial plane from the Twin Cities, while some of you will fly in a friend's private plane back to Cincinnati.

How many periodicals would be interested in some kind of story related to your trip? Hundreds! Let's do this systematically. Turn first to the Consumer Publications section in the latest edition of *Writer's Market*.

Your Market Potential from A to W

ANIMAL PUBLICATIONS such as *Cat Fancy* might be interested in your efforts to find the perfect kennel for Butterball while you're traveling. Is there a story in the neighbor boy and the tropical fish for *Tropical Fish Hobbyist*—either in print or online?

ART PUBLICATIONS like *American Art Journal* or *Art Papers* would be likely to publish something on Cincinnati's Taft Museum, the Walker Museum of Art in Minneapolis, or Carl Milles's thirty-six-foot onyx Indian statue in St. Paul.

ASSOCIATIONS, CLUBS, AND FRATERNAL MAGAZINES are very concerned with the ideals, projects, and activities of their sponsoring clubs or organizations. Any of these become excellent markets for the freelancer familiar with the area where the organization will be holding its next convention or the area where the group sponsors a particular project.

Even stories on the environs of a convention city are popular with association editors. If the Elks or the Lions, members of Kiwanis or Rotary, or one of the other associations happen to be planning a convention or trade show in Cincinnati, Louisville, St. Louis, St. Paul, Minneapolis, or even some nearby city, wouldn't some of its members be interested in extending their convention trip with a vacation in the area? Aren't you the logical one to tell them all about it in the association publication?

AUTOMOTIVE AND MOTORCYCLE SECTIONS mainly list those publications concerned with the vehicle as a hobby or sport. Publications in the travel, camping, and trailer section deal with the vehicle as transportation or shelter.

Is the friend with the private plane an aviation personality? Or will the trip be an especially interesting or unusual experience? If so, perhaps *Air Line Pilot* or *Plane & Pilot* would take a story.

BANKING PUBLICATIONS should be considered. Often these are addressed to those senior enough to have optional income. And what are most of these people saving for—travel, of course!

BLACK PUBLICATIONS might like to hear about your trip, especially if you're black.

BUSINESS AND FINANCE PUBLICATIONS—eight pages of them— might need a special angle.

CHILD CARE AND PARENTAL GUIDANCE MAGAZINES might find travels with a toddler a worthy story. *Parents Magazine* and many others would welcome your advice.

COMPANY PUBLICATIONS (also known as house organs) are sponsored by a particular company to keep employees, customers, stockholders, salesmen, and dealers aware of what's going on in the organization. Some companies publish several magazines—one for customers, one for stockholders, and another for employees, for instance—while others distribute the same periodical to everybody. Does the organization you or your spouse work for publish a house organ? Would the story of your trip find a good home at one of them?

CONSUMER SERVICE AND BUSINESS OPPORTUNITY PUBLICATIONS should not be overlooked. Actually, money is such a universal subject—everybody wants to know how to make it, save it, spend it to best advantage—that a financially oriented travel article is likely to sell almost anywhere.

EDUCATION PUBLICATIONS? Select one that looks for travel articles that show the educational value of the experience for the child.

ENTERTAINMENT? You should be able to find a periodical that will take a story on old-fashioned melodrama, Dixieland bands, or Mardi Gras Night.

FOOD AND DRINK is another lucrative category. Perhaps your meal experiences will be appropriate for inclusion in *Bon Appétit*—or maybe *Cooking Light* or *Food & Wine*.

GENERAL INTEREST AND MISCELLANEOUS PUBLICATIONS run the full gamut of reading material, and practically all of them publish travel stories in one form or another. The editors advise that articles "offer a service to readers and encourage them to take some positive action such as taking a trip ... tell us about the people, activities, or events that make the location special."

Travel-sophisticated readers of *Travel + Leisure*, and *Condé Nast Traveler* need an entirely different focus and tone from the focus and tone for readers of *Reunions Magazine*, which, as the name implies, is primarily interested in reunions of families, classes, military groups, etc., and whose online content is somewhat different. It's up to you, the writer, to discern these differences and pinpoint ideas that will appeal to the specific audience. *Smithsonian Magazine*, an intellectual monthly, might be interested in your tale. So might *Open Spaces*. But they would want quite different stories.

National Geographic Traveler writers guidelines state that a story must capture a place's essence in a way that inspires readers to follow in the writer's footsteps—and equip them to do so with useful destination information.

Another natural idea could be a story relating to contemporary American life—something that is upbeat and positive. Many publications look for "narrow scope" destination stories, similar to the type of thing Don McLeese did in "New Orleans: We're Playing Its Song." The story really wasn't about New Orleans at all, but about the music of Bourbon Street. What will you find on your trip that will give you the sharp focus you need for a story like that?

Reader's Digest, at the top of the pay scale, sometimes runs original "armchair travelogues." But most *Digest* articles, whether original or reprints, have a message far beyond "My Trip." When Charles Kuralt's "Prettiest Places I've Ever Seen" appeared, the description of a fantastic summer night on an Alaskan glacier, with the northern lights putting on a memorable show, was appealing. But toward the end of the article he speaks of the pilot who took him there, perhaps accidentally: "He sized us up as a couple of guys in a hurry who would benefit from a night to slow down and look around."

While this is a personal experience, written in first person, an earlier piece, "Take a *Real* Vacation!" is an advice article, where "I," the author, am telling "you," the reader, what you should do. The message is similar—take time to slow down and have fun—but it's more strictly structured. Steps one to five, describing common vacation problems and their solutions, and eight additional tips result in a final message clearly stated: "When you get right down to it, you *do* have time for a good vacation, and you *can* afford to take one. So let yourself go!" Is there something in your travel experience that will help your reader? Can you share that experience with her, either as a personal narrative or as good advice?

HEALTH PUBLICATIONS? Well, if your mother-in-law is even slightly incapacitated, *Accent on Living* or *Arthritis Today*, under Disabilities, might be interested in how she gets along. *Natural Health* and others all have something special to say to the reader. Can you help them say it? All kinds of articles on health and fitness are very popular right now—a trend likely to stay. A whole covey of fitness magazines, from *Shape* to *Weight Watchers Magazine*, will encourage you to tell about the fitness equipment and health and fitness classes you come across on your trip.

HISTORY PUBLICATIONS are another possibility. *American History* welcomes suggestions for illustrations, but usually doesn't buy photographs. *True West* limits its coverage to "anything west of the Mississippi River," so you'll have to be careful which riverbank you're talking about if you try to do a historical piece for them.

What about the Nauvoo, Illinois, Mormon community or the Indian battles at Dubuque, Iowa, or the Indian games in Lacrosse, Wisconsin, or other vignettes of history encountered on your trip? How about periodicals dedicated to antiques?

HOME AND GARDEN PUBLICATIONS (of which there are many) run some kind of travel article every month. Each travel article is, naturally, geared to that publication's readers. While *Better Homes and Gardens* frequently runs travel stories, they are always family oriented, fact filled, and related to something the reader can imitate. A fall issue juxtaposed two possibilities for winter vacations: "Some Like It Hot," a roundup of warm weather possibilities, from Palm Springs to Freeport; and "Some Like It Cold," with best tips for skiers, snowmobilers, and ice skaters. Both articles give advice on how to get the most for the money. Could you work out something around a theme like "It wasn't so expensive, after all" or "How to cut costs on a family vacation?"

INFLIGHT MAGAZINES have been affected by the shakeup in airline carriers. They still provide an excellent mid-range market for the travel writer, though, *if* you can figure out who the players are and what they are playing. What we call inflights—and their advertisers—court the affluent business travelers who make up over 50 percent of the plane's load, so it's a special kind of travel material. No first-person accounts, no camping out with the children, no long-winded sagas for what may be a fifty-minute ride.

While the trend is toward shorter stories, inflights don't ignore the fact that people who fly to a destination sometimes use other means of transportation once they get there. United Airlines' *Hemispheres*, for instance, did an extensive feature on "Walking England: A Coast-to-Coast Trek Across a Land of Love and Legend." *Hemispheres*, like many other inflights, has regular departments that cover business and investments, art and entertainment, food and golf, shopping and personal growth. And every month they publish a feature, "Three Perfect Days," about various cities, which purports to be an insider's guide to what and where to see, do, eat, stay, and enjoy. How about "Three Perfect Days" in Minneapolis or Cincinnati?

Even commuter airlines have their own inflights these days, and a publication called *Frequent Flyer* is distributed to those who fly so frequently and so unexpectedly that they have need for an *Official Airline Guide*.

IN-ROOMS, magazines similar to inflights, are produced by many large hotel chains, both in the United States and abroad. From time to time, waterborne inflights have appeared, produced by various cruise lines—this is something to check into. Nothing too "heavy" in any of these, and nothing too blatantly commercial. Just pleasant reading as you relax on a plane or train, in a room, or aboard ship. You could probably find a dozen subjects that would work into short pieces for this market.

JUVENILE PUBLICATIONS use travel material in two ways—stories introduce young people to the experience of traveling and they teach about children from other countries and other cultures. Many of them emphasize the values in other cultures, helping young people to realize that other people are different but not inferior. *Cricket*, *Highlights for Children*, and any of the Scholastic magazines would be good candidates for the travel experience from the child's viewpoint.

LITERARY AND LITTLE PUBLICATIONS take up over 30 pages of listings, many of them initialed, beginning with *AGNI* and ending with *ZYZZYVA*. These, along with their online companions, provide a number of opportunities for self-expression and recounting of personal experiences. Many, however, pay only in contributors' copies. The writer who feels a desperate need to get his or her travel thoughts in print might consider these as beginning markets.

MEN'S PUBLICATIONS still thrive. With the right angle to your trip story, you might find some aspect for *Esquire*.

MILITARY PUBLICATIONS? In addition to the purely professional periodicals, a number of these are interested in historical pieces, like features on little-known battles, ancient warfare, and weapons of war. How about something on those Indian battles in Dubuque?

MUSIC in this area is often spectacular and may inspire you to search for one of the music publications or one of the theater, movie, TV, and entertainment publications as markets for your stories. In music, especially, you have a wide choice for reviewing the entertainment or interviewing the entertainers.

THE NATURE, CONSERVATION, AND ECOLOGY SECTION—popular topics right now—features many publications. Some such as *Nature Canada* are environmentally oriented. Others, like *National Wildlife Federation* and *Wildlife Conservation Magazine* are more generalized.

Sierra and *E/The Environmental Magazine* often publish well-documented exposés on environmental issues of national importance. *Natural History* emphasizes the biological sciences and anthropology. All, of course, publish materials that interest their readers.

What ecology-oriented events and adventures are you finding on your vacation? Do you see groups of people walking along the riverbank picking up trash? Have you spotted, and photographed, a rare bird? Are developers cutting down fruit trees to build houses? Does one of the lecturers point out the wildlife in the water and along the banks? What is the history of the levees—good or bad? How do ships dispose of garbage and minimize the environmental impact of passage along the river? You can probably think of a dozen other article ideas that would fit into one of the ecology magazines.

NEWSPAPERS AND THEIR WEEKLY MAGAZINE SECTIONS are among the best travel markets in terms of volume, although their pay is often modest. You can, however, usually sell the same piece over and over again, marking it "exclusive for your circulation area," and sometimes it builds up quite a nest egg. Better still would be to make an arrangement with a syndicate, but that's sometimes harder than it appears. Newspapers will often have special theme issues, such as the *Los Angeles Times* with its annual issues for International and Europe; Alaska; Canada and the Pacific Northwest; Summer Vacations; Hawaii and the Pacific; Mexico; Cruises; and the Caribbean.

Many weekly travel sections run annual vacation issues. The travel writer can ask for a schedule of the issues planned, and act accordingly.

MAGAZINE SUPPLEMENTS AND SUNDAY SUPPLEMENTS often produce a travel edition in early spring and a vacation-resort edition shortly before school closes. Often the editorial material has some connection with the areas, accommodations, or means of transportation being advertised. Be sure to check with their writers guidelines for submissions and check their yearly list of themes.

Many newspaper editors insist on a degree of exclusivity, notwithstanding the fact that their checks may be disappointing. However, appearance in some publications adds to your reputation. For instance, publication in the travel section of the *New York Times* is very prestigious (they want all rights, by the way). At the *Times* they say, "Write what you have to, and then get out," but most newspapers insist that a writer keep under their maximum word length, usually about eight hundred words, hardly ever more than fifteen hundred, sometimes as short as three hundred. More and more newspapers are accepting color photographs now (for discussion of photography, see Chapter 14).

Monthly and bimonthly magazines, incidentally, have in-depth issues on specific themes, too—a certain area of the world and all its various charms, or a certain activity, like skiing or golf, and all the places it can be pursued. If the area, the site, or the activity is familiar, find out about these in-depth or theme issues ahead of time and see if you can fit what you know into what they want. Get in touch with suggestions before you begin your trip. It's highly likely that some editor will be planning an in-depth issue or a complete roundup of recreational activities in the area you'll be traveling.

PHOTOGRAPHY PUBLICATIONS might also welcome your story if you're clever with a camera. Photographs are an important plus value for any story, so keep your camera handy. Perhaps the picture-taking possibilities will give you ideas for writing, too.

POETRY AND PUZZLE SECTIONS are so specialized you'll have to work extra hard to tempt them. Wouldn't it be fun, though, to drift through a somnolent afternoon, sitting in the shade composing verse or constructing a crossword puzzle?

REGIONAL AND CITY PUBLICATIONS have, as you know, been booming, multiplying, and expanding. They're sorted by states, but they don't always stick precisely to their own areas in the stories they publish. They do, however, try to publish articles that will interest their readers.

Practically all regional and city publications say they want history, nostalgia, humor, and travel pieces, and many would like photo essays. Understandably, *Chicago* magazine has a more urban outlook than *Wisconsin Trails*, but most of them speak of their readers as upper-middle income, college educated, and interested in the arts and in travel to nearby areas.

RELIGIOUS PUBLICATIONS include magazines of all denominations. The material doesn't have to be *too* religious in theme, but it can't be *anti*-religious. Here again, each periodical is especially concerned with its convention site or the area of a special project. Some of the religious magazines pay very modestly; others are competitive with general publications. Saint Paul's Cathedral, styled after Saint Peter's Basilica; the Mormon buildings in Nauvoo, Illinois, built by Joseph Smith and his followers; the buildings of the communal society at New Harmony, Indiana—all would fit into a religious publication.

Another travel writer says he has revised some of his nonselling travel articles to emphasize the religious peg, thereby making them appealing to this group of magazines. He wrote about religious statues adorning an Arizona site that were built by a man fulfilling a World War I vow, and a pueblo once destroyed because its inhabitants professed Christianity. Study the religious markets. You'll get lots of ideas from your travels for stories that might appeal to them.

RETIREMENT PUBLICATIONS, as we have said, gain in importance as the average lifespan increases. More and more citizens retire earlier and live productive and interesting lives for longer periods of time. Travel is an important part of those lives. The "Cadillac" of retirement magazines, *AARP The Magazine*, the voice of the American Association of Retired Persons, has a huge circulation and pays very substantially. They publish separate issues for younger and older retirees. While there's considerable emphasis on promoting AARP trips, other travel material also appears in every issue. What travel-related stories could you write for them? Previous issues have contained nature-related articles about life along India's River Ganges; another article is entitled "Can We Afford the Wilderness?" and a photographic roundup of bridges, called "Magnificent Links," is featured in still another issue.

Dozens of publications, many of them church sponsored, welcome travel material that is slanted to those over fifty. These are not for rocking chair seniors but for people with a desire to enjoy their well-earned retirement or pre-retirement or semi-retirement in an active way. They want to travel a little bit slower, to stop and smell the roses, explore a small village and linger at a sidewalk café.

Additionally, newspapers addressed to seniors proliferate in all parts of the country. Some are weekly, some monthly, some quarterly, but they all accept freelance material, and they are all interested in travel. Pay here is often low and slow, but it's something to keep in mind.

RURAL PUBLICATIONS are interested in organic gardening, rural living, homesteading, and natural foods. Will you see stories along the way that would be suitable for one of them? Perhaps you'll buy eggs at a dilapidated farm just purchased by a young couple beginning to restore it, or you'll notice a hundred miles of roadside vegetable stands with signs advertising their wares as organically grown, and you'll stop to interview several of the farmer-greengrocers.

SPORTS AND OUTDOOR PUBLICATIONS beckon, with everything from bow hunting to baseball, from water sports to wrestling, each snug in its own category.

Field and Stream and *Outdoor Life* are excellent targets for your travel experiences. En route did you encounter any unusual hunting and fishing laws? Did you, yourself, have an extremely successful fishing session with new or unusual equipment?

Sports Illustrated is a wonderful market because of its *weekliness*—it uses four times as much material as a monthly! Sometimes what it uses it amazing—everything from "Sail a Slow Boat to See," a charmingly illustrated journey along the canals of France, to an early-in-this-century story of two small boys who crossed the continent on horseback, to the origin of Australia's theme song, "Waltzing Matilda," to "America Is Formed for Happiness," a story from the diaries and letters of British travelers who toured the colonies before the Revolution. A history teacher friend says *Sports Illustrated* publishes "some of the best history articles around."

If your travels take you where some sport will be holding a championship meet, you may have a story. The idea is, of course, to urge those interested in the sport to attend the championship event. *Skating*, for instance, began its story "On the Oregon Trail" with:

> Portland, Oregon, host to the United States National Figure Skating
> Championships next February, is more than just a city, it is an idea, an
> experience. Portland is a potpourri, spiced by variety. But Portland has
> something else undefinable but perhaps best-called personality.

It doesn't take much insight to figure out that this was written by the Portland Chamber of Commerce—but it does prompt the freelancer to look out for future championship areas. Naturally, you'll have such events as the Olympic Games, the World Series, the Boston Marathon, and other major sports events calendared early. Perhaps next year one of them will be part of your travels.

TEEN AND YOUNG ADULT PUBLICATIONS are for teenagers thirteen to nineteen, and many have a religious orientation.

Some of them, however, are good markets for travel material "from a student's angle": how to budget, what to take, where to go, etc.

TRADE, TECHNICAL, AND PROFESSIONAL JOURNALS offer a huge number of possible markets, too. These publications are produced for people in a certain trade, industry, or profession, and while their emphasis is on technical expertise, many of them fill their pages with interesting, only slightly related stories as well. Does your trade or profession publish a journal? Some education magazines, for instance, like travel stories the teacher can use in the classroom and those that help the teacher plan her own vacation. Your story could work either way, couldn't it?

Photography trade journals are good markets for the travel writer photographer. Trade journals within the travel industry rely heavily on freelance material to help the travel agent find—and sell—the best possible vacations. Travel, camping, and trailer publications, on the other hand, appeal to the buyers of those vacations. They cover a broad range. In addition to AAA publications, other automobile clubs, both U.S. and Canadian, publish similar magazines. Insurance companies and oil companies vie for the traveler's attention. There are several newsletters of travel advice, and a whole host of possibilities among the RV and camping publications.

As one editor states, "Freelancers are very important to national special interest publications, since it is economically unfeasible for magazines to have staff writers cover such a broad geographical area." He says that in addition to articles written by experts, he also needs travel pieces with an enthusiastic approach. During your RV trips to and from Cincinnati, will you find something to approach enthusiastically?

Don't overlook those house magazines, purchased in bulk by travel agents to send to their best customers. They need stories that lure the frequent traveler into planning yet another trip; and the trip has to be of the type to generate travel agents' commissions. These periodicals come and go, but while they're publishing they make good markets, so seek them out. Contributions to travel newsletters can be winners too!

Since some travel magazines are geographically oriented—the North, the South, the East, the West, Mexico, Canada, the Caribbean, etc.—your adventures would have to fit in with the area they cover. *Islands* is a wonderful magazine, and even if you can't create an article for them this trip, keep them in mind for another time.

Condé Nast Traveler says its service information is presented in a "tip-sheet style," but its destination stories are literary. It thinks of its readers as "affluent, well-educated, and sophisticated about travel." What part of your experience might interest those readers?

WOMEN'S MAGAZINES present probably the greatest diversity within a category. You doubtless know the big traditional publications, all of which use travel stories sometimes.

For some, though, the focus has greatly changed, and it's especially important to read several current issues before formulating your ideas for a travel article for one of them. *Woman's World* is a weekly, and it uses a lot of material. But it's a different kind of material from what you'll find in. The pitch to *Cosmopolitan* would be quite different from the pitch to *Family Circle*. *Vanity Fair* is entirely different from *Good Housekeeping*.

Essence is addressed to the African-American woman, *Chatelaine* speaks to the Canadian woman, *Radiance* is written for the large woman. Many women's publications, both online and off, cultivate businesswomen or religious women. *Bridal Guide* and *Modern Bride* use a lot of material on possible honeymoon destinations. *Redbook*, no longer one of the biggest buyers of travel material, has changed its focus slightly. The *Redbook* "young mother" may be in her late forties, and their other special sections are geared to the mother past thirty, as well as the mother under thirty. But if you think your family's vacation would interest other families, it's worth an inquiry.

Although these women's magazines are very different, all of them might be interested in a unique version of how to save money while traveling, how to pack, how to select accommodations, how to make your sightseeing arrangements, and other general themes that can be slanted specifically.

Whether you travel closer to home or farther away, the travel story you write can be published. Nearly all the publications we've mentioned here are listed in *Writer's Market*. And practically all of them pay *something*. We're not really mercenary, and we don't feel a writer's soul should have a price tag, but on the other hand, a travel writer is a professional and is entitled to be paid a fair price for a job well done. The trick, of course, is finding the right periodical for your particular story and studying the markets before you mold your material. This will pay big dividends in terms of selling what you write. Recognizing the wide world of travel writing markets can turn the story you write into the story you publish.

The Online Market

In today's world "publish" may refer to an electronic outlet as well as to the printed page. And there *are* writers out there "publishing" in cyberspace for money. The potential is tremendous. Again and again the current explosion of online "content" is compared to Gutenberg's invention of movable type.

A pioneer in electronic travel writing, Lee Foster insists it's possible to make a good living traveling and writing about it today. "My overall trajectory," he says, "has been to go out into the world, live out the raw travel experiences, then come back and publish them profitably ... in congenial print or electronic situations."

Lee and other online writers suggest several directions for the freelance travel writer to explore. One way is to approach the travel product manager at a commercial online service with an appealing proposal showing content you are prepared to provide. If accepted, you will receive a percentage of the revenue that the online provider collects from viewers of your material. It is possible, of course, to also prepare and collect examples of this content on a computer disk, which can then be sold in the same manner as a travel book.

Although CD-ROMs are becoming less and less popular as travel resources, you may still find a CD-ROM a good outlet for your travel experiences.

If you have enough to say, with photographs and graphics to illustrate, you can publish your own CD-ROM and either distribute it yourself or find a national distributor. It's more likely, perhaps, that you'll hope to sell content to some other publisher of travel-related software, such as Topics Entertainment. Study a CD-ROM catalog at the library or online to see what has already been published and who is publishing what. Then you can get together the facets of your adventure to try to fill an electronic void. Another opportunity for profitable publishing involves an information database service on the World Wide Web. This kind of arrangement gives free browsing to the viewer with payment to the writer only when his or her article is downloaded.

Arranging for a home page on the Internet provides infinite possibilities, many of them as yet unexplored. You can fill your Website with your own travel material, permitting viewers to browse, and then download for a fee, payable to you directly. You can also use the site to advertise and sell other materials you have available, such as books, disks, or CD-ROMs; or promote yourself as a writer, speaker, or professional in another capacity. And you can sell advertising space to "outsiders" whose goals don't conflict with or compete with yours.

Still another Web connection offers you the opportunity to provide content for online publications. Some of these, which proliferate daily, are stand-alone electronic magazines like *Slate* (www.slate.com). The *Air Affair*, for instance, focuses on recreational aviation. Others are electronic extensions of print publications such as *Condé Nast Traveler* or *Outside*. Your agreement with the commercial site organizer will either result in outright purchase of your material or will provide you with a percentage of the revenue from every viewer.

Writing an ongoing online travel column is a money maker, and every once in a while a writer's publication will contain an item like, "Yahoo! is looking for writers and illustrators to submit original humorous columns." A number of travel writers report on assignments they have received or resales of previously published articles resulting from their participation in appropriate online forums or chat rooms.

Unfortunately, not every writer is being recompensed for the exposure of reused material online. This entire issue of copyright and contract law is sometimes a murky area, as technological advances introduce new problems. As time goes by, more and more travel writers may think in terms of licensing their work rather than selling it, and all of them will become increasingly aware of what rights they are actually offering.

While we know that books, magazines, and newspapers are here to stay, the travel writer cannot afford to overlook the additional possibilities of online publication.

E-Marketing for Travel Writers

As time goes by it will become more and more evident what kind of travel writing will succeed with twenty-first-century technology. Right now we need to be observing, testing, working, and thinking creatively about how our travel writing fits in.

Lee Foster publishes a weekly travel destination article on CNN. At his Foster Travel Publishing Website, fostertravel.com, he has over two hundred worldwide travel destination articles with photos available for leasing by web or print publishers. He usually researches and writes a couple new destination pieces a month. He also uses the Website to promote his travel apps, guidebooks, and travel stock photo library.

While not all travel writers are positioned to take as much advantage of the new technology as Foster does, we all need to become aware of the possibilities. We need to assess the online information available and ask ourselves, "What is missing? What could I offer to fill the gap?" When we look at various Websites, again we ask ourselves, "How would my idea fit in here? How can I fine-tune it for presentation to a publisher?"

Whether you're looking at a Website, features for a commercial online provider, stories for an e-zine, an app database, or CD-ROM, you'll need the same skills necessary for print publication, but you'll be using them in a slightly different way. One e-zine editor says she has a natural bias toward people who can put together information in an interesting fashion. While she doesn't demand that the writer become a producer, she welcomes the one who has an idea for the entire feature, combining visuals and sound with words, and is able to provide links for the main story.

Online magazines tend to have small staffs. In one way, this is good news for the freelancer—the editor is glad to have help with all the facets of online production. In another way, it's bad news—nobody on staff has time to massage the idea, so if it isn't "right on" in the first place, it will earn a negative response.

Online journalist Kalia Doner says you should become familiar with the tools that will manipulate your words so that you understand words are only part of the package. Web zine editor Rachel Hager agrees, but encourages writers to make proposals of all kinds, which her staff at *Parents* will "hammer into desirable form."

Each online zine has its own format, its own goals, and its own needs, but in planning original work for online publication there are several caveats to remember. One is brevity. Since it's harder to read a computer screen than a magazine page, travel articles are usually shorter, more focused, more specific, and often lighthearted. On the other hand, much of the material accepted for cyber publication is more service oriented than we find in print travel magazines and newspapers.

Use your search engine to research online travel zines.

Links to Links

Many online articles have links to other information. Links are something like sidebars—suggesting additional stories related to the main story—and the same author at the same Web page may provide these, or they may be provided by an entirely different author on a different Web site entirely. And since the reader can begin at any one of these links, each has to be autonomous. A Thailand web page, for instance, links to a Lonely Planet book, which links to a story and pictures about an elephant and its *mahout*.

The possibilities for pictures, animation, sound, and audience interaction are unique to the Internet, and as a prospective author, you have to consider them. However, illustrations take longer to download, and surfers become impatient; so you need also to consider the time necessary for the graphics and hope the site gives the viewer a choice to view a selection without graphics if desired.

A slightly different audience reads travel material online—a younger, more technically savvy group. And while more women buy books and magazines, more men surf the Internet. Naturally, the advertisers are aware of this, and this awareness dictates the focus of the editorial material. It also means that those members of the publishing community who make their way into cyberspace to complement their printing presses are not always successful at directly translating printed material there.

Electronic Media: New Opportunities Abound

Another characteristic of online writing is individual response. It's easy to tell if anybody is reading the travel material you are writing because the new technology tells how many "hits" each piece in an online zine receives. You can also evaluate your effectiveness by noting the response on message boards and other interactive media. Then, too, material remains at the Website for a long period of time and is not always replaced weekly or monthly.

A substantial amount of travel material, in addition to the pedestrian publication of airline schedules, prices for cruise packages, and ads for car rentals, makes its way to the Internet.

December issues of e-zines predictably feature articles advising how to avoid the crush at the airport, telling the untold (?) story of *The Nutcracker*, reminiscing about favorite holiday destinations of the past, and telling readers "How to Survive Holiday Visits from Relatives."

At the *New York Times* Website, the Travel section says it's "designed as a resource for business and vacation travelers alike," and it regularly offers five collections of features selected from its regular weekly travel pages: What's Doing ("In Sydney, Celebrating as Summer Arrives"); Frugal Traveler; Practical Traveler ("Learning About the Art of the Concierge"); Business Traveler ("International Gift-Giving Can Be Worthwhile"); and Q-and-A, with a variety of tips and trends.

Online newsletters and columns are another way of entering cyberspace with travel material. K. L. Smith's *SeaLetter Cruise Magazine* (sealetter.com) for instance, is essentially a promotion for the various cruise lines, but it encourages readers to send in reviews, trip reports, and other articles. For this sort of thing, there's no pay for the writer, but it's a start! And you may manage to arrange a contract for producing a travel newsletter of your own.

Online writers can download samples of their material into library files, and again and again we hear of writers who receive wonderful assignments from "writer wanted" ads on message boards or from chatting with others on writing forums. Lisa Iannucci, who has profited greatly from logging on, makes several suggestions for gaining recognition in this area. She urges you to visit many forums, introducing yourself with such words as "travel writer" or "author of," to read all messages, to reply to possible writing assignments in whatever manner is suggested, and to keep in touch with editors who post online requests, reminding them again of what you can do for them. There can be many advantages to lurking online.

Many Websites welcome proposals for forums or Q-and-As, with you as online moderator. Who would you interview in your forum? What would your theme and your goal be? Make a proposal, after you think through what you could offer that is presently missing. Because there are no rules yet, you can be as creative as you wish.

Lee Foster optimistically believes that "the Internet presents the purest vehicle ever in the history of publishing." He says it's the first time that independent content providers have been able to attract a worldwide audience without the burden of heavy capital costs. If you decide to establish a Website, it's wise to employ a knowledgeable Webmaster to get started. For example, the Webmaster will help you put certain key words, called "metatags," at the first page of your Website so that the search engines will find your page when people are looking for your travel subjects.

You can generate revenue from your Website in several ways, such as selling space to advertisers or sponsors, as Foster has done with the banner ad at the top of his site. He says his largest income is through leasing his writing/photo content to Web or print publishers. He also receives a small sum from "affiliate" relationships with commercial sites such as Lodging.com and Amazon.com.

A Website can also sell your services as a speaker, teacher, or travel consultant. Perhaps you'll choose some combination of all these possibilities.

How about book publishing online? If this possibility interests you, you can easily explore its potential for the travel book you have in mind. Your computer will lead you to many of the entrepreneurs who have established various forms of **e-books** and print on demand books. E-books are electronically downloaded to your media device; print on demand prints out a hard copy of your book. The author pays a percentage of the sale price for each book sold. CreateSpace.com has step-by-step information on formatting your book into either an e-book or a print on demand book.

One of the advantages of online publishing is the possibility of developing both print and electronic versions of the book and marketing both, as Foster has done with *Northern California History Weekends*.

What They Pay for Cyber Writing

Pay for writing online content varies considerably—from nothing at all to more than fair. In general, at the better-paying e-zines, it compares to medium-market print magazines, about a dollar a word, sometimes quite a bit more. On the other hand, *Travel Watch* expects a writer to submit four unpaid articles that are acceptable, and then they will decide whether you should be on the paid or unpaid staff. You might invent a travel quiz that would be a link to your story that would pay much more than that per word. Or you might be so eager to promote your skills as a presenter of travel lecture programs that you would be glad to write a related piece with no remuneration expected.

Foster feels that he has been fairly paid for his online work. The clue, he says, is thinking in terms of leasing, rather than selling, your writing and photographs, preferably on a non-exclusive basis. He suggests selecting Websites where there is a definite revenue source, such as substantial ad revenue or major travel purchases.

Whatever you do, though, it is very important to have a clear understanding with the editor, the publisher, the Website provider, or the person with whom you are dealing. In cyberspace there are many opportunities for misunderstanding. If all your correspondence is via email and the company you're working with goes out of business, what then? Be sure to get everything on paper, including the physical address and phone number of the people who are going to pay you. Get it written down—exactly what is expected of you and exactly what is expected of them.

We're talking here about a whole new world in which the writing industry is changing dramatically, and it is up to travel writers to protect themselves against print publications that insist on electronic rights also, for no added remuneration. Writers don't know yet what the future holds, but when their contracts talk about relinquishing their rights for all media, known as well as yet unknown, they are being cheated.

Of course you'll hope to combine all facets of your online and print publishing as Lee Foster has. This may take a while, but if you look at your travel writing seriously, it can happen.

The Nuts and Bolts of Marketing

Whether it's online or in print, selling the stories of your travels is still a matter of finding the right audience for your ideas. Pore over marketing information with the unexpected in mind. Don't try to compete with the hundreds of travel writers who are trying to sell typical destination pieces to *Travel Holiday*. Think, instead, of an offbeat feature that would appeal to *Travel Holiday's* readers. A tennis vacation to *Glamour*? Maybe. A cruise article to *House Beautiful*? Perhaps. But if you have any unusual game recipes, try an outdoor magazine!

You'll find, as you become more familiar with the field, that market research will occupy a large part of your time. Try to do it as efficiently as possible.

That word "mileage" is a very important one, and often online publications give us the best opportunity for resales or for publishing rewritten material. The five or six pieces to which you have sold all rights still offer the possibility of being rewritten. With a new title and using the leftover research, they can be submitted to some other publication.

With an itinerary sheet for each of these possibilities and marketing materials within easy reach, Louise goes to work. When she speaks of marketing materials she means, of course, the marketing manuals; the torn-out suggestions from writers' magazines; samples of the publications themselves, with paper clips alerting her to special approaches; online information and lists of online editors; twenty or thirty letters from editors encouraging further discussion; and what seems like half a ream of disorganized notes to herself: "Try H. B. on Corms. in 6 mos." or "New ed at P. G. Try Bar RF?"

Keep Track of Details

Open a word processor document or spreadsheet on your computer and list all your working publication titles, alphabetically by country, followed by "query" for those publications that prefer it, and "send" for those that want to see the complete manuscript right away. "Send" might be further broken down into "email" and "hard copy," depending on the publication's preference.

Then go through the editorial correspondence, if any, noting on each article's itinerary which ideas or finished pieces have attracted an editor enough for her to say, "We're overstocked now, but try us again on this in six months," or "Have you anything else on Indonesia? We're running a Bali piece this month, but we could use another Indonesia story in February," or "We're holding your Denmark article and the three transparencies."

Naturally, you would give strong marketing preference to publications and sites where you have sold previously, and even to those where you've had a near miss.

Next, study the marketing lists and marketing manuals, juggling your ideas around in your mind. When you come to a market you think is suitable for one of your ideas, write the name of the market under the working title.

The Crossfile Is Ready

You have a crossfile of markets for each idea and ideas for each market. Now comes the careful scrutiny. Here are twenty ideas suitable for *Paradise Magazine*—which three or four should she select for the query? And here is that Caribbean cruise idea with twenty possible markets for it—where should you send it or query on it first? Begin with the idea for which there are fewest possible markets and the market for which there are fewest ideas, and continue matching and cross-matching from there.

Taking into consideration pay, prestige, and likelihood in an indefinable combination, you'll end up, the following day, with orderly itineraries for each of your forty ideas. Send immediately any articles that have already been written to the first market on the itinerary if that is suitable, or query on it if that's what the magazine requests. On the still-to-be written articles, send queries, marking on the itineraries and in your "out" book (which tells what has gone where and when) what you're doing.

Does this sound like a lot of trouble? It is at the time. But the information acquired on "Marketing Days" lasts many months. If your submission comes back, you'll know immediately where to send it next. If a query letter or email results in a negative response, query the next market on the itinerary. Replies to all these queries usually result in enough go-aheads and assignments to keep you working full speed until next Marketing Day, which may be anywhere from six months to three years later, depending on how much traveling you do, how many other projects you have, and the usual variables of writing and marketing.

Of course, you must be constantly updating, as you read marketing information and listen to the experiences of other writers, and adding to or subtracting from your idea list.

Sell Your Story Again and Again

Now that you've figured out where to sell your story, it's time to think of where to sell it *next*.

No travel writer can afford to take a trip and write only one story from it. Georgia Hesse, former travel editor for the *San Francisco Examiner/Chronicle*, advises that at least five different stories should come from each destination. If you do the research you should, you have made too great a time investment for a single story to suffice. So before you even leave on the trip, begin to think of what you will write and how you will get additional mileage from it. While you're traveling you'll see more mileage possibilities, and you'll find still more as you do your post-trip market research.

How can you sell your story more than once? There are a number of ways. Sometimes you'll use a combination of them and find that one article becomes almost an annuity for you as you go on selling the material again and again. The most familiar method of collecting several checks for the same research is to sell only *one-time rights* to each story buyer. There isn't room here to go into a full discussion of copyright, but it's well to remember that the 1978 copyright law favors the author, making him the recognized copyright holder. (However, some publications today insist that the writer sign a "work for hire" agreement, thereby making the publisher the copyright owner, which is contrary to the spirit of the law.) Resales are available to the many publications that have no objection to simultaneous submissions or the submission of previously published material. Usually these are religious magazines (the Methodists don't care if the Catholics are reading the identical article in their publication), regional periodicals (Texans might be interested in taking a trip on the Great Lakes and so might Floridians, and neither one cares what the other one is reading), trade journals, company publications, and association magazines (where no individual is likely to encounter the same article twice, since he's not likely to be a hairstylist and also a fireman).

But if there's any doubt in your mind that simultaneous submission might give less than full value to your editors or your readers, be sure to check it out with your buyer ahead of time. Newspaper and Sunday supplement editors usually don't care if you submit to their colleagues in other parts of the country. When you send something to them, mark it "Exclusive Your Area," and don't send it to a competing newspaper. Nino La Bello, based in Europe, sometimes manages to sell the same story to three hundred newspapers around the globe. Even if you sell first rights to the first buyer, you'll still make money on additional sales of one-time rights.

Subsequent publication is another way to get greater mileage out of a single article. When *Reader's Digest* condenses an article from another periodical, it pays the periodical and the author. Sometimes the *Digest* will help you place the article in another magazine so that they can later excerpt it if they feel the story you originally submitted to them isn't strong enough for a *Digest* original. Other magazines also sometimes excerpt from each other; books are condensed or excerpted or serialized in periodicals; articles are collected in anthologies. International reprints and translations are an excellent mileage maker for the author.

Syndication is a good answer to multiple sales, if you can interest a syndicate in your material. Sometimes sibling publications, especially trade journals put out by one publisher, will share some of their non-technical copy.

Payment Without Publishing

Can a negative editorial decision extend your mileage? A publication may offer a "kill fee" if the finished article does not turn out to be what they need. The kill fee is usually about one-fourth to one-third of the agreed upon price, and the article, of course, then belongs to the writer and can be resold.

If an editor takes your story and pays for it on acceptance, and then many months go by and it isn't published, chances are there's been a change of editors and/or a change in editorial policy, and your piece will probably never run. If you ask if you can have it back the answer is usually yes, and then you're welcome to sell it again.

If editors keep your article and/or photographs for an unreasonably long time without making a decision, they sometimes pay a "holding fee" if they decide in the end they can't use them. Sometimes the holding fee is substantial, as it was at *Smithsonian* magazine.

Another mileage-maker is an outline. Some publications, as we've said, prefer an outline to a query. And sometimes they'll buy the outline—leaving the writer free to sell the actual story elsewhere, with the outline money as a bonus. When Louise sent an outline on Malta to *Aramco World*, the editor wrote that he was planning to travel to Malta himself and would write his own story. However, he said, he liked her outline so much he wanted to buy it. Then she was free to sell the story elsewhere—the outline money was pure bonus.

What Do You Do with Overflow Material? Sell It!

Sometimes you have a lot more material than you can possibly use in one article—unless your editor's willing to let you make the article ten thousand words long. Actually, if you have enough solid material for ten thousand words, you should be able to write at least five or six articles on that subject without plagiarizing yourself. Some of the basic facts you'll have to repeat in each one, of course, but if you make the beginnings and the endings all different, vary the emphasis and the anecdotes, and tack on new titles, you'll have five or six distinctly different articles. You'll find this superfluity of material to occur especially in subjects involving lots of live research, where you have an unlimited source of anecdotal material from interviewing a variety of people.

Using the overflow is a good way to gain mileage. After you write the first article, gather up the bits and pieces you have left and concoct another story from them. Juvenile writer Mabel Watts says to be careful about doing this, though. After a trip to the British Isles, she sold one story with a Scottish background; then she used her leftover research for another story. But the editor to whom she submitted it said, "You sound like the old Scottish lady who threw all the leftovers into the haggis!"

Often, though, you can get another story out of the overflow of material or a spinoff from the one you're working on. Many of the spinoffs Louise has sold have been fillers or featurettes, such as the one to *Ladies' Home Journal* about how to avoid coming home from vacation to a houseful of dirty laundry, and the one to the *Denver Post* supplement on the origin of the English word "meander." When research for an assignment on Spain and Portugal led her to the many Iberian areas connected with Christopher Columbus, a Columbus Day story fell easily into place.

New Life for Old Themes

Sometimes you'll expand your horizons years later, when you update and change a travel article written long ago.

Often your mileage expands with the years. As you grow and change and become a better writer, you're inspired to re-treat ideas you now feel you didn't do justice by, and through your growing expertise an entirely new story emerges.

In your zealous quest for mileage, be careful, though, not to violate anybody else's rights. Sherman Grant says it's difficult to sell a story to an additional publication when the people you interviewed agreed to talk to you as the representative of the specific magazine that assigned you the story.

Other Ways to Increase Mileage

Other ways you can make mileage from your research are: rewriting an adult article as a juvenile piece, or vice versa; by using your travel background for a short story, a juvenile story, or a play, or taking the background from one of them for a travel article; by expanding a local story (usually by working out a "geographic spread" through additional research) into a national article; or by converting a national article, such as Louise's *Weight Watchers* piece on travel charm bracelets, to a local one, using local people and local anecdotes for an additional sale to a Sunday supplement.

Larry Holden speaks of seasonal articles that can be used year after year, when that season rolls around again. He refers not only to holidays but also to special times, like tornado season, about which he frequently writes. Fanny-Maude Evans has done that with her research on lightning, which also has a "season."

Holden speaks of "blending" and "paring" for increased sales, too. Blending means taking bits and pieces from several stories you've previously written to make a new story. Louise snipped tidbits from several advice articles on how to save money and how to have a good time on your trip and added new material for an article on "How to Get the Most Pleasure from Your Travel Dollar." Paring is the opposite of blending. If you've written a definitive article, you can often slice out a specific section and sell it as a short separate article, once you've changed it around a little.

As you think about it, you'll probably come up with additional ways for stretching mileage from your research. There simply aren't enough hours in the day for a travel writer to be continually researching new articles, and it's not necessary. Research thoroughly in the first place. Then write your story as well as you can each time. Willa Cather advised long ago, "Give your best every single time. Don't hold back and save anything out for 'next time.' 'Next time' will take care of itself."

Selling the International Market

Sometimes you can spread your message internationally—and increase your profit, too—by selling to English-language publications in foreign countries. When you're overseas you'll naturally survey the kiosk displays of newspapers and magazines and select a few to send home in your big envelopes, along with the foreign inflights and in-rooms you pick up. This is the best way to obtain foreign publications to analyze as possible markets; but you can also send for sample copies or buy an issue or two at a large bookstore or news-stand at home. Airports can be good sources.

In *Writer's Market* you'll find an occasional foreign periodical, but the two major sources listing foreign periodicals are the *International Literary Marketplace* and the multi-volume *Ulrich's International Periodicals Directory*, both published by Bowker. *International Literary Marketplace* is divided by country, with information on periodicals, publishers, and relat-ed matters listed under each country. *Ulrich's* begins its Travel and Tourism pages with *AAA Chicago Motor Club Home & Away*, but continues with *AIM* (Adventures in Mexico Newsletter); *Angling Holidays in Ireland*; *Asia Magazine*, published in Thailand; and *Auberge de la Jeunesse* in French. It goes on through the alphabet giving editors' names, addresses, and circula-tion figures.

Whether your special interest is jungle animals, international business, Catholic shrines, scuba diving, black travelers, or oriental art, you'll find an international magazine in the market for your work.

The *Australian Women's Weekly* buys material similar to that which appears in US and Canadian women's magazines and often runs articles on international, as well as Australian, destinations. Other foreign publications that might make good markets for you are not only in the South Pacific, the British Isles, and South Africa but include countries around the world that publish in English or translate from it.

Although payment from these periodicals is practically never as high as in the United States, they usually have no objection to previously pub-lished material. (The pay may be lower because the country's size trans-lates to a smaller circulation than that of a North American magazine.) If you can sell the same piece over and over, that's mileage and worth doing. Don't use up all the profits in postage, though; ask if email submissions are acceptable.

How to Market Overseas

Usually it's best to first send a query or an outline to a foreign market (email is perfect for this purpose). Then, if the editor wants to see the article, perhaps accompanied by photographs, it's easy to send the manuscript and photos via email. Check with the editor as to which format she would like the documents to be in.

What kinds of travel stories are likely to sell to foreign markets? Both foreign stories *and* North American stories. If you have something on the area the publication covers, wonderful. Many foreign editors would also welcome pieces about areas you know well.

Michael Sedge, a well-known Italy-based writer and photographer, emphasizes the importance of researching, in print or online, the culture of the country whose publications you're planning to approach. Do Muslim periodicals prohibit reference to alcohol, dogs, pigs, and body parts? Are European shoppers, accustomed to visiting a different store for each purchase, unaware of Walmart and Target? Do the Japanese cringe in embarrassment when an author carelessly mentions shoe-shod walking indoors, soaping up in a public bath, or backslapping greetings among friends?

However, most subjects that sell well in North America sell well in other countries, too. Sedge likens his global successes to cutting a pie into many slices, and he often sells the same story many, many times, in different countries. He does recommend eliminating colloquial expressions—and converting inches and feet to metric measurement. Most foreign publications tend toward British usage and spelling rather than American. Although they probably won't reject your excellent article just because you've called them trucks and elevators instead of lorries and lifts, or spelled what you expect them to send you as *check* instead of *cheque*, make it as easy for the foreign editor as you can.

Countries likely to have English-language publications include:

The Bahamas
Bangladesh
Bermuda
Denmark
Egypt
Fiji
Finland
Gibraltar
Greece
Hong Kong
Iceland
India
Indonesia
Ireland
Israel
Japan
Kenya
Korea (South)
Malaysia
Malta

The Netherlands
New Zealand
Norway
Pakistan
Panama
The Philippines
Republic of South Africa
Singapore
Sri Lanka
Sweden
United Kingdom
Western Samoa
Zimbabwe

Explore the foreign markets as you plan your strategy for getting the most mileage out of your research.

The "Back-of-the-Book" Market—A Great Place to Begin

Now let's look at a few market possibilities perhaps you haven't thought of. Some of them can be mileage markets, too. Have you wondered about those oddly numbered pages in many magazines—P1, PS4, G9, C12, or W31? And have you wondered why the stories on those pages never appear in the table of contents? Those are "back-of-the-book" stories. They may be located in the front of the book or the middle of the book, but they're still back-of-the-book stories. And that is a good market for the travel writer.

This market exists because nearly all national magazines accept regional advertising. That's the advertising on pages P1 and G9 and C12. Sometimes the letters have special meaning only for the publication, but at *Travel + Leisure* you don't have to be Sherlock Holmes to figure out that "C" stands for California and "W" stands for West, and both sections appear in the magazine sometimes. Because the ads don't entirely fill these pages, editorial material is required, and it's an entry-level opportunity. *Travel + Leisure* puts it tactfully:

> You might break in with a short piece for the front or back of the book.
> The regional pages don't pay as much as our national articles,
> but it's a good way to start.

Now this doesn't come right out and say, "Our regional editions are open to amateurs," but it does get across the point that slightly less polish is required. In other words, it's a good place for the less-experienced writer to begin.

Back-of-the-book stories don't have to be geographically related to the region represented; a New York edition had a feature on San Francisco's Carousel Museum while a California edition devoted a number of pages to "Getting to the Core of the Big Apple."

Ladies' Home Journal's back-of-the-book section appears often and carries such features as "Family Fun at Deer Valley." One recent issue has back-of-the-book stories on "Travel Scam Alert," "Sun and Fun in San Diego," "The Art of Packing Light," and "Prospecting Montana's Gold West Country"—all of them very simple and straightforward, between five hundred and a thousand words. *Better Homes & Gardens, Good Housekeeping,* and many other general magazines have similar back-of-the-book sections specializing in travel briefs.

How do you tell the editor you're sure your article isn't good enough for the national section so you're only asking him to consider it for the back of the book? Obviously, you don't. If the *Writer's Market* listing suggests you send regional material to a regional editor, then you'll do so. If the publication masthead lists a regional editor, you'll act accordingly. Otherwise, let the travel editor or the articles editor, or whoever is in charge of that kind of material, decide where your piece should go. (You'll follow instructions in the listing, of course, as to length, photographs, and whether or not to query.)

Other special magazine and newspaper sections may be better markets than you'd think for different types of travel material. *Good Housekeeping's* "The Better Way," for instance, often features such subjects as trip and vacation insurance, better gas mileage, tips on packing a car for travel, and other loosely travel-related subjects. They want "just the facts, please" for this section—*they* adapt it to their format.

Look for special departments in all publications, and try to bend your ideas to fit into some of them. Remember that short pieces give you **clips** and credits, too. While advertorials, those special advertising sections with considerable editorial material, are not for amateur travel writers, here, too, opportunity may beckon. Usually the writer's fee jumps higher for an advertorial.

What Are Your Other Markets?

Let's look at some different types of publications that use travel-related material of one sort or another.

Have you noticed the recent proliferation of travel newsletters? Mailed to subscribers, whether singles, seniors, or families, these purport to give the traveler the inside dope about hotels, transportation, restaurants, etc. A large percentage of this information is supplied by other travelers, who get paid for it. Travelsmartnewsletter.com, for instance, says it's partially freelance written and pays for candid advice on good travel values. There are several others of this type. They want the information to come from personal experience, but not always written in the first person. They need "mentions." If you've had a really good or really bad experience, you could detail it briefly, and consider one of these newsletters. Most of them prefer queries. They'll send report forms, if you like.

If you want to keep busy while traveling, but don't want to embark on a full-scale career as a travel writer, or you want something to supplement your career as a travel writer, consider providing hotel reports and/or ship inspections for travel agents' reference books. The pay is infinitesimal, and the editors are sometimes difficult to work with, but it's a handy plus if you're in the right place at the right time.

Many magazines and newspapers run regular sections covering lifestyles and cultural situations in other areas of the world. While these are not really travel-oriented, they provide the travel writer with an opportunity to use some of the material observed.

Some kind of "trip sharing" column is often a feature of both print and electronic publications. You tell about your trip in an informal manner and perhaps send a photograph. Some of them pay and some don't, so inquire first. Both newspapers and magazines occasionally run special contests for travel articles or photographs, and sometimes the prizes are substantial. Keep on the lookout for these. They often add mileage.

We've spoken of *Guest Informant*, which is one of the hardcover, four-color books placed in hotel rooms around the United States. Hotel rooms in foreign countries often have books of this type, too, in English. They use travel information only on the city in which they appear, and since it's such detailed information, you could work on one only for a city you're very familiar with. But they do use freelance material, so look into it further if you're interested.

Writing for *Guest Informant* is something you could do without leaving home. Let's look at a few other stay-at-home travel possibilities.

Stay-at-Home Travel Writing

A magazine like *American Demographics* is interested only in statistics on where Americans take their vacations and what kinds of trends are evident. One like *Incentive* magazine takes material on travel that firms use as rewards in motivational promotions.

You can interview travel agents for travel trade journals. There are a number of travel trade journals, some monthly, some weekly, and they do use freelance material on various phases of the travel industry. A woman in Sacramento, California, lamenting the fact that she doesn't get to travel much, contacts the Sacramento Convention Center to find out which groups, such as Rotarians, Presbyterians, etc., will be meeting there soon. Then she writes the editors of their publications with suggestions for travel stories on Sacramento.

Another possibility is writing brochure material advertising travel lecturers. The last brochure writer who interviewed Louise was producing such purple prose she asked him what qualifications a brochure writer needed. "Oh," he said, "you have to know how to exaggerate a little." Opportunities for writing publicity and advertising copy in travel-related fields increase every day. Whether you're writing about the objective of the travel—the restaurant, hotel, whatever—or the person who is going to tell others about those objectives, try not to exaggerate more than "a little"! Writing guidebooks, on your own area or elsewhere, perhaps something like "State Parks of New England," often provides good income for the travel writer. The stay-at-home can devise travel puzzles and quizzes, as well as cookbooks, too. Manuscripts for computer libraries are another way to go. In this digital age, travel-related apps are becoming more and more popular. What is an app? Its short for application: a program for a smartphone, computer, or other electronic device. We'll go into more detail in Chapter 16.

Travel lectures and radio and television programs, on the other hand, are the province of the active traveler. Juvenile and young adult audiovisual materials are another market for the returned traveler. In addition to the magazine and newspaper articles and adult and young people's books on travel, we mustn't overlook the value of the travel background for other types of fiction and nonfiction for all ages.

You can see the tremendous importance of market research and what a variety of possible markets are available. But we keep coming back to the same precept: "There is no such thing as writing *generally*." Everything you write must be slanted to the reader for whom it's intended.

Whether online or in print, look for the unexpected sale, but be sure you're approaching the right audience.

CHAPTER 6

Prepare for Takeoff

You'd think those who travel for a living would always be on their toes about what they'll need: letter-perfect in their preparations, and ready for the summons to adventure. However, now and then surprising situations arise.

Jacqueline forgot her driver's license once on a trip to Italy, during which time she planned to rent a car. You can imagine her reaction when the agent at the car rental office refused to rent her a car without one. She begged and pleaded to no avail. No driver's license—no car!

Georgia Hesse, then travel editor of the *San Francisco Examiner*, wrote a bittersweet column about meeting her friend the travel editor of the *Chicago Tribune* in Sri Lanka. His arm was red and swollen. Why? Because he had delayed too long in arranging for a necessary shot. Georgia was amused at the time, but admitted she found the situation less amusing a few days later, when she arose at 3:00 a.m. for a trip across the island of Mauritius to make a 6:00 a.m. flight to the Malagasy Republic. Authorities refused to let her board the plane. Why? Because she had no visa for Malagasy. When she'd looked up the requirements in San Francisco a week earlier it seems she'd mistaken Malagasy for Mali.

Whether you're going to Malagasy or Mali, whether your journey is to the next town or across nine time zones, do as much homework as you can when you're getting ready to go. Otherwise you're likely to be disappointed in dozens of wretched little ways—and plenty of big ways, too.

Check and recheck that your passport is up to date and in your day bag. Make sure your driver's license, money, credit cards, tickets, visa(s), and all documents you will need on the trip are also in your day bag.

Planning Your Trip

Most of us do our planning online these days. It's fast and easy to Google a specific destination and open an amazing amount of data. As you narrow down your search to a particular area or town, there are links to hotels, restaurants, points of interest, and history.

If your "getting ready" involves planning with a travel agent, be honest with her about how much money and how much time you really have to spend. What do you really want to see, and how do you want to see it?

A good travel agent will advise you on what is the best way to get where you are going. She can also make reservations not only for your flight, rail, boat, or car, but also for your hotel, museums, and tours.

Ask, "What is the 'half day of sightseeing'—is it four hours or only two and a half? Does this price include all gratuities? Will my sightseeing tours be in English *only*? Does a 'driver guide' know enough to help me with my research?" (Always request separate vouchers for each person and each item, so if you decide not to do something it will be easy to obtain a refund.)

With so much travel material online these days, it becomes easier and easier to plan your own trip. But whether you use a travel agent, accept a hosted trip, or do it yourself; whether you have assignments, go-aheads, or just something you want to see, always consider your sightseeing plan very carefully. It is the single most important feature of any trip. Sightseeing can be dull and dreary, hurried and half-baked; or, with intelligent arranging, it can provide maximum writing and research value as well as personal pleasure and enrichment.

Your sightseeing program is not something to arrange casually, trusting to luck that you will see the best things in the easiest way at the cheapest price. Too many people select the wrong trip for the wrong reasons. They ruin any chance of writing about their travels because they don't ask the right questions when they're getting ready to go. Sightseeing plans are geared toward particular people, particular places, and particular pocketbooks.

If you know the full range of what's available, you'll be able to select your own ideal plan, whether solo or in a group.

Get Your Objectives Straight

Ask yourself, "Why am I traveling? For adventure and discovery? Or for relaxation and diversion? What kind of readers will my stories appeal to? Why will *they* be traveling?"

There are other questions: Is the getting there or the being there more important to you? Are you traveling to find new ideas for your writing, or to give your ideas a rest? Are you pursuing the Holy Grail of some long-cherished dream? Will you be satisfied only if you see London's Old Curiosity Shop, the gravesite of Marcel Proust in the Pere-Lachaise Cemetery in Paris, or the Mark Twain Museum in Hannibal, Missouri?

Do you want to travel alone or in a group? Traveling solo allows you to set up your own itinerary, to explore and spend time doing whatever catches your attention. If you prefer a group there are tours for everything from Art to Zebras and tours geared especially toward writers and/or photographers (usually listed in spring issues of writers' magazines). There are also many work-play conferences. If well run, these can be stimulating and rewarding. As at a writers' conference, the shoptalk is valuable in itself and the entire trip is slanted to your purposes.

Maybe you've reached the status where an important editor calls you for a story assignment on the Alba White Diamond Truffle Fair in the Piedmont region of Northern Italy. He asks, "Can you make it to the airport by 3:00 p.m. for a flight to Milan? Your first-class air tickets and hotel vouchers will be waiting for you at the check-in counter at the airport. A chauffer will meet you in Milan and drive you to Alba. You will have time to relax and then join a small group for a special dinner featuring the White Diamonds. At midnight you and your group will go on a truffle hunt."

In such cases, your travel plan has selected you. Sit back and enjoy it. But if you're the one choosing what you will see and how and with whom you'll see it, be sure to consider what kind of person you are.

Gear Your Plans to Your Personality

Take into consideration your habits and your characteristics. *Your* sight- see-ing choice, if you like to get up early and be on your way by eight, will be different from that of someone who prefers to review the nightclub circuit. If you are compulsive about eating at definite times or need to rest after lunch in hot weather, you must take this into consideration. If you feel lonesome unless lots of other people are sharing your experience, or you're out of sorts when you have time on your hands, *your* sightseeing program won't resemble that of the person who's bored hearing someone else's opinion and gets disgruntled when every minute's arranged for. Do you like to laze in the sun, swim in the sea or pool, hike in the country, search for treasures in the markets, dress for dinner? Do you like to drive or be driven? Are you impulsive, eager to do what you want to do, when you want to do it? Do you detest regimentation? Remember what you like and don't like when you plan your sightseeing program.

Two writers comparing trip notes discovered that each had had a wonderful time traveling to the same area—although one covered every cathedral and museum and spent evenings at the theater, while the other shunned cities and tramped backcountry roads, staying at country inns in medieval villages.

Each had planned a sightseeing program that covered exactly what she considered a good time and liked to write about.

Each of these women traveled alone, because each was very sure of what she wanted to do and unwilling to make compromises. If you're an independent kind of person, never bored by your own company, consider solo traveling. Going alone, with a known traveling companion, or perhaps with several well-chosen ones, may work out best for you. If you and your traveling companion(s) don't agree about the ratio of time and money to be spent on various stages of the trip, you'll have to work out compromises. This is especially important when money is concerned. It's important to plan according to everyone's budget. If you want it to be a good trip, negotiate these matters *before* you go.

If you intend this to be a business trip for you, what will your traveling companion do while you're tracking down all the facts a travel writer needs? Your traveling companion may or may not feel the benefits are worth the sacrifice of your company, the early morning phone calls, the late-night research and writing sessions. Perhaps you can persuade him or her to become a part of the project—by taking photographs, for instance.

No matter how much information you unearth, and no matter how enthusiastic you *try* to be, you'll never convince your readers it's a great place if *you* aren't having a good time. So take into consideration your personality, the things you like to do, your special interests, and your physical condition. Consider, too: is this likely to be your *only* trip to this area? If so, perhaps you'll want to see the "musts." But sometimes the serendipity of just wandering the streets brings ideal fodder for wonderful stories.

The Pros and Cons of Tours

Discuss with your travel agent, with your prospective companion(s), or with yourself whether you want to join a tour group, or just amble unscheduled from day to day. Different traveling writers have different needs.

There's a tour to fit every possible interest or affinity. In choosing a tour, consider not only your assignments or planned stories but also your other interests and hobbies. Do you think you might find interesting and valuable a tour designed for those studying gourmet cooking, international theater, music festivals, local crafts, viticulture, or stamp collecting? Your pre-trip homework will probably be designed by the tour leaders, who will send you informative study material in advance. Then they will take care of most of the everyday arrangements, which the solo traveler has to work out for himself.

Do You Need a Guide?

Your "getting ready" preparation helps you decide on sightseeing arrangements of all kinds. Aboard ship, for instance, you'll plan whether or not to take the shore excursions. Some ports of call aren't worth a tour—just walking around will show you more than a bus ride would. Others have so much to offer that if the ship is in long enough you would do well to hire a private car and driver.

Traveling by yourself with a private car and driver is, of course, the most luxurious way to sightsee. If money is no object, you can tour the Everglades in an air-conditioned Cadillac limousine, complete with driver-guide and no worry about route maps or service stations.

Sometimes the money for a private car and guide is money well spent. Louise was in Milan only once, many years ago, between trains. Yet, she'll never forget *The Last Supper*—thanks to the knowledgeable young man who met her train, whisked her out to the refectory of Santa Maria delle Grazie, and then back to the station in time to catch the train for Lake Como. Because of his sensitivity, his awareness, his education in art, and his ability to communicate the artistic experience, Milan was expensive, but it was also a bargain.

Jacqueline and Cathleen Miller, a fellow travel writer, hired a guide to show them around the souk in Fes, Morocco. It was summer, and the city was filled with people from all over the world squeezed into the narrow alleys of the souk. The guide knew his way around and led them easily, stopping when they wanted to explore a stand or a store. He took them to a tiny restaurant tucked away on a small pathway. He knew the owners, who didn't speak English, but that didn't matter. They were welcoming and charming and brought out trays of delicious foods for Jacqueline and Cathleen to try.

When they told their tour guide they were planning to take a train from Fes to Casablanca, he suggested that a car and driver might cost about the same as the train. He went on to say the trains were very old, not air-conditioned, and often overcrowded. Overcrowded was definitely a turnoff for them, and they asked him to check with his friend about price and availability. He called one of his fellow tour guides who had a car and asked what the price would be. Sure enough, the price was almost the same as the train, so Jacqueline and Cathleen rode in a roomy, air-conditioned minivan along the scenic foothills of the Atlas mountains, stopping at a typical Moroccan restaurant the driver knew for a delicious lunch, and then on to Casablanca.

If you plan to concentrate on scenery, you won't need a guide, except for reasons of safety in wild and remote areas. Unless you feel compelled to know the height of every mountain and the depth of every sea, you can enjoy the

Appalachian Trail or Washington State's San Juan Islands without explanation. You move at your own speed, take all the pictures you want, and stop and eat where and when you feel like it.

Other times, the guide will be the key to your sightseeing program. Find out which sites have built-in guidance, such as the Panama Canal, where the "talker" comes aboard your ship and explains everything as you sail through the locks; or the French chateaux, where they hand out copies of information in your own language. Allow enough time for Gettysburg, where buses take you on regular guided tours of the battlefields, and Williamsburg, where the buildings are attended by the knowledgeable, costumed hostesses.

Today many museums, in cities from Paris to Hiroshima, lend or rent digital recorders with commentary on the exhibits in your native language. If you're touring some U.S. or Canadian national parks, or driving from San Francisco to Monterey or from County Cork to County Clare or to and from a variety of other places, you can buy CDs that will lead you through all major sights.

Apps for many locations are now available for your mobile device. Check with your app store for available destinations. Many of them use GPS to track your journey across town or across a region.

Please refer to the section on apps in Chapter 16.

Many large cities, as far-flung as Wellington, New Zealand, and Göteborg, Sweden, provide city tours in municipal buses, and Melbourne, Australia, does it with a harbor tour on a city-owned boat. The independent travel writer can build a sightseeing program around these possibilities.

For developing countries, however, where the language and even the alphabet is often extra difficult to American travelers, where facilities are expensive, where arrangements are complex and time consuming and distances are vast, you're usually better off with a doorstep-to-doorstep guided tour.

Consider Your Special Interests

Incorporating your special interests always makes travel more meaningful. An amateur genealogist talked for months about his exciting solo trip to study at the National Archives in Washington, DC, to seek out the tombstones of his Virginia ancestors. A couple traveling in East Asia made arrangements to visit the Hong Kong orphanage supported by their church, to which they'd been donating for half a lifetime. An artist inspected photographs of the areas she intended to see, so she knew in advance which would be the most interesting scenes to paint. These special interests later contributed to their travel stories.

Do you belong to a national or international organization? Write ahead to find out what's doing along your route. Not only Rotarians and University Women, but kite fliers, square dancers, model-airplane builders, fishermen, ham-radio operators, quilters, bridge players, and people tied together by practically any concern you can name have associations with many branches. Get in touch ahead of time for a warm welcome. This kind of "getting ready" homework is not only personally rewarding—it often leads to a story.

Perhaps you'll want to join an organization especially for the trip. Depending upon your age and orientation, such groups as the American Association of Retired Persons, Parents Without Partners, the Union of Polish Women in America, the Society of Painters in Tempera, the Youth Hostels Association, the Sierra Club, the British-American Society, the Irish Georgian Society, etc., as well as your professional or trade association, your alumni group, your church affiliation, and hundreds of other possibilities can lead you to travel friendships, travel discounts, and stories with plus value. Plan far ahead and send for membership information.

If you explore the various sightseeing possibilities, taking into consideration your personal tastes and desires, where you are going, and the type of sights you will be seeing, you can plan an ideal program within the framework of available time and money.

Whether it's your money or your editor's, you'll want to take advantage of financial considerations often given to those under twenty-five, over sixty-five, married, unmarried, teachers, students, military, doctors, patients, weekday travelers, weekend travelers, skiers, bowlers, joggers, and almost anyone alive and breathing. If it's the off-season, there's a special rate. If it's the right day you can go to the museum without paying. Days of the week and hours of the day can make a difference in the price of transportation, admission, and other travel writing needs. So look out ahead of time for whatever discounts or bonuses you're entitled to. And don't hesitate to ask, "Is this your best rate?"

Line Up Your Informants

As you think about your upcoming trip and what you'll be writing about it, think first: whom do I need to talk to for the stories I'll be working on? Then line up your interviews and appointments. In some countries you'll never get to interview anyone without a letter of introduction. Sometimes consulates and embassies can help you arrange business appointments; other times you can work through a company's branch offices. But it's imperative to search out the local customs and set all the wheels in motion early.

Will the person you need to see be available? Even if you're only traveling to the next town, check on the business days and hours so you'll be able to do what you need to do while you're there. Does an annual May Day parade block downtown traffic and close most business establishments? Is Election Day a legal holiday in that town? Do you need to speak to somebody at the school board office during a week when all school functions are on half-day session? Will the store you need to research be closed for inventory? Have all the farmers you planned to interview taken off for the Apple Butter Festival?

The farther you travel, the more critical the problem becomes because your actual transportation plans grow less flexible. One writer counted his single day in Buenos Aires a total loss because the taking of the census entailed a holiday that prevented him from finding the information to complete his story. Another travel writer, visiting Venice for an assigned photo essay on mosaics, found all the crucial people and places immersed in celebrating the Feast of the Redeemer. More than one surprised journalist has discovered that all of Australia races to a standstill on Melbourne Cup Day. And Japan celebrates a handful of holidays during Golden Week.

However, sometimes these changes of plans lead to other story possibilities. Jacqueline wrote an award-winning story about the Feast of St. Anthony in Lisbon, Portugal as a result of her plane from San Francisco to Chicago being delayed, causing her to miss her connection to the Azores. She contacted her tour leader and was told to fly directly to Lisbon; the group would meet her there in two days. When she arrived Lisbon was alive with festivities celebrating St. Anthony and sardines!

Holidays: A Plus or a Minus?

Both national and international holidays, like Papua New Guinea's Thanksgiving Day in August, Japan's Respect for the Aged Day in September, Hawaii's Aloha Week in October, and the "anything goes" Oktoberfest in La Crosse, Wisconsin, can be a plus or a minus for the travel writer. She has to work around the movable feasts, too, like pre-Lenten Mardi Gras in New Orleans, Carnival in Rio, or Charro Days in Brownsville, Texas-Matamoros, Mexico, as well as Ramadan, observed by all Muslim countries with a month of daylight fasting, and Kurban-Bairam, when everything is closed for family festivities. Travel writers may avoid holidays or embrace them but should always be aware of their existence.

If you're planning to be somewhere during a holiday—Good Friday in Seville, Carnevale in Venice, the Tournament of Roses in Pasadena—and you want to go there at that time *because* that's the story you want, find out first what will be the best vantage point. Then beg, bribe, or buy your way into that vantage point. Consider, too, that you'll want to take pictures, so if there's a choice of vantage points, pick the one at a good height for picture taking, with the sun in the right direction.

Try to ask friends who've been where you're going the best way to see the event. They may tell you that at Copenhagen's Tivoli Gardens you can rent a sort of periscope that lets you look over the crowd to see what's going on. Other friends may tell you to climb the steps to the rooftop restaurant overlooking the Djemaa el Fna square in Marrakech, where, for the price of a soft drink, you can see all the action. You can look down on and photograph for free the peddlers, the snake charmers, the storytellers, the water carriers with their tinkling bells and copper cups, and the mobs of fascinated bystanders.

The seasons of the year can be important to the travel writer. Naturally, if your story involves New England's fall color, the show of rhododendrons in San Francisco's Golden Gate Park, or the tulips in Holland, you'll have to take pains to be there at the critical moment. Sometimes, it's hard to second-guess nature. What week will the cherry trees bloom? What time will the fairy penguins parade up from the sea? Do your best to obtain accurate predictions from tourist offices, chambers of commerce, local residents, and frequent travelers to the area. Human beings, on the other hand, are more predictable. In August, when the French take *their* vacations, most Parisian activities shut down or fold up; during the hot summer months many U.S. East Coast businesses work a four-day week, or shorter hours some days, or different hours.

While off-season travel has many advantages—cheaper prices, smaller crowds, warmer welcomes—it can have its disadvantages, too. The excursion boats don't travel up the Hudson to West Point or up the Thames to Greenwich; the famous restaurant may be closed; the planes, the trains, the buses will run on different, less frequent schedules. Twice a year the arrival and departure of daylight saving time can change your travel schedule. The time change can cause problems with transportation. Jacqueline once was an hour early for her train from Paris to Marseille because she didn't know daylight saving time had ended. Nailing down these specifics is part of "getting ready."

Local Customs Can Affect Travel Plans

Even days of the week make a difference. One travel writing team spent three Sunday hours restlessly pacing among the benches of a Paris train station after discovering that the 11:00 a.m. train to Chartres didn't leave at 11:00 on *Sundays*. Another couple spent a long, hungry day aboard a Kuala Lumpur–Singapore train. Now they know—the dining car isn't always attached to the train on *Sundays*. In New Zealand and Australia you could starve on a weekend while the waiters and the dishwashers are out surfing and sailing, and if you insist on eating in a restaurant, you're going to pay extra for it. Your pre-trip homework will reveal that in those countries and in many others, as well as many major U.S. cities, Sabbath laws regarding the serving of alcoholic beverages dictate what time the restaurants will be open. What day *is* the Sabbath? In Muslim countries it's Friday. In Israel it's Saturday, beginning at sundown on Friday. Not only are all banks, business offices, stores, and restaurants closed, but transportation is limited as well. The wise travel writer confirms this information and takes it into consideration when getting ready to go. Museums all over the world tend to be closed on Mondays. Except some are closed on Tuesdays. Or Wednesdays. Or Sundays. A California journalist making a trip to New York for a special show at the American Museum of Natural History heard the museum was open Mondays but checked out their Website to make sure. It was a good thing—the Museum *is* open Mondays, but not until noon. Will you be doing research at libraries, museums, archaeological digs? These often require letters of introduction before they let you through the gates. Ask the most eminent scholars you know to attest to the excellence of your character and the importance of your mission.

Get Your Tickets Well in Advance

In some countries it's essential to have a "Reader's Ticket" to work at the national library, the public record office, the national maritime museum, or other research sources. Save on-trip time by sending ahead for these permissions. An audience with the pope? It's easier if you write ahead to: Bishop's Office for United States Visitors to the Vatican. If you're Roman Catholic, include a letter from your priest or bishop, or ask your local parish to help arrange the audience.

Whether it's for a story or just for fun, tickets to a special festival or event can add another dimension to your trip. But the Salzburg and Bayreuth festivals sell out a year in advance, and the every-ten-years Passion play at Oberammergau is reserved long ahead of time. Whether you're going to the opera in Santa Fe, the Mozart Festival in Burlington, Vermont, or the Old Fiddlers' Convention in Galax, Virginia, check availability and order tickets online or write for tickets as soon as you know your plans.

Do you want to review a Broadway show? Sometimes you can send a check and an SASE to the theater months in advance. (That's how Louise happened to have six first-class seats for a hit musical. By the time she saw the show, the tickets were selling for many times what she had paid.) Or you can go to the TKTS booth near Times Square for discounted tickets the day of the performance, but be prepared to stand in line. They open at 3:00 p.m. (earlier on matinee days), but right after breakfast the line straggles out to the street. Occasionally you can go up to the box office a few minutes before showtime and find turned-in tickets at the box office price. Or you can call or show up at a ticket broker's headquarters and pay a surcharge—which may be very substantial.

A new app for TKTS has a comprehensive show search where you'll find what is happening onstage in New York City—including show descriptions, performance schedules, theater locations, accessibility information, and links to official show Websites.

You Can Communicate Efficiently and Economically

Your telephone can be your passport to efficiency and economy. In big countries like the United States, Canada, and Australia, an off-peak call from west to east or an early-evening call from east to west still catches people during the business day. This often works for country-to-country calls, too, so the writer needing a telephone interview or wanting to make an appointment or check a fact with someone several time zones away can call at the cheapest rate.

Your smartphone may not work outside of North America, but many of the cellular phone companies offer service that includes international calling features. Check with your provider for availability and details. It's also possible to make an overseas cell phone rental arrangement with other companies such as Cellhire.

Email is a useful way to communicate. It's fast and easy to send and receive data. Even if you don't take your own equipment, you'll find what you need to use at one of the ever-present **cyber cafés**, and most hotels have business centers where they offer computer access, some free and others with a small fee. A **USB flash drive** is a handy way to store email messages and data. Or you can save the email and forward it to your own email address.

Text messaging is gaining in popularity to quickly and immediately send information back and forth. Check with your service provider for costs of sending text messages from where you will be located.

Cross the "T" in Document

What kind of documents must you have to travel where you're going? Passport? Visa? Tourist card? Apply for whatever you need in plenty of time, and follow the instructions carefully in filling out the forms. Check and recheck to make sure you have everything you need. Many times we've seen people in the airport prevented from boarding the plane because some "i" wasn't dotted or "t" wasn't crossed on their travel documents—or they had looked up requirements for the wrong country. (Incidentally, allow plenty of time at airports for inspection of those documents when you're traveling internationally.)

87

Jot down the numbers of your travel papers, as well as those of your credit cards and airline tickets, and put them in a different place from the originals. You might even wish to photocopy them. Saving the information on your computer or on a USB flash drive is also a good idea. If anything is lost or stolen, you'll have an easier time replacing it if you have the number.

Obtaining travel documents is now easier than ever for millions of Americans planning international travel. VitalChek, the leading birth certificate processor, and Zierer Visa Service (ZVS), the leading passport and visa expediter, have combined forces to make ordering passports, visas, and birth certificates as simple as going on the Internet. Go to OfficialTravelDocuments. com and PassportVisaExpress.com for assistance with all types of passports; they also can expedite visa applications to over three hundred countries.

When you visit most foreign countries you'll need a passport, and for some you'll need a visa, as well. If you travel a great deal you can apply for a forty-eight-page passport at no additional cost, so you'll have more room for the official stamps of entry and exit. If your plans change en route, don't worry—you can obtain the necessary visas in some other country as long as the one you're planning to visit has representation there.

Throughout your trip you'll often be required to identify yourself on various documents, and the phrasing of the information may be more significant than you think. In some countries, listing yourself as "journalist" or "travel writer" is like waving a red flag. Consider the political situation in some Third World nations. Perhaps it's better to stick with "businessman," "housewife," or "retired." Sometimes this becomes a sexist matter. When Louise and her husband debarked from a ship in Chile a few years ago, the immigration people wanted to know all of the *men's* professions— even those who were retired had to come up with something to satisfy the questioners. But the *women* were never interrogated. On each woman's debarkation card, beside the Spanish word "ocupación," was written the English word "laborer"!

You may wish to describe yourself as a "student" on your passport. Catherine Elwood did that when she was studying for her Ph.D. at Stanford University. One immigration inspector took a second look at her papers, Then a second look at her forty-year-old face. "Student?" he muttered. Then he looked her straight in the eye. "*Still?*" he inquired.

If you can prove you have been a full-time student during the current academic year, regardless of your age, apply for an International Student Identity Card (ISIC). Bring your current student ID card, a small picture, and a modest fee to a regional office of the Council on International Educational Exchange (CIEE), available on most college campuses, or send it to the main office. Allow at least three weeks for processing.

Identified students become eligible for student-priced charter flights and discounted air, rail, boat, and bus fares, reduced-rate car rentals, museum entries, tours, accommodations at student hostels, welcome services, and special travel insurance, as well as a variety of helpful publications.

If you study only part time and don't qualify for the ISIC, you may still find that describing yourself as a student will open many doors. Mature researchers Norm and Rose Grabstein, while working for advanced degrees in archaeology, found that writing in advance for permission to see restricted sites and beginning the letter, "We are students," usually led to the special permission they sought. When they asked to tour France's closed-off Lascaux caves, the French Conservation Service not only granted permission but warned that visitors have to walk through disinfectant to protect the art and suggested they wear expendable shoes and clothing.

Your Appearance Can Be Important

As a travel writer you should *always* plan to wear clothing you don't care too much about. But the *type* of clothes can be important when you're searching for a story abroad. In many countries clothing customs require covering some specific part of the anatomy. In Saudi Arabia, women who do not conceal their arms and legs risk fines, imprisonment, or expulsion. In Jerusalem's ultra-Orthodox Mea Sherarim district they risk stoning and spitting. At the Vatican a Swiss Guard refuses admission to women considered immodestly dressed. (Formerly a nun posted at the main door to Saint Peter's lent plastic raincoats to women with bare arms and legs, but too many took the raincoats as souvenirs.)

It's all right for women to wear long pants at the Vatican, but at the Meteora, the cliff-top monasteries of Greece, they must wear skirts or dresses. To enter the African republic of Malawi, those skirts or dresses must cover the knees. Malawi, incidentally, is one of the many countries that imposes its own grooming standards on the length of male visitors' hair and beards. If immigration officials consider them too long, the airport barber stands ready with the shears.

Golf courses and tennis clubs all over the world are becoming increasingly strict about players' apparel. If you show up in cutoff jeans and a tank top with an advertising message, they won't let you play.

Men must cover their heads at Jerusalem's Wailing Wall, as well as at any Orthodox synagogue, and paper skullcaps are usually provided. Women, however, should come prepared with scarves of their own. At the Wailing Wall, married women of all faiths cover their heads, as do all women, married and single, in the churches of many other religions.

You should think ahead, too, to the parts of you that will be uncovered while traveling. At Muslim mosques and Buddhist temples all over the world, as well as many other buildings in Asia, you'll be required to remove your shoes. You will, of course, inquire in advance about climate and activities that would influence your clothing choice. Try to take clothes that won't make you too conspicuous and outfits and separates that will do double or triple duty for many kinds of occasions.

Your pre-trip research will not only help you conform to local dress customs but will also alert you to differences in manners and mores you'll want to observe. Whether it's a matter of kissing the hand, kissing on both cheeks, arriving early, arriving late, eating with your fingers, or sending flowers to your hostess, you as a travel writer will want to blend into the local environment.

Attend Carefully to Pre-Trip Details

It shouldn't be necessary, but maybe it is, to remind the travel writer to try out *everything* at home. Break in your new shoes. Make sure your alarm clock works reliably. Does your laptop do everything it should? How about your mobile devices? Do you have extra or rechargeable batteries (and a charger that works in the countries you will be visiting) for electronic equipment? Do you have the proper plug adapter for the electrical current? Do you have plenty of memory chips/smart cards for your **digital camera**?

If you plan to do any shopping on your trip, think about which brand of computer, photographic lens, binoculars, wristwatch, etc., is most easily serviced back home. Will you really know a good buy when you see one? How much duty will you have to pay? And what time do the shopkeepers take their siestas?

If you'll be driving in another country, get your International Driving Permit from the American Automobile Association, which is valid for one year, and costs fifteen dollars. Two passport-size photos are needed. If you don't have any photos, they'll take your picture for a small extra charge. Usually, ten or fifteen minutes takes care of the whole procedure. If you're an auto club member, inquire as to what membership privileges carry over to other countries: Emergency road service? Legal advice? Lists of club offices? Estimates of road conditions?

The American Automobile Association Plus membership offers emergency medical transportation coverage as well as twenty-four-hour emergency traveler's assistance, and other travel benefits, worldwide. In the British Isles, where U.S. auto club memberships *are* honored, the British Automobile Association not only patrols the highways and byways but also provides the driver with information about what times big trucks and buses jam the narrow, winding roads so you can avoid them.

The travel writer at the wheel does all he can to ensure against an empty fuel tank. If your gas tank registers even half-full and you see a service station, stop and fill your tank. Most gas stations now have twenty-four-hour access. By using your credit or ATM card, you can fill up at any hour of the day or night. Be sure to check which type of fuel your car runs on.

If you're driving your own car, of course you'll make sure it's in top running condition before you take off. If you're driving in another state or another country, look into speed limits, traffic rules, etc. Trucks, campers, motorcycles, bicycles (and probably burros) are also subject to certain regulations and restrictions, so find out what they are.

Check with your insurance carrier about what additional auto insurance you may need. Check, too, about health and accident insurance, trip cancellation insurance, baggage insurance, and perhaps a floater on your camera equipment.

At home or abroad, arrange for good maps. But don't be misled by them. Sometimes what appears to be an easy hundred-mile drive is really two hundred miles of winding mountain path. Learn the names of major towns along your route and also your compass directions—your particular destination may not appear on the highway signs. A GPS is a good way to map out your destination. Most rental cars are now equipped with them, and many mobile devices have a built-in GPS. There are many of these devices available that can be programmed for the country you will be traveling in, so check with your service provider for details. There are also an increasing number of apps available for countries and cities around the world. It's also a good idea to obtain good country and city maps. Then you'll be able to mark the path you took down the mountain at Delphi, the sites of different treasures, and exactly where you were standing when you took that dramatic picture with the wide-angle lens.

About Matters of Money

In addition to your purely professional planning, it's important to know, too, that local customs vary greatly as to when the banks are open. ATMs are readily available all over the world, but some out-of-the-way places might have very few, and some none at all. You can easily research worldwide ATM locations through Google.

Give thought to how you will handle your travel funds when you're getting ready to go. ATM cards and debit cards can be very helpful to carry in your wallet. The major advantage to using your ATM card is that there are many banks with automatic teller windows that will allow you to withdraw money in the local currency. Many are open twenty-four hours a day. Check with your bank about the service charges, usually minimal, for these transactions, as well as the limit of cash withdrawals allowed per day.

It's a good idea to carry more than one ATM card. Jacqueline was using a bank ATM in Lisbon, Portugal, on a Sunday afternoon. The ATM released the amount of money she requested, but when she pressed the button to return her card, nothing happened. She pressed again—nothing. She went to a nearby police station and in halting Portuguese explained what had happened. The police officers were very friendly and sympathetic, but said there wasn't anything they could do. She would have to return the next day when the bank was open to retrieve her card. Luckily she wasn't leaving town until after lunch the next day so it was easy for her to return to the bank. The moral of that story is: if at all possible, only use ATMs when the bank is open. If Jacqueline was unable to return to the bank, she would have had to cancel her card. That's why it's important to have an alternate source of funds or another ATM account.

Let your bank know you will be traveling, including destinations and the period of time you plan to be away. Some banks have been known to freeze accounts when transactions are made far away from your home.

If you're applying for a new credit card, allow plenty of time to receive it before you leave for your trip. If it's an old credit card, and you are suddenly charging expensive air tickets and cruise deposits, be sure to call the company and explain even though it's within your credit limit. Otherwise, they may think it's a scam and refuse the credit. Mention, also, any foreign countries from which you expect to make charges. Leave some money in your checking account and take along your checkbook, too. Some establishments give discounts for cash or checks.

Can You Learn the Language?

If you're planning an overseas trip, you may want to learn, or brush up on, a foreign language. At least listen to CDs or a language app every day, and practice your pronunciation. While every travel advice writer emphasizes the importance of learning "please," "thank you," and "Where is the bathroom?" in all the languages of your itinerary, it's also important to learn directional terms. Although non-English-speaking people may think they know the difference between "right" and "left," it's best to check the directions by repeating them in their language. How do you say "around the corner" in German? "Fourteen kilometers" in French? "Down the hill toward the sea" in Greek? "Back to the Imperial Hotel" in Japanese?

If you'll be interviewing somebody in a foreign country, even if that person speaks English, you'd do well to look up ahead of time translations for the key words you'll want. Look up words you'll need at the front desk of your hotel, at the camera repair shop, at a restaurant. English is a difficult language, and often people who have mastered a few words don't really speak or understand as much as we think they do. There are a wide assortment of foreign language dictionaries and phrase books available at your local library or bookstores, as well as foreign language apps available. Hal Gieseking suggests also learning the words in every language for "Is the service charge included?" Then you'll know whether to tip the waiter and the housemaid the traditional amount or just leave a little spare change.

There are many voice translation apps available, which can be much easier to use than flipping through your language dictionaries to find the words you want. Simply Google "language translation apps" for a variety of links. One of the excellent ones is Jibbigo. When you speak into the microphone on your mobile device, the program translates your speech into the language of choice and actually speaks back in that language.

How Healthy Are You?

It would be foolish not to candidly consider your physical condition as you get ready for your trip. Writers are often sedentary people. If you sit at a keyboard day after day, you're likely not to have much stamina in the legs and feet. If you've hardly walked around the block all winter, your heart, lungs, and muscles will protest when you have to hurry between widely separated airline counters. There's a lot of walking involved in any trip—far more than the writer may be accustomed to—so you have to begin early to get ready. Serena Bartlett, author of the *Grass Routes* guides, advises that

> preparing physically for travel can be as important as planning itineraries
> or packing your bags. Even if you're off to research meditation retreats in
> Japan, considering the experience ahead and how it will be different from
> your regular activities is crucial. That's not to say you'll need to shine up
> your crystal ball, but some forethought and exercise can go a long way
> to increase your comfort and flexibility in new situations. For me, travel
> writing has a lot to do with flexibility—being able to embark on the
> adventure ahead without too many barriers. Don't let yourself get in your
> own way by skipping some kind of training—let's call it exhaustion pre-
> vention insurance.

> Start by sketching out your trip. If it is a long trip will you have to haul
> your bags to multiple locations? Are there several transit connections?
> Will you be based in one place or moving beds every night? The transi-
> tions in travel can be the most laborious, but a day in a travel writer's
> life isn't necessarily a breeze either. One day I began by interviewing a
> baker before 6:00 a.m., checking out the scene at two popular parks
> before work hours (and when there was good light for photos), sampled
> dishes from three breakfast spots, completely navigated—by foot—two
> rather dynamic city neighborhoods, joined in a flash mob at the other
> end of the city, talked with a local journalist from the city paper, jaunted
> through an art museum, sampled three more eateries, toured the inside

of a historic theater, went to a pub and finished off with some nightlife exploration. There are no two days alike, and certainly few that are this hectic, but if I hadn't prepared for all the action I would have missed out on opportunities to further understand and discover the environment around me.

To ready yourself for a research trip start by amping up your daily walking. If you're the right-brained type you can get a pedometer to track it. If you can, walk in the morning and at dusk—getting into a pattern helps. Try at least a mile each outing if that's realistic for your schedule. As the trip gets closer I start carrying a small packed backpack with me. Begin your walk or run with a warm-up routine to get your heart rate elevated and your blood flowing and finish off with stretches to avoid soreness and inflexibility. Start and finish your day with stretches while on your trip as well. This can even help dampen the impact of shifting time zones. I find that endurance activities like this best match the rigors of big trips, but doing activities you love can also be part of the regime. Swimming is my thing, and planning for a trip helps remind me to get in the pool. If you run or climb or do yoga—whatever form of movement excites you will help in preparation.

If you intend to carry a heavy purse, camera case, or flight bag, haul it around at home, gradually adding items, so your arm and shoulder muscles won't be screaming with pain your first day of sightseeing. If you'll be bicycling, dancing, or rock-climbing on your trip, practice before you go. For really rigorous trips you need rigorous training.

Diane LeBow is a well-known travel writer who often goes to exotic places, and has trained Morgan show horses, ridden a camel across the desert, and scuba dived around the world. A mountain biker and a backpacker, she says, "The key, as for any of us, whether travelers or not, is consistent and reasonable physical activity and eating habits, not simply before the plane departs. Each day I walk for at least thirty minutes or use the elliptical machine at the gym (which gives a total body as well as aerobic workout and doesn't strain the joints), or swim along with water stretches and exercises. I try to practice interval training, i.e. really push myself for a few minutes at a time until I've raised my heart rate, with any of these exercises. I eat pretty healthfully, limiting carbs and sugars."

If your trip is to an exotic location, extensive, and/or physically challenging, arrange for a complete physical examination and obtain all required shots in time to recover by departure day. See your dentist, too. But don't let him fill, extract, or work on a root canal within twelve hours of an air trip. As a Midwestern dentist explains, "Whenever a tooth is opened, a small bubble of air may enter. Then that trapped gas expands as you're airborne. Changes in atmospheric pressure can leave you stifling screams of agony."

Do you worry that you may need a doctor while away from home? In the United States, just do a Google search for the county medical society. In foreign countries, American clubs usually have lists of U.S.-trained doctors and dentists.

If you have a need for regular lab tests, don't let that stop you from going on your planned trip. You can get your tests performed easily and quickly in many foreign cities.

A few years ago, Jacqueline's blood had to be tested every two weeks to make sure the blood-thinning drug she was taking was doing its job. She was planning on being in Ireland for just over two weeks, so Tourism Ireland provided her with the name and address of a hospital in Dublin that could run a blood test. She showed up at the hospital with her doctor's request and was in and out of the lab in no time. The results were faxed to her doctor and were on his desk the next day.

Much of the world provides free health care for its citizens, so, depending on where you go, you may or may not even get billed for the work. If you visit a pharmacy or private doctor, you probably will be charged for services, however.

But it might be wise to be prepared with a list of well-trained English-speaking physicians on twenty-four-hour call. IAMAT, a non-profit organization, not only supplies lists of qualified physicians, but its twenty-four climate charts cover the globe, detailing specific climatic conditions throughout the year, advising on clothing, and outlining the state of sanitation and water safety.

AAA has Medivac insurance through its Plus program.

Travel Assistance International helps with all kinds of problems before, during, and after your trip.

Medic Alert protects you by alerting others to information about your special conditions, medications, or allergies. The organization sells identification bracelets and necklaces that specify the wearer has a medical condition that might not be apparent and provides a twenty-four-hour number to call for the patient's medical history.

A traveling doctor contends that poison ivy, poison oak, and poison sumac have "ruined more vacations than the combined effects of bad weather, missed travel connections, and inconsiderate guests." Learning to recognize—and avoid—these is another precautionary pre-trip preparation. Find out some of the other botanical hazards in the area you'll be visiting. Are there animal and insect hazards, too? Those travel writers who are extremely allergic to the bites of bees, mosquitoes, sand fleas, or other common insects will want to inquire carefully about the area's fauna. It's a good idea to discuss these issues with your physician before leaving on your trip, in order to get advice and medication that would be needed in case of a crisis.

Dealing with Jet Lag

While travel writers often require treatment for itchy eruptions, tired backs, over-walked feet, gastrointestinal disorders, respiratory complaints, heart and blood pressure problems, accidents, sunburn, insect bites, and heat exposure, the complaint you're most likely to have is jet lag.

Although there are many hints on how to prevent jet lag, nobody has really found the answer. If you cross more than two or three time zones, you'll feel it. Don't add boredom to fatigue. During long airport waits and endless rides, bring books to read, either hard copies or downloaded onto your mobile device. There are a huge number of games and movies available. Some people like to catch up on email or work on their laptop computers. Survivors of many cases of jet lag and auto ennui advise the traveler to get up or get out and walk around as often as possible. If you're driving, plan to stop every couple of hours, whether anybody's tired or not, and take along some nutritious snacks and something to drink. Don't try to drive more than eight hours a day, and quit before your reactions begin to slow down. You can't take a bottle of water through security at the airport, but you can bring an empty bottle and fill it once you pass security. It's very important to stay hydrated on a long trip.

Plan for Your Comfort

The travel writer should consider creature comforts in getting ready to go on a trip. Find out in advance how late your hotel will hold your reservation. Should you guarantee the charges on your credit card? And inquire about checkout time. Does the tropical beach resort shove you out at 9:00 a.m. so you're sitting all day in your traveling clothes, waiting for your evening plane?

Or will your room's previous occupants remain legally staked out until late in the afternoon while you're arriving at dawn, exhausted by jet lag? You may not have much choice in the selection of a hotel room, but if there is a choice, opt for the quiet one. Spurn the room with a door that connects it to the adjacent room (television and party sounds seep through the cracks) and the room that opens directly on the pool area (you'll hear the night owls swimming at midnight and the early birds trying to beat the dawn).

If swimming and tennis are important to your story, make sure the pool and the courts will be in service while you're there. Mealtimes are worth knowing. Is seven a normal dinner hour at your destination? In Ireland it's too late. In Spain it's too early. If you're the kind of writer who can't work on an empty stomach, important pre-trip inquiries will be about food service on trains, motels with twenty-four-hour restaurants, and meals served on flights.

If you have special food needs, find out in advance what kind of restaurants you should look for.

Many of the airlines no longer serve complimentary meals on some of their routes. Be sure to check on food service before boarding the aircraft. Some carriers sell boxed meals on board, and many food outlets set up kiosks near boarding areas to sell "take aboard" food items. It's also possible to pack a meal before leaving home. Just make sure you discard any uneaten fruits before leaving the plane. Many countries have restrictions about bringing in fresh food products. Check this out before you go and plan accordingly.

However, if your carrier does have food service, let the airlines know of any special dietary requirements when you make your reservations, then double check twenty-four hours before you leave. They'll provide you with an ulcer patient's meal, a low-calorie meal, a vegetarian or diabetic meal, hamburgers and hot dogs for your children, or whatever else you need.

Are You a Frequent Flyer?
Be sure you're using your frequent flyer miles to your best advantage. Make an overall plan for them. If you belong to several programs, should you consolidate? Do you have some miles that expire this year? Would you have a more comfortable trip if you used your miles to upgrade to business class or first class? It's generally considered that frequent flyer miles are worth about two cents each, so act accordingly.

If you are charging expensive travel costs to a credit card that gives frequent flyer miles, inquire as to whether there is a limit on the miles that can be awarded for any one purchase. If your credit card has that limit, it may be better to split your charge over several dates or several credit cards. Do you have a favorite airplane seat? Obtain the chart from the airline (these are often available on the airline's Website or check SeatGuru.com), and reserve your seat either online or by telephone several weeks in advance, if possible. The window seat is best if you're taking pictures, but the aisle assignment may give you a little more legroom. Try to avoid seats against the bulkhead that don't recline fully. If you occupy a seat in an emergency row, you must be prepared to assist in case of emergency.

Any time you can avoid a connecting flight, do so. The chances of missing your connection, losing your luggage, or just plain hassling escalate each time you change planes. Check and double check whether your flight is non-stop or whether it's direct, which involves a connection. Airlines often use the same flight number for the connecting planes—but it's a connection, just the same.

Weather, as we know, can be crucial to the traveler. While the weather likely to greet you at your destination is important, it's even more important to find out what the weather is like at your plane's point of origin and at any point where it may touch down en route. Winds in Chicago, snow in Boston, or even an unusually hot day in Los Angeles can cause significant delays, which may affect your ongoing plans. If you can avoid flying during the busiest flight hours of a holiday weekend, you'll be glad you did. And you'll be glad, too, if you can arrange to leave and arrive at some time other than rush hour on the highway outside a big city airport.

Most major airlines have apps you can download to your mobile device to aid you with flight status, terminal, and gate information; download mobile boarding passes; and get a variety of other handy information.

Jacqueline's friend John told her he was flying to New York from California, and he used his iPhone to download an app from Delta Airlines. He said it was easy to check the status of his flight, download a boarding pass, and pay a lower fee for his bag. All he did at the terminal was hand over his bag and let them scan the bar code on his iPhone.

Be Ready to Field Questions

Most places you travel, a brigade of well-wishers stands ready to help the travel writer with personal or professional problems. But sometimes when people discover you're a travel writer, they want *you* to help *them*. They expect you to be expert in many fields and know something about anything they might ask you. Sometimes they have hard questions they've been waiting to ask people for months, and when you show up, they expect you to answer.

So one of the most important pre-trip preparations is getting ready to answer the questions people will ask you. Whether it's in the next room or across nine time zones, the people you meet will be interested in what it's like where *you* came from. A little thought and a little homework will make it possible for you to present logical and informative answers. Some questions, of course, like those about power shortages, First Amendment rights, racial discrimination, inflation, strikes, unemployment, sometimes don't *have* any easy answers. But try to be prepared so you can present the facts without floundering.

Pondering answers to probable questions is part of getting ready for your trip. So is planning your sightseeing program. And if you set up your business appointments in advance and arrange for your professional and personal comfort when you're getting ready, it will pay off in pleasure and productivity once you start traveling. Preplanning makes it possible for you to find plus values, and when all the pieces fit together for you as a traveler, you can begin to act like a travel writer. So think ahead, get ready, and *go*!

CHAPTER 7

Hitting the Road

There are several things a travel writer must carry—even if you have to leave behind your toothbrush and clean underwear.

The first necessity is *something to show you're a writer*. Take along membership cards to travel or writing organizations, a press card if you have one, and a walletful of printed business cards that will serve to introduce you as a travel writer or journalist, especially if you're going overseas, where business cards are an even more important appurtenance than in North America. You'll be surprised how many doors those little pasteboards will open—everything from the press box at the horse races to a private tour of a government child-care center.

With professional credentials you take on a professional air and encourage professional respect.

Don't Forget Your Camera

The second essential tool is your camera. Now you may be thinking, "Oh, my camera isn't very good—it doesn't have all those fancy gadgets," or "I'm not very good—I'm not much of a photographer," or "I don't have time to take all those pictures—I need to see what's going on!" Carry a camera anyway. Not only do photographs help you sell what you write but also even if they aren't of salable quality, they'll help you write your story. The very act of taking a picture forces you to focus sharply, to concentrate on what you're looking at, to see it more clearly. And when you get home you'll discover details you might have forgotten. Jacqueline didn't remember, for instance, the way the sardine scales looked iridescent, almost translucent, as the fisherman held them up for her to inspect.

She was reminded when she downloaded her photos and saw that she had captured the colorful fish scales.

While you don't want photography to overwhelm the trip experience, the advantages of taking pictures far outweigh the disadvantages. You don't need to be an expert photographer to strengthen your memories of a trip through photographs. In most cases, a modern camera demands only that you point it at the subject and hold your breath for an instant to keep the camera still as you shoot. The camera does the rest.

You don't have to invest thousands of dollars in photographic equipment. A medium-priced camera, even operated by a beginner, can provide salable illustrations. Even the cheapest disposable camera, operated by a beginner, will provide useful pictures to help you recapture the feeling of where you have been.

Digital cameras have pretty much taken over from film cameras these days. They vary in price, and their features can be confusing. If you are going to buy one, make sure it has at least 5.0 megapixels. Many digital cameras are so tiny they easily fit into your pocket or handbag. They have the added advantage of being able to display your images immediately so you can make the necessary changes to the format if you aren't happy with your results. Small digital-media cards, which can hold numerous images, are a wonderful alternative to carting around multiple canisters of film. For the more advanced photographer, all major manufacturers offer more sophisticated digital cameras. Many have the same features and benefits as film cameras. Do a bit of research before buying and consider your needs and talents before making your purchase.

Take time before you leave home to learn about your new camera and how to use it. Just make sure to pack the manual along with extra regular or rechargeable batteries (don't forget the charger that works in the country you are visiting) and a few media cards.

Jacqueline knows a colleague who photographs his suitcase from several angles just in case it gets lost. Then he can show the people at the lost baggage desk what the bag(s) look like.

Videos are wonderful, of course, and the cameras are lighter and less expensive than they used to be. You will have to decide whether the extra weight and expense will give you enough extra pleasure and enough additional exposure as a first-rate travel writer.

(See Chapter 14 for further photography advice and information.)

Take Along a Recorder

The third indispensable item in the travel writer's luggage is a small, lightweight recorder, or a recorder attachment for your mobile device that is capable of voice or surrounding-sound recording. Most mobile devices have a recorder built in. There are even mobile devices that can translate spoken word into written word using an app called Dragon. (For information on apps, please Chapter 16.) Our willingness to tell the microphone more than we'd ever put on paper makes a recording device very handy.

Don't forget, though, to take brief, on-scene notes so you'll remember what to tell the recorder. It's better yet to take the recorder along when you're sightseeing, and develop the habit of dictating into it everything you're seeing and everything you know about it. You'll never have to wonder later: How high are the foothills? Is the church on the same street as the school, or around the corner? Why did the ship founder on the rocks? How many people can play on the golf course? When did they serve the sherbet—before or after the meat?

Always tell your recorder the answers to the reporter's traditional Five Ws—*who, what, when, where, why*—and add the *how*. You can, of course, record the sightseeing guide's complete spiel, if you like, and if the guide has no objection. But keep in mind, voices in the open air do not carry as well as voices indoors, and voices with strong accents will reproduce with the accents exaggerated. So perhaps you'll want some written notes, too. Do take the time to mention on the recorder where you are and identify the person you are talking with or the name of the street where the street sounds are coming from. Certainly you will use your recorder to capture street sounds, as native music, the yodelers, the bagpipers, the church bells, the muezzins' voices calling from the minarets, all come to life again when you replay your recordings. It's a good idea to take it along to interviews you've scheduled along the way—asking for permission to record, of course. Here, too, it will be easier to remember what the historian said, what the fisherman said, what the bank president said, and what the lace-maker said, if you have it recorded rather than trying to unscramble it from scribbled notes.

One man used his mobile device recorder and camera to great advantage when violence erupted in Egypt. He was caught in the gunfire and the bombings, which he was able to record. He also dictated a description of his plight and, later, of his dramatic rescue. Then he uploaded the photos, transcribed the spoken data, and emailed them to a network newscaster in exchange for a substantial sum.

Even if the information on the recorder itself is not salable, it may provide you with deeper insights and endless enjoyment.

You can download foreign language apps to your mobile devices. They can be great for supplementing the refresher course you've been studying. But if you're in a country where English is often garbled and directions are complex—a country like Thailand, for instance—have the hotel concierge or a knowledgeable guide dictate the directions for how to get where you're going in his own language. Then you can play the directions back for the cab driver or someone on the street that is trying to help you. Also be sure to have dictated the name of your hotel and how to find it.

As mentioned in Chapter 6, there are apps for your mobile device that will speak the translations out loud.

Travel Diary or Journal

A travel diary or journal is essential. Some journalists use small notebooks to jot down information, ideas, and experiences as they go along. Others use fancy writing journals. Jacqueline likes to use a 6" by 8 ½" spiral-bound notebook with lined pages in which she pastes her itinerary, important facts, phone numbers, addresses, etc. She carries her notebook wherever she goes on the trip so she can easily jot down information or make small sketches of interesting details that she sees along the way. In the back of the notebook she pastes an envelope about the same size as the book so she can insert business cards, receipts, and ticket stubs.

Special Needs of Travel Writers

If your story is to grow out of your backpacking, mule riding, or wagon-training trip, you'll need to take along the appropriate equipment. If skate-boarding, house boating, motorcycling, or caravanning is your style, you'll need to be outfitted still differently. And if you're thinking of taking your four-wheel drive into the bush, you may want to follow the advice of Michael Bargo, Jr., who suggests in *Four Wheeler* that you carry along "all the spare parts you know how to repair." Every travel writer must take the supplies he needs for his own distinct traveling interests as well as the more general items we all find essential. Here is a checklist of things pertinent to the travel writer's trip:

1. *Mobile device.* A mobile device can be a smartphone/computing device, or an electronic notebook/tablet, typically having a display screen with touch input and/or a miniature keyboard. These devices can eliminate the need for taking along your computer, a recorder, and piles of paper research materials. You can also download apps.

   What's an app? *App* is short for "application," which in this case refers to a software application—in other words, a software program. But an app is not just any old software program—it's a special type of software program and typically refers to software used on a smart-phone or mobile device such as an iPhone, BlackBerry, **iPad**, or Android phone.

There are hundreds of apps available, from foreign word translators to walks around different cities. For more on apps, please go to Chapter 16.

2. *Assignment sheet.* Don't laugh! In the confusion of taking off, it's easy to forget which editors said "yes" to what, and which ones said "maybe." You probably have ideas of your own about what trip stories you'll surely write, and you'll want to keep an eye out for the stories in which editors expressed interest, but when it comes to arranging your travel time this sheet will ensure you're allowing enough for the firm assignments.

3. *Itinerary.* Unless it's a real "spur-of-the-moment" excursion, have several copies of your itinerary distributed among your luggage. Put a copy in the casing of your luggage tags, including hotel names and dates—it might prevent your lost luggage from being sent home at the very beginning of your trip. Jacqueline emails her itinerary to herself and leaves it in her in-box so she can access it in case of emergency.

4. *Address list.* Addresses (street and email) and telephone numbers of those people you plan to call or see on your trip and those you may need to call or write to at home. These can easily be stored on your mobile device.

5. *Tickets, vouchers, and confirmations.* Check, and check again, to be sure you have your tickets for transportation, theater, sports events, or whatever else you've arranged. Check on your vouchers for lodging, food, sightseeing tours, or other items you may have prepaid for and your confirmed reservations for everything from the Uffizi Gallery in Florence to the campsite at Yosemite.

   Many airlines allow one to download boarding passes to mobile devices, saving the worry about misplacing paper tickets and vouchers.

6. *Documents.* Your photo identification, press pass if you have one, and credit cards as well as membership cards, essential health records, letters of introduction, and whatever else you need. Notify your bank if you'll be using your ATM card overseas—a series of withdrawals from unexpected places may cause enough suspicion to have them block your account. And be sure to take along the Entertainment Card appropriate to your travel area. You've probably already used it for discounts on your hotel reservations, but you'll want it for meal discounts, too.

7. *Travel literature.* Condense all pertinent information into the margins of one guidebook. Then tear out and discard any parts of the guidebook that don't apply to where you're going. There's no use carting along South America when you're only visiting Chile and Peru. If you arc using a bor-

rowed guidebook, photocopy the sections that are relevant to your trip. Don't forget, though, to take along those city and country maps you've been studying. There are a fast-growing number of apps with information about many travel destinations, along with points of interest as well as hotel and restaurant recommendations.

8. *Postcards and snapshots.* The people you meet enjoy seeing pictures of your town, neighborhood, house, family, pets, car, and holiday celebrations. These are easily downloaded to your mobile device. Books about your area, as well as the postcards, become treasured gifts.

9. *Small change.* Regardless of the financial plans you make with debit cards, regardless of what country you're in, always begin each day with a pocketful of small local change so you won't be paying ten times the price for a newspaper or have the cab driver tell you he can't change a twenty-dollar bill or have to choose between tipping five cents or two dollars for a five-dollar service.

10. *Alarm clock.* Bring this especially if you distrust hotels' wake-up systems or stay where they don't provide that service. Jacqueline, her sister Judy, and another friend were taking the night train from Paris to Saint Raphael in the south of France and missed their stop because the night porter forgot to wake them in time. Judy had slept in her clothes, so she was able to grab a couple of their suitcases and get off the train before it started to move on. Jacqueline and her friend were left half dressed and cursing their bad luck and that porter. They were able to get off the train in Cannes and take another back to Saint Raphael, where Judy was anxiously waiting. Now Jacqueline always travels with a small battery powered clock, but is slowly getting used to relying on her mobile device as an alarm.

11. *Flashlight.* This is very important if you awaken in a strange hotel room or at a strange campground, disoriented, in the middle of the night. It's also important when you sightsee in caves, catacombs, and other dim areas like Egypt's Valley of the Nobles, where the illumination—sunlight ricocheting off a pocket mirror—barely permits you to see the frescoes *with* your flashlight. Take along a pen flashlight, too, so you can jot down your thoughts in a darkened theater or write up your middle-of-the-night inspiration. A small portable book light (with a clip that attaches to your book) is also a good idea. It can double as a flashlight if needed. Traveling by car in North America? Tuck a hundred-watt bulb or Tensor lamp into your suitcase. Motel rooms seldom provide enough light for a travel writer.

12. *Magnifying glass.* This is indispensable for reading maps, essential for buying jewelry, and wonderful for viewing nature's or a museum's treasures.

Jacqueline has a magnifier with a built-in flashlight to illuminate maps. This is ideal at night or in low-light situations.

13. *Batteries.* At least one complete set of extras for everything you're taking that requires batteries. If they are an unusual type, take two sets. Although small batteries can be found for sale nearly everywhere, they're rarely available at midnight, when you're telling the tape recorder what you saw today; or at noon, when you're shooting a flash picture inside the cavern, three miles from the souvenir shop; or at five in the morning, when you're shaving before an early flight.

14. *Glasses.* While every traveler needs to take care of his or her eyes, the travel writer must be especially vigilant about possible eye-related problems. If you wear glasses or contact lenses, take along an extra pair and your prescription. Take sunglasses and a sun hat to keep your vision clear on bright days.

15. *Plastic bags.* These, especially the "zipper" ones, are handy for carrying everything from your backup batteries, dirty underwear, and cosmetics to your shoes or a wet bathing suit. Take a small supply in all sizes.

16. *First aid kit.* While every traveler has his own special "can't do without," it's generally a good idea to have such items as small bandages, mild pain relievers, and cough drops, as well as insect repellent and sunscreen.

17. *Swiss Army knife, scissors, bottle opener.* Be sure to put these items into your checked baggage only. Security will not allow you to carry these and other forbidden items in your carry-on luggage. Check with your airline for a list of restricted items.

18. *Ear plugs and eye mask.* These make sleeping easier in noisy circumstances from the all-night disco across the street from your hotel to the crying baby on the airplane.

19. *Shawl.* Cathleen Miller always takes a soft woolen shawl that does double duty, keeping her warm on long flights and serving as an evening wrap that dresses up any outfit.

Recommended Overseas Take-Alongs

The travel writer who goes abroad should also take along:

1. *Documents.* Your passport, visas, press pass, tourist cards, International Drivers License, and whatever other foreign travel documents are required for the countries on your itinerary.

2. *Extra passport photographs.* Use these for extra visas or other official documents.

3. *Currency converter.* Available on mobile devices, for changing the value of dollars to guilders or pesos, etc.

4. *Foreign language phrase book.* Bring if appropriate. Even handier is a language translation app for your mobile device.

5. *A short wave radio.* This is a plus under some circumstances and may be worth taking if you're heading for faraway places and need to keep up with what's going on in the rest of the world.

6. *Binoculars?* Perhaps. Animal sighting and ship identifying would be among their uses.

7. *Extra notebooks.* Along with pens and refills, highlighters, paper clips, rubber bands, and that product of a thousand uses—cellophane tape. It's often hard to find what you need away from home, and the search uses up lots of travel time.

Will You Actually Write on the Road?

You'll notice that we haven't said anything about laptop computers. While some writers won't stir without their laptops, many find that using either a computer in the hotel's business center or at a local cyber café works just fine. Jacqueline doesn't like the added worry involved in carrying her laptop on some trips. She suggests uploading your thoughts and information on a borrowed/rented computer and then emailing them to yourself. To access files that she has worked on at home, she saves the information onto a USB flash drive that easily inserts into a borrowed/rented computer. If you'll be in one place long enough to really pound a keyboard, by all means take your laptop, especially on a cruise or to a resort. If, on the other hand, you're planning a series of one and two-night stays, you may find lugging it is more trouble than the productivity is worth. If you do plan to take along some electronic or electrical helper, be sure the wiring on the ship or in the hotel is compatible and/or will be adequate for your recharging purposes.

Some writers may feel it's more important to take along their research resources than their writing tools. Many save their important information to a USB flash drive. They are small and easy to carry around in the traveler's day bag, and can easily become the travel writer's best friend. Some journalists email their important data to themselves. A growing number of journalists leave their computers at home and are now using their mobile devices to collect and store information and writing.

Sometimes you can borrow equipment from the ship's purser or the hotel desk clerk, or they'll let you use what they have in the office after hours. More and more hotels, airports, and other travel facilities provide Internet access in one way or another. For a list of cyber cafés near your destination, log on to www.cybercafe.com to locate the most convenient ones all over the world.

The Travel Writer's Wardrobe

In addition to whatever professional tools you take on your trip, you'll want to give some thought to your travel wardrobe. Insist on comfort. A travel writer's concentration should not be on his mirror. Naturally, if you're going to the Arctic, you'll pack a different outfit from one suitable for the tropics. Will you need après-ski clothes or protection from mosquitoes and sunburn? If traveling to a variety of climates, dress in layers so you can put on or take off without bother.

Unless you're going to watch the polar bears mating on the ice cap, take only a lightweight, all-weather coat or jacket that will fit easily over a bulky sweater and has lots of pockets. In overheated airports, stuffy bus stations, airless hotel lobbies, unventilated vehicles, and warm rooms, you'll carry your jacket more than you'll wear it. Outdoors, if necessary, snuggle into a sweater beneath your coat. For every time you say to yourself, "My teeth are chattering—I wish I'd brought a heavier coat," there'll be ten times you'll say to yourself, "Why did I bring this coat at all—it feels like I've lugged it ten thousand miles!" The lighter the coat, the more muscle power you'll have left for other necessities.

For women, a few well-chosen color coordinated pieces of clothing are recommended. You can jazz up a plain top and skirt with a colorful scarf or shawl for evening. Tuck in a pair of rubber flip-flops or lightweight travel slippers and two pairs of comfortable, well-broken-in shoes, one pair of sturdy walking shoes and one pair that could be worn to a nice restaurant in the evening. (Ladies: it is wise to leave your stilettos at home!) The travel writer with the hurting feet won't be the travel writer with the prose that dances.

For guys, besides necessities, throw in a pair of long pants and a tailored dress shirt, as well as shorts and t-shirts. Shoes for guys are important too. Take along a pair of rubber flip-flops, one pair of athletic sandals, and a closed shoe for more formal occasions.

Again—be comfortable! Don't let what you're wearing get in the way of what you're working on. Unless your trip is built around a posh event, like a coronation, a jet-set wedding, or an opera premiere, the travel writer has far less use for dress-up clothes than for casual everyday wear. So put your fanciest duds back in the closet. Even cruise ships are planning fewer formal nights, but they do suggest bringing your workout clothes. Your guidebooks may tell you the kinds of clothes you'll need, but the best source is somebody who has traveled to that place or in that manner.

The Question of Luggage

When deciding what kind of suitcase(s) will best contain your necessities, consider how you'll be getting where you're going. If it's by public transportation, check out in advance the luggage specifications of each carrier. If you're driving, test the limitations of your baggage space, and give some thought to this problem when ordering a rental car. The trunks in many of the economy cars outside the U.S. can be very small.

If you're going by air, avoid paying luggage charges for bags that are over the weight limit by inquiring how many and what size checked and carry-on pieces are permitted for each leg of your journey. Sometimes local airlines, used for brief hops, have more stringent restrictions on the amount of luggage allowed, but may relax the rules if you have an ongoing ticket for other destinations. Airlines often make special arrangements for such special items as skis, golf clubs, and fishing rods.

Even without camouflaging the weight or bulk of their possessions, women travel writers need pockets in jackets, shirts, skirts, and pants, and many travel writers find that carrying a shoulder bag gives them a convenient container for extras such as a water bottle, maps, cameras, mobile devices, and spare batteries. Pockets and bags leave hands free to wield a pen, tune a recorder, or focus a camera. On a long trip, start out with an additional soft-sided suitcase inside your luggage. Fill it as you go along, and send it home with everything you find you can spare. It's easier to unload a little way into your long trip, as you discover what you aren't using, or need to send back items you purchase along the way. If you are a U.S. citizen, mark the send-home package "American Goods Returned" or "Used Clothing and Effects" for duty-free passage.

Since porters are almost non-existent, be sure your luggage has wheels. Never take more pieces or bigger pieces than you can manage by yourself. Above all, be sure your carry-on case has wheels. This is the case into which you're always stuffing the heaviest, bulkiest items—the telephoto lens, the hiking boots, the bronze sculpture you bought Aunt Hattie, the duty-free perfume, and Gibbon's *Decline and Fall* to read on the plane. This is the bag you're always carrying yourself through the labyrinth of airport corridors and the jungle of arrival and departure lounges. You can download e-books and apps for Amazon's Kindle and Barnes and Noble's Nook and have access to more and more material to read on your mobile device or computer, therefore leaving heavy books at home.

In any event, always identify the *outside* of your luggage with a tag that hides your name and address from the casual viewer; but put full information on the inside of all baggage. For quick identification, tie two strands of colored ribbon or yarn, in identical combination, to the handle of each suitcase and carry-on bag. Keep a mental count of how many different parcels you should have with you at each stop, so a click in your brain will alert you—something's missing! Remind yourself frequently, "I should be toting two things. Why do I have only one?"

When traveling overseas, find out the luggage and customs regulations of each country on your planned itinerary. Although most countries aren't too rigid about enforcement, it's expedient to know how many special items (cameras, electronic equipment, etc.) they officially permit you to carry in.

The All-Important Day Bag

Jacqueline carries everywhere what she calls her day bag, containing tools and items she will need for the day. These include: her iPhone, a small wallet with a copy of her passport, her driver's license (if needed), some local currency, a credit card, business cards, and her press pass. She puts in her travel journal, pens, maps (if needed), a tiny flashlight attached to her key ring, camera with extra battery and media card, a bottle of water, sunglasses, reading glasses, a zipper-lock bag containing a couple of bandaids, insect repellant, sunscreen, lip balm/lipstick, and a small pill box containing her necessary prescription drugs along with several Tylenol-type pain relievers.

The bag itself is a lightweight, medium-sized messenger pouch that she wears across her body Girl Scout-fashion, with her left arm protecting it from pickpockets. The bag has several zippered sections so things can be organized and easily found: keys in here, cell phone in there, etc.

The travel writer is first of all a traveler. With each trip you will become more adept at planning so you don't drag along too many things you rarely use and you can manage without the things you left behind. The comfortable, well-equipped but unencumbered traveler is the one likely to find the story with plus value.

CHAPTER 8

Sense and Sensibility

You have arrived at your destination. You are well equipped and well prepared—on the scene at last. It can be a little intimidating as you look around and wonder where to begin—there's so much to see, hear, smell, taste, touch, know, and enjoy.

Sometimes you start by looking for particular information to flesh out specific ideas or to fit specific markets. Other times you approach the travel experience with an open mind, waiting for your story to find you. In big cities or small villages, homes or palaces, temples or cemeteries, deserts or rain forests, the travel writer is always exploring, sampling the action, seeing for himself whether there's anything worth writing about.

You have to remain aware and alert, continually searching for ideas and information. Even "relaxed," on holiday, your mind is always working. One travel writer, who says 100 percent of his wanderings are related to writing and selling articles, admits that even short trips to attend weddings or visit his parents provide the basis for future travel pieces. That's because he's always on the lookout for the potential story.

Other times the story seems elusive, and you have to create the plus value. Jacqueline traveled to the top of Mt. Etna in Sicily fully expecting an exciting show of red-hot lava and swirling steam. She was disappointed when she got there because Mt. Etna didn't seem to be doing anything. Not even a small wisp of steam came out of the crater. The story she planned to write fell flat, but while wandering around the small shops that lined the rest center and parking lot she found her story in an unexpected place. Being flexible is important. Expect the unexpected and realize that even the best plans can sometimes fall apart.

Give yourself a goal of finding at least five stories on each trip. It's not that hard. For example, you could write about the place, the food, the arts, or interesting people you might meet; the marketplace; festivals, fairs or other public events; scenery; what makes that place so special. See? We've given you several ideas that can make interesting and saleable stories. We're sure you can enlarge that list once you get to your destination and perhaps cross off some items as well.

Look for That Special Angle, Other Stories, Too

Usually the best stories cover all the ordinary things as well as some special, unique angle pieces. Search out the details of your story, but also remain on the lookout for additional stories. Often you'll see something more interesting than you expect.

"Sometimes the best story ideas come from the little happenings that fall through the cracks in the itinerary floor," says Dee Henri. She tells of traveling to Nova Scotia in a forty-six-person bus that stopped unexpectedly at a tiny roadside cafe. The single young waitress-cook was overwhelmed, simply unable to serve so many cold, hungry tourists; whereupon the passengers made themselves at home in the kitchen, opening cans of soup, brewing coffee, and serving each other. "The spirit of the lunch stop was more impressive than the sights we saw," says Henri.

Orientation Comes First

A brief sightseeing tour is often the best way to orient yourself to the place you are visiting. Try for an aisle seat, close to the front, so you can see and photograph both sides and be first out when the bus stops. Sit or stand near the guide. Don't be bashful. Ask questions. If you're overflowing with questions—too many to ask—try to determine which answers you'll be able to find elsewhere, and then ask the other ones. Use your portable recording device to record the guide's information and answers to your questions. If the guide is a good one, write down his name, address, and email address in case you have a question to ask later. If the guide is a *very* good one, write a complimentary letter to his boss to encourage excellence in tour guides.

Don't rely completely, however, on everything the tour guide says—or even on the written information at the monument you are examining. James W. Loewen's *Lies Across America* explains that the log cabin where Abraham Lincoln was supposedly born was actually built thirty years after his death, and George Washington was nowhere near Valley Forge the winter he was depicted praying in the snow. Check your information carefully. There is nothing worse than having an editor find errors in your article.

Whether or not you take subsequent tours, do use public transportation for sightseeing. Procure a good map of the bus or subway system. In some cities you can download apps containing maps of the city, bus, or subway schedules along with points of interest. If you are in a hurry in a big city, take the subway. But if you want to see the people and the neighborhoods, the kids walking home from school, the housewives pinching the fruit at the greengrocer's, the workers relaxing on front stoops, look for surface transportation. In addition to buses, trolley cars, and trams, consider the jitney, the shared taxi so popular in many areas, or horse-drawn carriages or rickshaws. Bicycles and motorcycles give you still a different view, as you actually become part of the street scene. Riding a funicular or a cable railway or even sitting in the top section of a double-decker bus presents another perspective—farther removed, more telescopic.

Don't Miss the Offshore Perspective

Whenever you can, go by water. Practically all riverfront or lakefront areas offer waterborne transportation. From Westminster, for instance, you can take a water bus along the Thames downstream as far as Greenwich, upstream as far as Hampton Court.

The boat on Lake Geneva is a floating kaffeeklatsch. Mrs. A. embarks in Geneva, saving three seats for her friends; Mrs. B. comes aboard ten minutes later from the dock of a lakeside house; Mrs. C. boards at a small village five minutes away; then they order coffee and cakes, so they're all ready when Mrs. D. joins them at the next boat stop. The four chatter in rapid-fire French all the way to Montreux. The travel writer may not understand a word they say, but their appearance, their postures, and their gestures offer intimate insights that flesh out the story.

One of the world's biggest transportation bargains is a ride on a ferry-boat. While on assignment in Turkey, Louise remained on deck as the ferry that leaves from Istanbul's Galata Bridge sailed past the elegant Dolmabahçe Palace and the frowning fortifications of Rumeli Hisar and Anadolu Hisar. The ferry zigzagged between European Turkey and Asiatic Turkey, letting off and taking on passengers and cargo at dozens of docks. Water traffic of all kinds crisscrossed the Bosporus around them. After debarking in Sariyer, where the restaurant sent a fisherman out front to catch her lunch, she took a bus back to Istanbul. The half-hour ride through fields, orchards, and peasant villages taught her much about rural Turkey. On-the-spot "research" aboard the bus and the ferry provided background for a number of stories.

Nothing Beats Shoe Leather

When given the opportunity, don't turn down a journey on a camel, an elephant, a mule, a donkey, or an ostrich.

Camel rides across the Sahara or mule rides through the Alps can make for interesting articles focused on the method of transportation, but often such episodes are just one sentence of a story. Exotic conveyances can help you get the feel of a place, but overall, the most satisfactory type of transportation for a travel writer is shoe leather. On your own two feet is the best way to catch the most intimate glimpses of everyday life, as well as close-ups of parades, fiestas, and wedding processions.

To really know what a place is like you have to see its most important landmarks several times, at different hours of the day. Some sights, like the Taj Mahal or the pyramids, are always surrounded by rapt tourists at special times—sunrise, sunset, the light of the full moon; but even the modest plaza in a Mexican village looks different and feels different at dawn, at noon, and at twilight.

Notice what they call their plazas and squares and how they name their streets. Is the town laid out with First Street and Second Street intersecting A and B and C? Or are the streets, the squares, the gates, the areas named for famous people? What kinds of famous people? Politicians? Generals? Writers? Artists? Musicians? Entertainers? Millionaires? Sometimes it's the date that's important—Mexico City's Avenida 16 de Septiembre (named for the Mexican Independence Day) or Buenos Aires's Avenida 9 Julio (a crucial day in Argentina's struggle for liberty).

The place names give you the flavor of the community. California's San José and La Jolla as well as New Orleans's Bienville Street, Chartres Street, and Beauregard Square evoke the areas' origins. Be sure to note interesting names to use later in stories or titles. Or write an article about the names themselves. A newspaper story, datelined Norway, Maine, explains how such a true-blue Yankee state happens to have place names ranging from Madrid, Moscow, and Mexico to Paris, Poland, and Peru. Other travel writers have studied the history or patterns of street names or town names in certain areas and have come up with salable stories. It's a good idea to take photographs of street name signs if at all possible. For some strange reason, street name signs are often almost hidden or not there at all in parts of Italy.

Other clues to what the people of an area consider important can be found in their parks. Often there'll be trees planted by well-known people, or noteworthy political or military figures. Prime ministers and rear admirals are invited to plant trees in parks all over the world. In whose honor were the fountains, statues, or other monuments erected? Are there more playing fields or formal gardens? Is there a toddlers' playground? Has the city attempted to provide green space for its citizens? Is there a bandstand? What about wedding sites? Is there a special rose garden or gazebo for weddings?

Some museums have special information they hand out for school children's field trips. Get copies if you can. Many experienced museum goers recommend that you begin at the end—at the gift shop. They say you'll find the experience more rewarding if you first browse through the available guidebooks and check the postcard display for the showstoppers.

There are apps containing maps and information available for an increasing number of museums. See Chapter 16 for more information about apps.

The travel writer needs to look for the universal as well as the specific. Never be a mere name dropper, enumerating the airports and train stations you've waited in during your trip. Instead, cultivate the essence of the places of transportation so you can interpret them for others, like noticing the beautiful art nouveau Le Train Bleu Restaurant at the Gare d'Lyon in Paris or the art gallery at the Schiphol Airport in Amsterdam.

What If It Rains?

A very significant question to ask your tour guide, your bus driver, or any other local expert—a question not often answered in your pre-trip research—is, "What is there to do if it rains?" If the downpour drowns out your planned activity, your travel umbrella was capsized by the wind, and your traveling companion has the sniffles, what is your fallback option? Often there's some very interesting alternative—you just have to know about it. Then you can even write an article about what to do when fog and drizzle envelops Ayers Rock or the Adirondacks.

Tune In to Details

Improve your travel stories by *noticing*. Observe the trees and shrubs and flowers. Are the gardens well kept or weed filled? Are there plants in the window boxes? What kind? What colors are the flowers? Are the buildings well maintained? Is there trash on the sidewalk? Animals wandering in the streets? Iron bars on downstairs windows? Graffiti everywhere? Are there street peddlers? Hawking what? Lots of advertising signs? Promoting what? Are the people on the streets well dressed or in rags? You learn a great deal when you *notice*.

We should notice with *all* of our senses. We need to remind ourselves later how it sounded—the clear chorus of church bells, the hoarse groans of the foghorns, the echoing footsteps of a solitary walker, the cascading of stream water over rocks, the shrill sound of a single bagpipe.

What do we smell? Fish frying? A rose bush in full bloom? Damp wool? Incense? Cedar trees? Hot tar? Bread baking? Coffee roasting? The smells are part of the place—and part of the story. Take your nose on a journey as you go. Notice the smells and make note of them. What was enticing, what was dreadful, and what made you want to taste whatever it was that smelled so good?

What are you seeing as you look around? The green of the trees? The pastries in the bakery window? The people passing by? How are they dressed? Are the streets wide and congested, or are they narrow passageways that allow only foot traffic? What type of architecture are you seeing?

Taste is important. Does clam chowder taste different in Boston than in San Francisco? Try the reindeer steak or bird's nest soup or the borscht. Taste combines with the sights and sounds and smells when you eat a hot dog slathered in mustard from a street vendor in New York, or tamales on a street corner in Mexico City, or drink coconut milk on a palm-shaded beach in Barbados, etching the scene on your brain. Absorbing local color is not enough. *Record* it. If you don't have your recorder along, jot down reminders in your notebook. Take photos of everything that will remind you of your experiences as you travel along.

Do your feet feel cobbled streets or dusty roads? Will your fingers trace the pattern of a New Orleans balcony rail or an Arizona pueblo? How does it feel: the rough, unmortared stones of the seawall? The cool, smooth touch of a marble banister? The feel of an aged redwood railing?

Meet the Local People

Visit a family at home if you possibly can. Practically every country has a program that encourages local families to extend hospitality to visitors with similar hobbies, professions, interests, or whatever.

Better still, take along the names of friends of friends, relatives of relatives, and even acquaintances of acquaintances. Any opportunity to see how local people live provides the travel writer with invaluable background material for stories. It's within the family circle that you really grasp the people's relationships with each other, their relationship to their government, and their relationship to the rest of the world, whether they live in mansions crumbling in shabby gentility or in overcrowded apartments with wall-to-wall sleeping bags. The food they serve you is important in more ways than your observation of its type. How it's served is a clue to the people's lifestyle. So is who is eating. Do the women do the serving but not serve themselves? Is the oldest person present served first? Are the children at the table? Do the people speak freely about their government's shortcomings or parrot "everything's perfect" slogans? Sometimes when you dig a little deeper, long-held images are shattered. At a Moscow apartment the college professor's wife complained about the difficulty of obtaining eyeglasses in the former Soviet Union. The American visitors wondered how she had managed to procure the ones she wore. "Oh, *glasses* you can get," she said. "But it's impossible to find any designer frames."

Eat where the locals eat. Sit and sip at a sidewalk café. Order the house specialty. Talk to the waiter. Don't rush. Observe. Eavesdrop. Stare. Strike

115

up a conversation with people sitting nearby. Don't be afraid to talk with strangers. Of course, you must use your good judgment before starting a conversation.

Seek out old-timers to spin yarns about yesterday. You'll often find these people, who are, as John Wright says, "priceless" to the story, at the local mom-and-pop café. Search for a restaurant that's "a step above a greasy spoon, but a cut below fancy nonsense."

Sometimes you might even find surprising connections with the locals. Jacqueline went into a tiny *deposito di tabacco* in Taormina, Sicily to buy a postcard stamp and was charmed by the proprietress who was a tiny old woman, wearing her reading glasses over her regular glasses and wrapped in a lovely old shawl. Although the shawl was somewhat tattered, the beautiful workmanship was still evident. Surveying the goods for sale, Jacqueline discovered a big display of an Italian chewing gum with her son's (who is a model) photo on the packets. When she pointed to the photo and told the woman it was her son, the woman grabbed up several packets and announced to everyone in the shop that Jacqueline was the mother of the *uomo bello!*

Picnic in the park. Let the sun caress your shoulders. Listen to the squeals of the children somersaulting on the grass. Watch the grandfathers pondering the next move in their eternal chess game. Taste the vanilla ice cream. Listen to the calls of the local birds. Throw back the errant ball that comes your way.

Go to the grocery store. Is it a supermarket, selling everything from laundry detergent to fresh fish, from shampoo to tennis shoes? Are the displays of canned goods veiled in layers of dust, their prices so high in relation to wages that the display is merely decorative? It's fun to buy small grocery items to bring home. Jacqueline bought several kinds of paprika in Hungary and local sea salt in Portugal, a tube of anchovy paste in Venice and a string of chili peppers in Albuquerque.

Go to the outdoor markets too. You have to start before dawn at Bangkok's Floating Market, where mangoes and bananas, coconuts and papayas are bargained for and bought from boat to boat, and you, drifting through the kalongs and canals, are poled right into the center of the action. Start early, too, for Curaçao's colorful Schooner Market, where dockside customers haggle with vendors in sailboats for fresh fish, exotic vegetables, and flashy fabrics. Go early, also, to Singapore's Chinatown, where customers dicker for snakes and lizards to brew into virility-producing broths; to North African souks, where they sell spices and grape leaves and tiny cups of strong, sweet Turkish coffee; or to Pennsylvania Dutch markets selling pig stomachs, Amish pretzels, and old-fashioned sweet bologna.

Stop in at the boulangerie, which lures you with the seductive smell of crusty bread and chocolate tarts, and the charcuterie, where the aging lamb is flanked by a pair of peacocks and a selection of wild hares.

You may be surprised at some of the places where food is sold. Ferryboats which cross international boundaries may cater to long lines of people who've taken the ride for the groceries. As soon as the boat's commissary opens, the passengers crowd around, eager to buy coffee, liquor, and whatever edibles and potables are scarce or expensive in their own country.

Soak Up Local Color at Laundromats and Shops

You will also get a realistic view of the people at the laundromat. Who's there? Career singles from the rooming houses in the next block? Camping families with muddy duffles? Senior citizens? Louise remembers a stormy day in Southern California when the first mate of a small ketch commandeered all the dryers for her life jackets, cushions, bedding, foul-weather gear, and dock lines. On another day, halfway around the world, in Alice Springs, Australia, an aborigine woman lugged into the laundromat bag after bag of blankets, towels, and clothing—enough for every washing machine in the place—as five children marched behind her, licking dripping ice cream cones that were getting their shirts into condition for next month's wash. Puerto Vallarta's main "laundromat" was on the edge of town—rocks for scrubbing, riverbank for drying. Immediately behind the washing area, at the city-built playground, the children of the laundresses sang as they scrambled down the slides or swung out over the sharp stones.

Check out the department stores. Do they feature more dress patterns and sewing notions than ready-mades? More work shoes than ski boots? Electric orange juicers or manually operated orange juicers; or no juicers at all? Luxurious linens or low-end, serviceable sheets and towels?

What does all this tell you about the people in this community? How about the local shoppers in the department store? Are they queued up for a special bargain or because some household item, heretofore in short supply, has just been received by the store? Are people carrying plastic bags, string bags, elaborately decorated shopping bags? Do they look well dressed? Fashionable? Are they swathed in furs or shivering through threadbare wraps on a cold day? Are most of the items in the store manufactured locally? If not, where are they from? What other services does the store offer? One huge Tokyo department store not only presents kimono fashion shows and demonstrates the art of flower arranging but also provides lessons in the use of knives and forks—for chopstick users who want to learn Western ways.

Don't stop with the department stores. Visit the specialty shops, the bazaars, the souks, the flea markets. "Shopping" is more than a frivolous pastime when you're searching for your story.

Even beauty parlors and barbershops abound in clues to an area's reality. One travel writer says he's had his hair cut in countries around the world. He feels that barbershops give him insights into what the country is all about. During Louise's own first time in Cairo, sixteen different people worked on her simple shampoo and set, from the young girl who handed her a plastic-bagged comb, brush, and towel to the man who, two hours later, wielded the hairspray can. How to tip? Egyptian and European ladies were going around dispensing the equivalent of one cent to the teenager who brought the coffee, five cents to the shampoo girl, two cents to the young boy who removed the rollers, and ten cents to the maestro who set the hair, etc. That bit of local color found its way into one of her stories on Egypt.

Join the Congregation

While many of us are naturally reluctant to intrude upon the religious rites of others, Louise has often stumbled into a ceremony and been invited to stay: a prayer meeting in a Turkish mosque; a christening in a Greek church; a coming-of-age ceremony at Saint Peter's and another one, very different, at the Wailing Wall in Jerusalem; a Buddhist funeral in Japan; a Presbyterian wedding in Brisbane. Religious ceremonies always provide special insights. Be sure to look up your own religious affiliates when you travel. You'll not only meet pleasant people, but you'll probably be invited to attend a coffee hour after the service, a congregational potluck supper, or the annual Sunday school picnic.

Do you feel you could never bear to see a bullfight? You might find it less gory and more interesting than you expect. And the real show is the people around you and how they act and react.

Ballgames bore you? Don't be too sure. Whether it's sandlot or World Series, with a little pre-game explanation you'll understand enough of the action to understand the other spectators' enjoyment.

Too old for circuses? No, you're not. Applaud the elephant ballet and shiver in fear for the high-wire artists along with the rest of the audience. The successful travel writer not only attends the event, he observes the crowd. Watching the people around you often leads to a story angle. Louise's article about the Boxing Day race meeting in Auckland, New Zealand, focused on the female spectators' hats. In an era when women everywhere practically never cover their heads, these stunningly dressed kiwis all wore their millinery proudly. Louise guessed there must be a reason, so she asked the woman in front of her in the buffet line.

It was an annual contest, the lady explained, sponsored by Auckland's milliners, with a prize—a vacation in Australia for two—given for the most attractive hat at the meeting.

The best part of participating in local entertainment is your opportunity to see the people of the area relaxed and having a good time. You learn from watching them, talking to them, joining them in joy, fear, amusement, grief, devotion, satisfaction, or anxiety.

Your readers will want to know how many people were present at any kind of public gathering—parade, concert, ballgame, political demonstration. This figure is not only important in gauging the popularity of the concert artist or the political candidate but it lends meaning to the occasion. Are there a hundred people waiting in line for the art show to open—or only a dozen? Are there a hundred demonstrators waving signs—or a thousand?

A quick way to estimate the number of people in attendance is: if the crowd is seated, count the number of seats in a row and multiply by the number of rows. If it's a restaurant, count the number of tables and the average number of seats at each table; then consider carefully the degree of fullness of the room. (If the number of seats is common knowledge, all you have to do is count those that are empty.)

Professor Herbert Jacobs of the University of California offered this formula for estimating standing crowds. First measure (or estimate) the length and width of the area in feet; then add the two figures together; if the people seem to be moving around fairly easily, multiply this sum by seven; if they're tightly packed, multiply by ten. Thus, an area 100 by 150 feet—a sum of 250 feet—contains approximately 1,750 freely moving people or 2,500 tightly packed people. Learn to "eyeball" an area measurement: Outdoors, is it bigger than a football field? Indoors, is it as long as three bathtubs or wider than two full-size beds?

Welcome Chance Meetings

While you're traveling, encourage chance encounters. Speak to the person sitting next to you on the plane, train, or bus or in a restaurant. That person may turn out to be a pleasant traveling companion; and he may be the very person you need to alert you to an important story breaking along your route. Or he may be from a distant country, with ideas and insights that introduce you to that country in a way that years of reading never could.

Jacqueline and her sister Patty were visiting the Tower of London, laughing and making comments on the treasures on display when they noticed a tall fellow trailing them. Turns out he was an American and in London all alone. They invited him to join them and spent the rest of the day seeing sights and then eating a bangers-and-mash dinner at a traditional pub until finally he escorted them to their train, which was departing for France. They entertained the other waiting passengers with goofy antics and sang every train-related song they could remember. Jacqueline wrote a funny story about that adventure.

Getting lost may be one of the very best ways to see an area. Local people love to show you the route, and the experience often leads the travel writer down interesting bypaths. While struggling with his high school French in France, John Pollack remembered Ben Franklin's advice to let others do *you* a favor if you want them to like you. He went around asking strangers to photograph him with his camera. This led to interesting conversations, vast amounts of inside information—and a huge collection of dull pictures.

While he was able to practice *his* French, in many countries people like to practice *their* English. When an English-speaking person asks for directions they're delighted to help. Never hesitate to ask questions. All over the world, people young and old like to show off their surroundings, and will often take an unbelievable amount of trouble to lead you to something they think you should see. Often the "something" is more charming, less crowded, richer in beauty and meaning than the well-known sight nearby.

A stranger's description and a nudge in the right direction might lead you to the Roman ruins under the city of Barcelona, or to exquisite secluded beaches, exciting but little-known galleries, and hole-in-the-wall restaurants with tasty regional menus. Always listen to local people's recommendations. Pay attention when somebody says, "Don't miss seeing ..." or "Be sure to stop at ... "

Make use of every person-to-person opportunity. Sometimes you'll need special help while pursuing your on-trip research. But finding the individual who can give you the exact information you need isn't as hard as it sounds. Your at-home research provides a starting point. Ask each source to suggest other sources. Jo Combs likens it to "unraveling a ball of string—find a starting person, and he will direct you to others, who will help you find still others."

While your embassy or consulate might assist in arranging interviews with people you need to see overseas, usually they won't do it until you actually arrive in the country. They've found too many people change plans at the last moment. (Remember, if you need the services of a translator, the interview will take twice as long, so budget your time accordingly.)

Cultivate "People" Resources

The hotel concierge prides himself on being able to answer practically any question or solve any problem. Ask him for advice and printed information as soon as you arrive. Lois Kirchner forgot to do this at the Park Lane Hotel in London. Only as she was leaving did she discover she could have walked through nearby Green Park to Buckingham Palace and witnessed a leisurely and uncrowded Changing of the Guard.

In Paris, the concierge at the Hotel du Louvre told Jacqueline about a tunnel under the dreaded Étoile roundabout and how to find it. She had been terrified at the idea of driving around that famed traffic hazard. She had a fear of getting into the circle of cars and not being able to get out, and was very happy to be able to avoid it.

Others can help you, too. Question the saleslady, the flower seller, the cobbler, the proverbial man in the street. The more people you talk to, the better feel you'll get for the place; the more you know about it, the better the story you'll write. The dining room maitre d' led one writer to a French organization that dates back to the Druids and gave her the name of a book on the legends of Brittany that was exactly what she needed for a forthcoming story.

Go to a bookstore and ask if they have anything on local history. Listen for folktales and stories of local heroes. Jot down the names of people and places you'll be able to look up at home.

Be sure to buy local newspapers and magazines (many foreign countries publish English editions also) to find out more about the local scene, as well as events of interest. Read the want ads. Tune in to local radio and television programs.

Even though you've done your research in advance, you may want to pursue some special interest while traveling, and you'll find librarians everywhere glad to help you when you show sincere purpose. When Winifred Johnson spent four months in Jackson, a town in California's Gold Country, she visited the museum so often that the curator set aside a special room for her to work in. On days when the museum and the library were closed, docents took her on tours, showing her memorabilia the more casual observer doesn't get to see, some of it from the time of the Gold Rush itself. She did her research in 1850s newspapers and in private homes, whose owners heard about her project and invited her to visit.

James Winchester also found more help than he expected. Trying to complete a *Reader's Digest* assignment about Russian trawlers off Newfoundland, he was ready to give up when he heard on his rental car radio that the Russian oceanography ship working with the trawlers had put into port with a sick seaman. He hurried to the pier, though he didn't really expect to be allowed on the ship. He was, however, welcomed aboard. Many of the crew spoke English. The captain himself took Winchester on a complete tour. Whenever they came to a locked door the captain sent a seaman for the key. While they were waiting—and there were many such waits—they had a glass of vodka, bottoms up. Winchester was happy to report that he upheld the dignity of American journalism by remaining on his feet all day.

Alcohol Can Be a Problem

You will have to work out your own rules about alcohol. Will your hosts be insulted if you refuse? Will you be too sleepy to get your story if you accept? Should you stick to Perrier? A refreshing beer? Wine with lunch? And how much?

There aren't any "standard" answers. In many situations the drinking of alcohol to toast almost everything can be daunting. Individual circumstances and your own personality will dictate your response when alcohol is served. But do take into consideration the mores of the people you're with. Strict Muslims would be deeply offended by your invitation to "stop by the Hilton Bar for a drink." But if your Viennese hosts take you out to Grinzing to a *Heuriger*, a "new-wine" garden, they'll be insulted if you don't taste the new wine. However, tasting doesn't necessarily mean drinking an entire glass of the wine.

If you, yourself, are opposed to alcohol, don't make an issue of it. If everybody else is drinking, order fruit juice or a soft drink. Toasting is a very important activity in some countries, with rigid rules, but you can participate with an empty glass. The important thing to remember when toasting is to look into the eyes of the person(s) you are toasting with as an acknowledgement of their existence.

Check into alcohol-related etiquette for the place you are visiting and establish a pattern that seems comfortable to you. In general, remind yourself that every day is a working day for the travel writer, and a professional manner is imperative.

Knowing what to look for, what to listen for, what to think about, and how to use your other senses are the travel writer's secret weapons. Take advantage of your on-scene position as you gather material for the stories you've already planned—and the stories you didn't plan because you didn't know ahead of time how terrific they could be.

CHAPTER 9

Follow the Reader

Who is your reader? The avid traveler or the armchair traveler? The younger, active hikers or the older, easy-going travelers? Sometimes addressing a particular type of traveler will be important in your stories and articles. Keep your reader in mind when you query an outlet or when you actually write the piece. The approach used on a story for *Backpacker* magazine might not appeal to the AARP crowd. Readers—and editors—really appreciate that special information that comes from your personal research. Put yourself in your readers' place. Remember, you are their advance man. While you're there, get all the information your readers might need or want, and record it carefully, so you can pass it on. While you might not use all the information you gather, it will help you conjure up images that will help your readers get an understanding of just what the place is all about.

For example, tell them, "Windy San Francisco street corners make the woman with the wraparound skirt wish she'd worn something else," or "If you're going on a house boat and you like to work crossword puzzles, don't forget to take along a pencil," or "Theater ushers and restroom attendants in many countries expect to be tipped." Explain to first-time ship cruisers that glamorous evening clothes aren't really necessary and that nobody "dresses" the first and last nights or whenever the ship's in port. Mention the fifty-six-degree temperature at Carlsbad Caverns, and the fact that 11,400-foot Cuzco is apt to be cold in the evenings and early mornings, even if it's shirtsleeve weather at noon in nearby Machu Picchu. Remind them that August is when much of the population of Europe goes on vacation so many restaurants and shops will be closed. The weather in many European countries is sizzling in August and sometimes into September. Because of all the stone and water, Venice can be freezing in the winter and steaming in the summer. Remind them that although it may be summer above the equator, it's winter below the equator. These little tidbits of information can help the traveler decide when and where to go.

Suggest they have birth certificates notarized for Mexico, observing that a friend had to cancel a trip when she couldn't find a notary at the airport. Give them the benefit of your experience by encouraging early reservations for camping space in California's state parks or for New Year's at the Williamsburg Inn. Whenever possible, investigate different travel styles while you're in the area you'll be writing about. Your reader may opt for accommodations, recreation, or sightseeing very different from what you, personally, would choose. You owe him the courtesy of checking out the entire scene. If you're staying at a youth hostel, go to the best hotel in town. (Make sure you are properly dressed. Katsu Miyata found this out when he attempted to duck into the Hotel Ritz for a drink while following in Ernest Hemingway's footsteps, wearing shorts, and was turned away.) Stroll through the lobby, order a snack in the coffee shop, window shop the boutiques. If you're staying at the plushiest hotel, check out the one-star around the corner, as well as the youth hostel, the YMCA, and the nearest campground.

Sample many types of transportation and travel experience from donkey carts in Greece to rickshaws in Cambodia to high-speed trains all over Europe and Asia. Try out the inner-city modes of getting from one place to the next. Ride the bus, tram, underground, taxi, and ferry. Sometimes the language can be a problem. Jacqueline found this out when she wanted to use the underground while visiting Budapest. The written Hungarian language is filled with consonants and as a result the station names were long and unpronounceable for her. So, using the first few letters in the various station names, she managed to make up her own versions and learned her way around the maze of the underground system. When in doubt, write down the name of the departure station and the name of the station where you want to get off.

Tell the "Bad" News as Well as the "Good"

Never use your keyboard to settle private scores or to get even with those who gave you a bad time. Both your praise and your complaint should be tempered by the knowledge that both the restaurant or the hotel and *you* have had good days and bad days. Before you write too bitterly about the atrocious lunch, take into consideration the circumstances that might affect your outlook: the fact that you're suffering from a heavy cold, the airline lost your luggage, and an unseasonable rainstorm beat against your windshield the whole twenty miles to the restaurant; the fact that it's the chef's day off and the storm prevented delivery of fresh produce. Then, if you can be humorous, rather than grim—write explicitly, but amusingly—the result is often an entertaining, informative article. Tell your readers the truth—but be sure it *is* the truth.

On the other hand, Jacqueline doesn't like to write about specific bad situations. She knows from experience that restaurants sometimes have an "off" day or are unable to procure specialty products. The chef got sick, the fisherman didn't catch what was wanted, the specific vegetable wasn't available. Things like that can cause havoc in the kitchen.

These days, choosing a hotel is a bit easier because most hotels have a Website where one can find lots of information, including location, price, details about the property, and often a map with the location indicated. If there isn't a map, you can go to MapQuest.com or maps.google.com, enter the address, and find out the location. If the hotel is located in an undesirable part of a city, you will have to decide if the inconvenient location is worth the cheaper price than a hotel that is centrally located. The star rating of hotels helps the traveler understand what is and what is not included, the overall ambiance, and amenities available. These facts are important if you are including a specific hotel in your article.

Check Out the Details

In addition to absorbing the *feel* of the place, you need to find and record the facts. Be sure your information is complete and accurate and current and includes all the cogent details. Keep careful track of mileage and costs. Be ready to tell your readers which landmark signals the turnoff or what track they should stand on for their train. Find out, so you can say authoritatively, the best time of year to take this trip and how long to stay at each place. Some publications prefer what they call "mentions"—the name and address of the hotel, the restaurant, the car rental agency, the sightseeing company. Some only want you to include mentions when you're being complimentary.

The wise travel writer, though, stows away the information, regardless. Your present editor may scorn mentions, but the next time you sell a piece on this destination, a different editor may cover your manuscript margins with questions you can't answer. The value of this is dramatized in Eleanor Bogart's article "Oh Yes, I Remember It Well," in which she tells of her plans to write a story describing all the streets she's loved. She has just returned from four days in St. Paul, Minnesota, and she will begin with Summit Street. Or is it Summit Avenue? Or Boulevard? Or Drive? Are the trees elms or maples? Are the houses really Victorian? Or earlier or later? Well, at least the Hill mansion she remembers. But was it brown or red? Stone or brick? It was four stories, she thinks—or at any rate, three. Surrounded by a fence. Was it wrought iron? She ends up unable to recreate Summit Street (Avenue?) because she didn't take five minutes to jot down or record the details. Using the Internet to Google some of this information can be helpful, but not always. Write down or record what you are seeing.

We all do that—think we know a place very well, until we sit down to write about it. While we're traveling it's all so *memorable*, we think we'll never forget. But we do. Make it a firm rule to scribble or record those supporting details you'll need later.

With the details firmly in mind you can go ahead and write without stopping to look things up. If you have all the facts straight you can concentrate on plus value and won't have to keep asking yourself, "Was it on the corner or in the middle of the block? Were the children wearing their school uniforms or their play clothes? Was it a canoe or a rowboat?"

A Note about Notes

Once you're home, you'll discover it's very hard to track down some small, but colorful and enriching, fact. You may find yourself spending vast amounts of time and money searching for a nebulous tidbit that you should have written down on scene—and never uncover it.

Paul Theroux says he never scribbles in a notebook in front of the people he's talking to. He doesn't like to arouse suspicion. Instead, he absorbs the conversation for about an hour, then hurries to a private place to make his notes, and amplifies the notes that evening.

You might want to organize your field notes by writing the solid information in order. The special little extras you might want for something else, either jot on a separate page or circle when they appear in the middle of more mundane information. When you tape your thoughts later you will gather together all these colorful little extras and remarks about them at the end of the more general information. Thus you're reminded that the schoolgirls wore dark blue skirts with white shirts and blazers in a Black Watch plaid; and the red rowboat called *Erma* had yellow trim, a human eye carved on the bow, and shiny brass oarlocks.

Using the recorder on your mobile device, you can easily and discreetly record an interview or dictate your notes. There are apps, such as Dragon, that will transcribe spoken words into text.

It's the details that bring a place to life and make the reader eager to visit it. Robert Schiller must have been thinking of his readers when he wrote "Storybook Prague" for *Reader's Digest*. He must have marshaled all his senses and digested all the details to tell so much, so easily:

Nestled below the castle is Mala Strana, the Little Town, Prague's loveliest section. Although most of its baroque palaces are now foreign embassies and government offices, the area has changed little since the eighteenth century. You must explore its winding alleys, exquisite little squares and courtyards on foot or you will miss the charming angels, eagles, chalices, keys and fiddles carved over the doorways, which told the postmen where to deliver mail in the days before houses were numbered. Cross the Vltava by the Charles Bridge, one of earth's most fascinating spans. Built in 1357, with elaborate Gothic guard towers at either end, it is lined with 30 sculptured groups of saints in ecstatic poses. Pious Czechs doff their hats as they pass the figure of Saint John Nepomuk, the "martyr of silence," who was tied in a sack and thrown into the river for refusing to reveal secrets of the confessional. The eastern end of the bridge leads into the Old Town. Here is the famous Carolinum, seat of ...

Do you, the reader, want to visit Prague?

Specifics ... Not Adjectives

Bill Peeples, for many years one of the editors of the *Los Angeles Times* travel section, was a hard taskmaster. He always asked the writer, "How *much* was the tip you say won the guide's lifelong devotion? What do you *mean* by 'remarkably inexpensive?' How *far* is 'an easy day's drive'?" Peeples says, "It's amazing how many writers don't tell the reader what they saw. 'There was a beautiful panoramic view.' Period. Paragraph. Perhaps they never saw it because they didn't really look. But what the travel section needs are specific details, not adjectives." Perhaps the writer could have said:

> From the lookout at the top of the mountain, vineyards filled the valley below. Their red/yellow and brown leaves left no doubt that summer was over. The air at the top of the hill was filled with the soft fragrance of the pine trees around us.

Peeples, as a writer, tells about Nantucket's shops, restaurants, rental vehicles, boats, and sports, and where to get more information. He must have kept his eyes open to give his reader this vivid a picture of Nantucket:

> It has been said that the shape of the island, an accumulation of debris pushed off the mainland by the last glacier, is like a sailor's hammock. A full one, with a sailor in it. If that is the case, Nantucket town is right where the sailor's hands would be if he were folding them across his stomach while he slept.

> Nantucket town, safely inside the jetties at the west end of a long, narrow harbor, is a place mostly of asphalt streets although three blocks of Main Street are cobblestoned. Main Street slopes up gently toward the north, a

wide avenue framed by tall trees that shade shoppers but let the sun shine through, too. . . .

Everyone watches as the moonglow becomes more golden. Then suddenly, as if someone held a ping-pong ball under the water and let it go, the moon pops up.

There's only one way you can write that way—*know* what you're talking about.

Your Reader Cares

Remember that your reader, whether armchair or active, is interested in the world as it is today. With Green Travel replacing the Grand Tour, it's up to us, who write about tourism, to share our insights with the reader. Who is doing what about protecting endangered wildlife? Where are the best research programs for preserving threatened ecosystems? How can one hundred species of ants coexist with the lure of tourist dollars?

Not all of your readers will have the opportunity to travel to the Galapagos Islands, but they'll all appreciate careful, accurate reports of what's happening with their environment. Incidentally, email is an excellent resource for conferring with others who are trying to enrich rather than destroy, so that you can write about ecology in individual terms. The hotel that donates its broken crockery to a university art department's mosaics, the city that actively encourages carpooling and low-impact development, the steamship line that homogenizes its potato peelings and chicken bones for fish food—these are all stories waiting to be told.

How to Use Sidebars

A sidebar is a block of information that runs adjacent to an article, often set off in a box or with a different color or typeface. It can come before or after the main body of the article or in the middle or alongside. Solid facts are needed for the sidebar, where information is expressed concisely, not necessarily in sentences, sometimes even in chart form.

If your story is interesting and moves right along, but you still need to work in more details, try using a sidebar. Magazines and newspaper travel sections regularly carry sidebars to major stories, headed "If You Go . . ." or "If You're Going . . ." The sidebars, or boxes, are filled with straightforward facts on how to get to the place in your story, how long it will take, how much it will cost, and how to get more information. Because of its conciseness and prominence, the sidebar needs to be rich in facts that matter, so collect the details carefully. Naturally you'll be guided in sidebars you plan by the layout style and content of your article. You'll want to tell your readers which airlines fly there, how they can proceed from the airport, and where to make a reservation. Additional sidebars, or perhaps additional paragraphs in the same one, will cover accommodations, restaurants, recreation, and sightseeing. Other publications will emphasize advice on shopping—what to buy, where to find it, how much to pay for it. Still others will seek something special, such as a historical vignette or an outstanding side trip.

Brief roundups often work well for sidebars, too—assembling a group of arts and crafts or artists and craftsmen, special upcoming events or annual festivals, for instance. How something works, or how it got to be that way, or what happened when, sometimes fits a sidebar. If there's a side trip you want your readers to know about, put it into a sidebar. Maybe the editor will like it so much, you'll have an opportunity to make the sidebar into a story of its own.

The sidebar has many advantages. It gives the editor leeway in layout, making it easier to schedule the piece. It helps the writer organize his material and tell his story in a readable manner, still confident that he's providing the necessary facts. It gives the reader in-depth information without slowing down the article itself. Many different kinds of material lend themselves to sidebars, and many pieces have more than one. To accompany a Nile cruise article for *Going Places*, a house magazine sent by travel agents to their best customers, Louise furnished three sidebars. One told of the many companies selling Egyptian travel, and how to get in touch; the second, of the various boats sailing up and down the Nile, their prices and accommodations, advantages and disadvantages; and the third delineated what to bring along—everything from binoculars and a strong flashlight to a warm jacket and an outfit suitable for camel riding. The travel section in the *New York Times* and many other newspapers run similar sidebars that include this kind of information.

One issue of *Travel + Leisure* featured as a cover story a one-page "Mediterranean Miscellany," with a quote from Lawrence Durrell boxed in the middle of the page, followed by two pages of consecutive sidebars, which included a map. The sidebars dealt with such subjects as "Daredevil Drivers," "Worth a Major Detour," and a chronology, showing what happened in the Mediterranean and when, from the Jewish exodus from Egypt in 1400 to 1200 B.C. to the death of Francisco Franco and the crowning of Juan Carlos in A.D. 1975. The boxes also gave the names and dates of Mediterranean born VIPs, alphabetically, from Aeschylus to Virgil; a quick rundown on art museums in Mediterranean countries; an explanation of the "ill winds" of the Mediterranean such as the mistral, which Aubrey Menen calls the "cold displeasure of God"; and a definition of such terms as "Riviera," "Costa Brava," and "Cote d'Azur." As you can see, the sidebars were even more "miscellaneous" than the article.

In another issue of *Travel + Leisure*, a six-page article on Philadelphia had five sidebars, one to a page. They dealt with the Liberty Bell's new home, where to find information at the Convention and Visitors Bureau, outstanding restaurants, a brief history of the old mansions and information on touring them, and a potpourri of scheduled special events.

Alongside "Nepal, a Trekker's Paradise," in an adventure magazine, is a box written by someone other than the author of the article, which is a common device. In this case the sidebar was written by Jim Whittaker, the first American to reach the summit of Mount Everest. It describes trekking conditions in Nepal, comments philosophically on the environment and economic impact of the popularity of trekking, and advises the would-be trekker in such specifics as making arrangements through a reliable organization and planning the trek for some time other than peak season for the area.

Sometimes a travel writer asks an expert like Whittaker to write a sidebar to accompany his article; sometimes he discovers after he's interviewed an expert that the material lends itself especially well to a sidebar, and he designs one that's composed of quotes from the interview; and other times the editor makes an arrangement with the expert to write a short piece on the subject of the writer's story and uses it as a sidebar.

Consider a sidebar, even if the publication doesn't normally use them, whenever it would help you round out your material without slowing down your story. If you wonder how to write and submit it—call it a sidebar, title it if you wish, and begin it on a separate sheet following the main part of your article.

Links provide wonderful possibilities for online media. You not only find additional information—you can actually access it with a single click of the mouse. An article on finding day spas abroad, for instance, provides links to information on health and fitness, family fun, getting fit, health on the go, family spas, outdoor health, swimming fitness, and other related topics.

Check and Recheck

Your reader will be quick to point out the slightest error. If you want to build a reputation as a travel writer, don't assume anything! Get the facts straight. Don't give him the chance to catch you in an error.

Once you have recorded a fact, don't mindlessly use it forever without rechecking it. Constantly update your knowledge so you're presenting as current a picture as you possibly can. Although Jacqueline always tries to do this, she still remembers when she arrived at the address of the beautiful Victorian hotel in Saint Raphael in the south of France she wanted to include in her story about unique hotels along the Cote d'Azur. She was horrified to find the hotel was gone and in its place was a group of rather sterile apartments.

Be sure you're recommending to your readers something that still exists. And be sure it's a travel experience the reader will be able to duplicate if she wishes.

The easiest way to write a travel article is to visualize your reader. Then say to yourself, "If I were that reader, what information would *I* want?" Your writer's eye, writer's ear, and writer's nose will uncover what you need. Your most urgent task will be selecting from this mass of material the items you want to use in your story *this time.*

CHAPTER 10

Getting Things Write

You may expect your story to write itself once you get home and listen to your tapes, look at your photographs, and review the printed material you've collected. But don't count on it. You usually need a many-pronged assault to compile the research for any story. If you're alert to the possibilities before, during, and after your trip, you can combine the various sources so they reinforce each other.

As we've said, your pre-trip research should include extensive reading—everything from brochures to the encyclopedia—and conversations with those who have been where you're going.

While traveling you'll interview people—in person and on the telephone. You'll observe everything with your careful writer's eye, ear, nose, and senses of taste and touch. You'll record your impressions with camera, notebook, and recorder. You'll collect concrete details as well as register the overall feel of the place.

You may plan your story while you're traveling (target market firmly in mind), or maybe you will even write it on the road—and find the check in your mailbox when you return. But other articles you'll wait to write until after you're home. Although we always try to gather the material we'll need on the trip itself, occasionally an editor wants a story one of us hasn't prepared for.

At this point Jacqueline would like to remind you that the Internet offers a plethora of information on topics from types of penguins at the South Pole to Chinese opera or the proper way to cook a Florentine steak. She recommends spending some time surfing the Internet for background information and research on any given topic, using search engines like Google.com, Yahoo.com, or Ask.com. Be sure you keep track of the Website URLs that have the information you want.

Talk About Your Subject

As you review your previous research and return to the library and expand your live investigations, don't forget to talk about your subject to anyone who will listen. You'll be surprised how many people will have something to add to your project, whether it's expertise in one facet of the subject or acquaintance with just the person you need to quote.

Notice we said *subject*—not *idea*. When people ask you what you're working on, or even if they don't ask, tell them in broad general terms about the subject you're researching. But don't go into detail about your concept and the clever words you'll use to implement it, especially if you haven't written them yet. There's danger you'll do such a good job in the telling, the freshness will be spoiled and you'll never get to the writing. So don't seek praise for your ability with words until those words are actually written and published. On the other hand, never be bashful about asking anybody—friend or stranger, face-to-face or online—"Do you know anything about Timbuktu? What have you heard about crossing Siberia by train? Do you know anybody who's had emergency surgery in Mexico? Have you heard of any families taking special vacations this year?" Keep in touch with people who helped you before and during the trip—tourist offices, travel agents, public relations people in the travel industry, superior tour guides, and interesting people you've met along the way.

In addition to consulting experts who've previously written about your area, search for experts on your own. Finding the individual who can give you the exact information you need isn't as hard as it sounds. Newspaper and magazine bylines, library files, corporate public relations departments, and trade and professional associations often provide a starting point. Some universities publish press contact booklets, which list expert sources on the faculty. Even if your nearby university doesn't do this, it shouldn't be hard to uncover your own authority.

The Internet makes research fast and easy. From highway conditions to checking on airfares to arranging hotel rooms, the Internet is the way to get information quickly, easily, and cost effectively.

Sidney Sheldon says he used the phone constantly for authenticating the backgrounds of his novels. He has obtained information ranging from the weather in New Orleans, verified by the local chamber of commerce, to the name of a train station in Milan, supplied by the Italian consulate in Los Angeles. However, with access to the Internet, he could have found out all this information without expensive long distance phone calls.

Turn to Your Files

Jacqueline likes to store information in files on various subjects on her computer or a USB flash drive. Use what's still valuable of the material in your files, but be sure to update for accuracy. When you come across an old quote from a good source, phone, write, or email for an up-to-the-minute opinion. Reread the written materials you used in your original research, visit libraries and bookstores, and surf the Internet to investigate new facts. If you began filling your file before you left on your trip, you'll have good resource materials to use when you return home. If you haven't done all the research you should have, now's the time to make up for it.

When you're wrapping it all up, consider the relative value of the research materials you're using. Take into consideration the author's qualifications, experience, education, and reputation, as well as the reputation of the publisher or sponsoring agency. Consider the range of the subject matter and the limitations. How up to date is the material? Does it seem accurate and unbiased? Is the book well indexed and well illustrated? Is the Website credible? Select carefully as you incorporate research material into your own story so that you are giving your readers the most valuable information you can.

Compiling all your notes and references from before, during, and after the trip can seem like an overwhelming job. Sometimes you just don't know where to start. One way is to make a copy of everything, then put one copy away as your master file. For the other copy you can use your computer's cut-and-paste feature, to move the pieces around like blocks to judge where they best fit into your story. If the situation changes after you've written your piece, do your best to correct your copy before publication.

Check and Recheck for Accuracy

As we've said, just being there is never enough—you have to flesh out your on-the-scene observations. You must check and recheck the information you've collected. For instance, a *Newsday* editor once wanted to know what Louise meant by "a mile-long avenue of ram's-headed sphinxes" at Luxor. "How many ram's-headed sphinxes?" he asked—a piece of information not easily uncovered.

If we want our writing to inform and assist our readers, we must guard against errors. Louise has had readers question a single word or name in a four- or five-thousand-word article. She casually mentioned, in an *Aramco World* piece, the names of the sculptors who contributed to the ornamentation of the Temple to Artemis/Diana, one of the World's Seven Wonders. A history professor wrote Louise a complimentary letter on the article, then commented cryptically, "Phidias would have been over 200 years old! Remarkable!" She found in her original notes a big red question mark after "Phidias" and then a scrawled "OK." The information came from a British Museum book written by the man who rediscovered the temple, and it obviously referred to a different Phidias from the one who ornamented Athens for Pericles. Louise was pleased to be able to send the history professor a photocopy of this impeccable source.

A friend wrote "Collecting from Country to Country" for an art publication, and a mutual acquaintance called with compliments on the article's accuracy. "I couldn't find a single thing wrong with it," she said. "Not a thing! I looked up everything, and the author didn't make a single mistake." While Louise and her friend chuckled, they both knew that she, like most readers, would have been quick to point out the smallest error.

Jacqueline once wrote a story that mentioned a Paris restaurant called L'Orangerie. She received a comment in a rejection from a major newspaper travel editor assistant reprimanding her for a mistake "because L'Orangerie is a museum and not a restaurant." Jacqueline was happy to send the assistant a business card from the restaurant L'Orangerie.

The satisfaction of feeling you've done your best to provide accurate information for your audience cannot be matched.

Shortcuts Spell Trouble

Whatever research methods you use, don't skimp or take shortcuts. So-called writer's block is invariably the result of too little research. If you know enough, you won't have any trouble putting it down on paper.

And never underestimate the intelligence of your reader. Don't depend on the forlorn hope that he won't know when you're bluffing. John Ball tells of a private screening of a two-million-dollar motion picture that showed a DC-8 taking off and then, a few minutes later, a shot, presumably of the same aircraft in flight, "Only this time it was a 727-200, a very different plane, with the power plants in the rear, not under the wings." When Ball mentioned this to the producer, the reply was, "Who will know the difference?" At the formal premiere of the movie, when the wrong aircraft came on the screen, the entire audience burst into laughter.

Members of your reading audience are wiser than you think. Whether or not you've done the ideal amount of pre-trip and on-trip research, be sure to do a good job on your post-trip research so you can give your readers the most accurate, up-to-date information possible.

PART TWO

CHAPTER 11

Asking the Question

In Jaipur, Louise's Indian guide proudly mentioned his publications in *National Geographic* and *Vogue. National Geographic* she could understand—but *Vogue?*

"How did you happen to publish a travel article in *Vogue?*"

"Oh, I sent them a query letter," he replied. "They liked my idea and told me to send it along."

This man had guided a group of American travel writers working on a Jaipur story, and they advised him about his own writing: "Always query first."

Your Most Important Sales Tool: The Query

Good advice. Those travel writers believed—and we believe, too—that the query letter or email is the most important sales tool in the travel writer's repertoire. Although it looks like an extra step in the writing process, it's usually the quickest path to publication.

What is this magic tool, the query letter? It is, as it sounds, a letter of inquiry: a letter inviting the editor of a publication to express interest in your idea *before* you proceed to research and write the article.

Sometimes your query will sell your story before you write it; sometimes it will elicit the encouragement that indicates you're on the right track; and sometimes it will help you see that this particular idea isn't worth pursuing.

In this chapter we'll consider why the query is such an important tool, what elements it should contain, and what it can do for you, including the where and the when (and the when-not-to) of query letters, as well as different types of queries and possible editorial responses.

Why Is the Query Such an Important Tool— What Can It Do for *You*?

It saves you the time spent researching and writing an article that is never going to sell. Although presumably you will study such compendiums as the *Readers' Guide to Periodical Literature*—either printed or electronic—and the publications themselves to see what has been written on your subject lately, you have no way of knowing whether your target market is currently considering or has recently purchased an article on the same subject. While you're riding your mule to the bottom of the Grand Canyon, your editor may be buying a Grand Canyon piece from somebody else.

These days many newspapers, magazines, and other periodicals have suffered a reduction of staff. Consequently many editors work alone or with only one or two assistants. Email is usually the best way to reach these overworked editors. Email queries can be accompanied by attached clips and/or photographs.

Another important reason for query writing is the chance it gives you to avoid the editor's taboos and to find his or her main interest. An objection to your subject matter or stance might make it pointless to send the completed article. But an editor may let you know that while he's not interested in the religious history of Aegean Turkey and won't permit you even to mention Saint Paul, Saint John, or the Virgin Mary, he's fascinated by the sixteenth-century Barbarossa brothers, pirates who pillaged Turkish beaches. He wants you to include every possible kernel of information about that era. Could you research and write your story in the direction he prefers? You'll never know *what* he prefers unless you send a query.

Come Up with Ideas

Don't waste an editor's time by asking "What can I write for you about my upcoming trip to Morocco?" Make a list of possible story ideas about Morocco and then query the editors.

If your plans are firm enough to solicit sales several months before your trip, you increase your chances of traveling with go-aheads and assignments. As soon as your pre-trip research reveals writing possibilities, suggest one or several ideas to your target market. Sometimes your insight will catalyze the editor into suggesting ideas of his own—assigning you to research them.

If the editor is in a hurry for your article, she'll tell you. She may suggest an approach, form, length, additional research sources, or other aids to enrich your piece. If you follow the suggestions, your manuscript will have a head start toward publication. Not only will you be able to mail it directly to the editor who encouraged you, but also when she sees it she will recognize the idea as one she liked. If you've used your story lead in the query, she'll also recognize the words. Having encouraged you to send it, she's ready to praise your piece at the editorial conference. She has a stake in your success. To ensure this recognition, many writers enclose or attach to an email a copy of the go-ahead or assignment when following a query with a manuscript.

Your Query Letter Is Your Showcase

The most important plus of the query letter is the opportunity it gives you to get organized. Obviously you can't write an appealing letter until you've thought through what your article will cover. Many times Louise started to write a query and found she didn't know enough yet to make a strong presentation. Several times she has discovered that what she had at first thought so fascinating didn't really make a story after all. On other occasions, trying to formulate the query proposal helped her find the focus for the finished piece.

While the focus should be clear in the query, it should be stated briefly. Without brevity, you lose your advantage. Most editors are too busy to search through a long letter to find just what you are proposing. We've all heard writers say, "My idea is so wonderful, so unique, so exciting, so stupendous, there's no possible way I could confine its description to only a couple of paragraphs." Our advice is to open a file on your computer and write out your idea(s). Then, go through the ideas, delete the weak ones, and then enlarge on the strong ones. After completing this, go through the descriptions and highlight the best descriptive words. Those words are the ones to use when writing your query letter or email.

The query is your showcase. To function as a sales tool it needs the aura of unmistakable excellence. It should sparkle with well-selected words and significant statements. The editor assumes that your finished work will be no better than your proposal.

The professional travel writer plans and polishes the sales tool until he is proud to send it out. Sometimes it's a good idea to begin the query with the hook you've devised for the finished piece. Designed to attract readers, it's also likely to attract an editor.

Your marketing book gives you the first clue as to who gets the query letter. You will find there the names of the editor, articles editor, features editor, travel editor, or someone especially assigned to deal with your type of material. Throughout the year, writers' magazines and yearbooks help you keep your marketing book up to date as they announce editorial changes. Another clue comes from the publication itself. Which staff member listed on its masthead is the one most likely to be concerned with your idea? But if you've had previous correspondence with anyone on the staff, you'll address your letter to that person. If you've had a recent nice rejection letter (we'll examine "nice rejection letters" in a minute), you may even want to refer to your previous idea in your present query.

Types of Query Letters

Sometimes it seems more appropriate to encapsulate your idea in the first paragraph of your query, briefly summarizing what your proposed article is all about. This opening paragraph in a successful query was used by one writer to woo the editor, although these exact words never appeared in the finished piece:

> Malta, one of the world's smallest independent nations, encompasses one of the world's oldest civilizations. A dazzling gem to fifty centuries of would-be conquerors, this Mediterranean paradise today offers excellent climate, unspoiled beaches, and interesting landmarks.

Another type of query can begin with a startling statement:

> One out of every ten Americans will die in a transportation accident. An article I have in mind would help your readers protect themselves and their families against transportation accidents on their vacations.

There are many ways to launch your query, but be sure you begin with a grabber that induces the editor to read on. As you concentrate on keeping the "you" big and the "I" small, remember the editor isn't interested in what he can do for you—only in what you can do for him. Your success may depend on how well you can identify with his outlook.

Whichever way you begin, somewhere in your query, in one concise sentence, indicate the thrust of your message. Indicate also what your viewpoint will be. Are you writing a first-person experience, a second-person how-to, or a concealed viewpoint destination piece?

Give hints about how you will develop your story. If your message is, "South Carolina is the cheapest vacation spot in the United States today," show the editor how much it costs for a superior hotel room and a good dinner, and how much you tip the cab driver. If you say it's good, as well as cheap, show why.

Toot Your Own Horn

Use examples that bolster the importance of your story and convince the editor that you are the only one to write it. Have you published in this periodical previously? In a sibling publication? In one or several big-name publications? Say so. Whether or not to include copies of published articles with the query is an individual decision—you're balancing between showing off your best and burdening the editor with additional reading. If the editor asks for tear sheets, a resume, or a credit list, of course you will comply if you can. Otherwise, the decision often depends on how appropriate the tear sheet or the credit list is to your present query, in terms of subject matter, style, and market.

What in your educational, vocational, or avocational background fits you to write this particular story? It may sound immodest to say: "Several recent trips to Turkey and extensive research make me well qualified to write this article for you. My historically oriented travel articles have appeared in *House Beautiful, Modern Maturity, Brides* magazine, and many other publications of national circulation."

But this is no time to be modest. The editor is probably also interested in knowing if you are just leaving for the site of your story or just returning from there. Have you been there often? A long time ago, as well as recently? Do you have relatives there? Friends? Special connections?

If you have access to unusual research sources or unique skills as a researcher, mention them. Queen Elizabeth invited you to Buckingham Palace to see her favorite flower arrangements? Cairo University's dean of archaeology guided you through the Valley of the Nobles? You have an extensive bibliography of original sources? Don't keep these facts a secret.

While you're trying to think of everything you can in your favor, it's not necessary—or desirable—to include a five-page curriculum vita. And don't include anything unrelated to the subject of the query. The editor is interested in you as a writer for this particular story.

The editor is also uninterested in your previous literary achievements if all they add up to is the assistant editorship of your high school yearbook or a sonnet published in a literary magazine long ago. On the other hand, it's foolish to confess in your query letter, "I have never written anything before," or "I have no tear sheets to send." If you have nothing significant to say, say nothing.

Query Do's and Don'ts
Your relationship by marriage to the publisher's second cousin probably doesn't matter either. The editor usually is not interested in your financial situation. Telling him how badly you need the money for the article is more likely to elicit antipathy than sympathy; and describing in your query the reasons you need the money is like talking yourself out of the assignment.

Attempting to ooze affluence, on the other hand, or embracing a "What's the difference?" attitude about finances, does nothing to gain editorial favor either. Never offer to work at a cut-rate price because you're "so anxious to break into print, I'll do anything—even give it to you for nothing." This not only indicates that you may have a low opinion of your own individual worth or value, it exposes your amateur standing. The time to discuss money is after the editor says he wants your story. That's also the time to discuss editorial changes. Do not, as so many amateurs do, tell the editor in the query, "Feel free to change anything you want to." She already feels free.

Be truthful and don't exaggerate, but don't be falsely humble. If you start your query with something like:

> You probably won't be interested in my idea, but I just thought I'd ask you anyway, because now that I'm retired from my job as a bookkeeper I have lots of free time, and I used to think when I was a little boy I'd like to be a writer when I grew up. I just took a trip to Catalina Island, but lots of people have been to Catalina Island, so you probably won't want my story. My sixth-grade teacher used to say I was very clever at telling little stories, but you probably won't think my writing's good enough.

The editor wonders why you bothered.

If you're not a regular reader of the target publication, don't say so. It's amazing how many would-be writers begin a query with "I never read your magazine, but ... " If, on the other hand, you've subscribed for thirty years, that's less important than a concrete demonstration of your familiarity with the magazine's contents.

If your selected market or a competitor has recently published something even slightly related to what you have in mind, it's wise to defend your originality and show how your approach, your idea, your information would be different—and therefore desirable. This letter addressed to the editor of *Better Homes and Gardens* begins with mention of similar material:

> Although you published a houseboat piece last year, I would like to suggest a more practical, definitive article on rental houseboating vacations. My article would be addressed to the hesitant—to those who would like a houseboat holiday, but are afraid they can't afford it or that they don't have the necessary skills to run the boat.
>
> While your previous article was helpful to the houseboater searching for destinations and activities, I had in mind something with more emphasis on life aboard the boat. Those who don't know much about outdoor recreation in general often wonder if they'll find comfort and enjoyment with a rented houseboat, and I would be prepared to answer their unasked questions with specific information.

A query addressed to the editor of American Airlines' inflight magazine begins:

> Although you naturally encourage your readers to travel to Cairo by air, once they get to Egypt they can have a wonderful time cruising the Nile by boat or traveling alongside it by train.

If your material is controversial, tell how you will show the other side, also. If you foresee objections to your idea, try to answer the objections before they arise. Be wary of sweeping generalizations and unverified facts—the editor may know more about your story than you do. Although it's all right to say "I have never seen another article on this subject," do not say didactically, "Nothing has ever been published on this subject," or "Not much has been published about this subject recently."

If you have a catchy title for your article, it helps the query. The words *new* and *free* are always attention getters. So is the word *you*. Remember, however, that the editor to whom you are sending the query is not the "you" to whom your article will be addressed. If you start your letter to the editor with "Are you hesitant about renting a houseboat or afraid you can't afford to?" you will give the wrong impression entirely. Editors say they are often offended by a query with this type of beginning. A good alternative would be "Is your reader hesitant ... are they afraid they can't ... "

Although a good writer should be able to shorten or lengthen any story according to directions, if your information is so limited or so extensive that the length of your manuscript is necessarily predetermined, suggest your projected length.

If you expect the publication to pay part of the expenses involved in obtaining your story, you'd better mention that in the query, too. If you're a newcomer to travel writing, the chances for expense money are slim. If you're a veteran, they're not much better. Sometimes, however, you can persuade an editor that although he cannot afford to send his personal representative halfway around the world on a story, he's getting a great bargain in providing you with a modest expense account. Explain that you'll be using a combination of other expense accounts, travel perks, and your own vacation funds. Be sure all arrangements are spelled out on paper before you leave home.

Photos Help You Sell

If you have illustrations or you can secure illustrations, say so. And help the editor to visualize them. Bert Goldrath thinks the key to his hundreds of magazine sales is the camera that is part of his *modus operandi*. "I research the picture possibilities first," he says, "then in the query I always include details about the photographs I'm prepared to supply."

Some publications like you to include a couple of sample photographs with the query, and they so indicate in their market listings. An editor of a military-oriented magazine sends out frequent letters reminding his contributors that "the cupboard is getting bare again." He asks for pictures plus a few sentences describing the story line. If he likes your photographs, he invites you to send your manuscript. Many other editors reply to preliminary suggestions with, "That might make a good story for us. Let me see your pictures, and I'll let you know whether or not to go ahead with writing the piece."

Do try to offer the kind of illustrations your target market desires. See Chapter 14 for tips on taking salable pictures, advice on securing illustrations from other sources, and information on how to send photographs.

The Book Proposal

If you're seeking an assignment to produce a travel guidebook, your preliminary queries to book publishers will be similar to article queries. When your introductory letter of inquiry elicits interest, you will probably need to develop a full-scale book proposal.

Presumably you'll select a likely publisher for the kind of book you have in mind, and you'll plan your approach to reflect a similarity to that publisher's existing list. If you propose something very different, it may or may not be appealing.

In any case, most successful book proposals include certain basic information, such as the proposed title and subtitle, probable length, format, potential readership, and probably a sample of your writing. Of course, you will include your own qualifications for writing the book and a description of what you can do to help promote it.

The necessary "selling handle" is a brief, enticing sentence or two that will make the buyer want to buy and the reader want to read. As Michael Larsen says in his excellent book, *How to Write a Book Proposal*, "The selling handle should broadcast the benefit readers will gain from your book." Larsen also recommends including a substantial chapter-by-chapter outline and one or more sample chapters as part of the proposal.

While the objective of your inquiry is always to arouse the editor's interest and cause him to ask for your book or article, don't oversell. In your query or proposal don't promise more than you can deliver. But *reach* in your query. Reach for an anticipation of excellence in your article. And within the article, reach for the best writing that's in you—and a little beyond.

Should I Send a Query or the Manuscript?

When do you send a query and when do you just go ahead and send the whole piece? In general, you send a query whenever the research is more important than the style. Although the query letter is an excellent tool that can provide a strong plus value for the travel writer, there are times when it cannot be used.

Most publications have Websites, so Google their names and look for "Writers Guidelines" somewhere on the individual Website. Carefully read the guidelines. Does your story fit with what the publication is looking for?

There are times when the material is so dependent upon the author's style, rather than upon the subject matter, that a query would be pointless. This is especially true of humorous, nostalgic, and personal experience stories. Sometimes, too, the story is very short, especially if it's intended for a newspaper travel section or as a magazine back-of-the-book piece. If the finished story is shorter than the query, or only a little longer, send the story.

As a general rule, send a query first whenever the subject matter's significance eclipses the style, unless the editor says he doesn't want one, or the length or timeliness of the story indicates otherwise.

If the publisher asks for the query (or, indeed, the manuscript itself) on a CD or online, of course you will comply.

When you query an online zine or attempt to become part of an online production, you first need to decide whether you are offering content, concept, or both. (When somebody else has the concept, the producer will often hire writers to fill in the content.) Your query will be similar to one for a print publication, but you will send it by email. Email queries have one tremendous advantage—the subject line. Be sure to begin the subject line with the word *query*, and then add the sharpest banner you can think of. Each word in the subject line is worth hundreds of dollars, and you only get about five words that will show up in the subject line. Choose VERY carefully which words will ignite the editor's interest so she will continue to read the body of your email.

Email queries are usually a bit more informal and should come right to the point. An email query to an online publication goes like this:

(Subject line) Query: Comedy of Errors on Mexico Cruise

Senior Editor (name)
www.salon.com

Although a comedy of errors, including late planes, lurid cruise ship, and lost documents, launched my Mexican Riviera cruise, it all worked out just fine. Watching the divers in Acapulco was a spectacular experience. Getting arrested in Mazatlan was less delightful.

Excellent photographs, both black and white and color, would accompany the article, in any format you prefer.

For more information about me and my credentials, please check out my Website at: _____

I look forward to hearing from you soon.

Cordially,

It's a good idea to have an automatic salutation in your email program with your name, address, phone numbers (land and cell), email, and Website and blog addresses.

When to Send Your Query

When do you send the query? You send it as soon as you've done enough research to make an attractive sales presentation. However, "enough" is hard to pinpoint.

It might take one writer on one subject a couple of hours to research enough material for the query, while another writer, working on another subject, might spend six months gathering enough solid facts to put together a salable story idea.

Your Query Must Instill Confidence

You want to be sure to always do enough research so the editor knows you know what you're talking about. You have to have enough facts to instill a feeling of confidence, because every editor is haunted by the fear that he will accept a story by an inexperienced writer that later proves to be untrue or inaccurate.

It isn't only the inexperienced writer he worries about. Some publications now insist on written verification of facts and sources from everybody. One editor explains, "We've seen too many freelance stories reporting on interviews that never actually took place."

For another publication, an imaginative travel writer even described an island that never existed. The editor especially liked his story of a small Caribbean island that supposedly never appeared on charts because it had been a secret U.S. Navy installation during World War II, and the Pentagon deleted it from all maps. The author described the island—discovered by him—as an Eden with a "happy native population virtually untouched by civilization."

Letters and phone calls from readers begged for directions to the island paradise. Only one protesting voice spoiled the climate of bliss. "It was Ernest Hemingway's brother," says the editor. "And he knew the Caribbean like the back of his hand. According to him, no such island existed or ever did exist."

When questioned about his sources, the writer, unabashed, replied, "I've always wanted to do a story about a mysterious, undiscovered island. But since there weren't any that I knew of, I just made the whole thing up." Can you blame editors for being wary?

So in your query, allay the editor's fears with what is clearly well-researched information. If there's material you expect to use but haven't yet verified, call it unverified, so the editor knows you know the difference.

Do Your Homework Before You Query

Never take shortcuts with your research. But don't fall into the trap of endlessly researching something that may never sell. Many writers do this. The research itself becomes so attractive they postpone writing even the query until they spend "just another couple of days" and then "just a few more" researching, and they somehow never get around to writing. "That's my trouble," says an archaeologist-writer. "Although I've managed to sell two popular articles on Pompeii, I have a dozen more archaeologically oriented travel stories written in my head. But before I send the query I always check and recheck—and then check again—every single word. Did the original source find exactly the same thing I did? Perhaps I should look for just one more original source? Eventually the whole thing seems sort of stale. I begin to wonder whether anybody else would be interested, so I don't bother the editor by inquiring."

This writer is losing one of the great advantages of the query. A query works best if you do only enough research to write the letter. Then if no one thinks your idea is as good as you do, you haven't wasted much time on something nobody's going to buy.

You will, of course, send some queries before you start on your trip. Others you may send while you're traveling, so it's a good idea to have a file on a USB flash drive of travel-related publications, editors' names, and email addresses so that when you stumble upon a story unexpectedly, you can query an editor immediately. Still other queries you'll send upon your return home, and some you'll send long after your return.

The Travel Writer Thinks Ahead

The travel writer learns to think far ahead. Some writers use special calendars to remind them to plan the "Old-Fashioned New England Christmas" story in March, to get ready for "Easter Week in Spain" at the beginning of June, and to start querying in December on "Give the Kids a Treat at Disneyland Before They Go Back to School." If your target market says it needs material six months in advance, add to that how long it will take you to write the finished piece, plus a couple of weeks for a response to your query. Then add a couple of weeks for unexpected delays. Do you have enough time? If it's already August and you don't have the story written, there's no point in sending a query about New England this Christmas. Begin, instead, to plan for next year.

If you have a travel story that's really hot news—something like a confirmed seat on the first space shuttle to the moon—you may want to telephone the editor for an early okay. Since telephone calls are seldom popular in editorial offices, try to find out when deadline times are, so you won't be calling at the worst possible moment, and always ask, "Is this a convenient time for you to talk to me?"

If the editor answers yes to your proposal, firm it up with a supporting email letter to protect yourself. Make it a pleasant, friendly letter, thanking him for the consideration and outlining your understanding of the arrangements.

Sometimes even a negative telephone call has value. As one prolific writer, who often telephones proposals, points out, "If the editor tells you no, he'll probably tell you why—which is important information for you to have."

If you are at the stage where you're making appointments with editors, make those appointments productive. Plan ahead. Prepare to discuss your specific ideas with the same care you'd put into a query letter. If you don't have enough facts yet to show the editor what you mean, do more research before you meet her. A social occasion where you vaguely inquire, "Is there anything I can do for you?" may be personally pleasant, but professionally it's a waste of her time and yours.

A *Field & Stream* editor says an oral query shouldn't be "so aggressive as to be obnoxious, but don't hesitate to ask." He reminds travel outdoor writers that once the editor has given the affirmative nod to an oral query, you're obligated to show the finished article to him first. He tells about a writer who discussed with him at great length a story about some lakes near his home. "The idea sounded good," he explains, "and I told him to send the article to me when it was done. I finally saw the story, but it was in another magazine."

Don't play games with the editor. If he seems interested in your proposal, let him see the finished product before offering it to somebody else. Otherwise, don't expect him to even appear interested in your next proposal.

Give the Editor Choices

Face to face, you'll probably discuss a number of different ideas with your editor. But most inquiries will still be by letter or email. How many ideas should you propose in a single query letter? Many professional writers oppose presenting more than one idea at a time. "You only compete against yourself," they warn. "Send one idea, and if the editor likes it, then send another. If he doesn't like it, still send another. But send them separately, one idea at a time."

Pre-trip query letters often evoke interest from editors. Then you can concentrate on the facets of your trip experience that interest your prospective publishers.

Query Mechanics

Regardless of the form you use, put your best foot forward in the query. To make your query work for you, make sure its mechanics meet the highest standards of excellence—including the correct spelling of the editor's name.

Remember, you have only one thirty-second chance to make a good first impression. The editor suspects your manuscript will be no better than your query.

Turning Rejections into Acceptances

Once you have gotten your query together, agonized over each word, carefully composed an email letter, and sent it on its way, what kind of reply is it likely to elicit?

Unfortunately, the most common type in the beginning may be a small letter or emailed reply with a message something like this: "Thank you for your proposal, which has received careful consideration. We regret that this material does not meet our needs at the present time, but we appreciate your interest."

Disheartening as these rejections are, overcome the temptation to click "Delete" or burn them in the fireplace immediately. Save them and file away in the proposed story's folder, either online or hard copy. If later you take off some writer's expenses on your income tax (see Chapter 17 for discussion of tax deductions), rejection letters are good evidence for the IRS that you're working on becoming a writer.

Learn to read between the lines of a rejection letter. Across the miles you can picture the editor regretting, just a trifle wistfully, that he must turn down your masterpiece of an idea in so casual a manner. If "Try us again" is part of the letter, that's definite encouragement.

Often you can turn a "nice" rejection letter into an acceptance by simply reading between the lines. Does the editor say your idea is too complex and would make too long an article for him to use? Amputate and re-query. Does he say he has too much material on hand now, but "try again in six months"? Mark it on your calendar. Does he like the subject area but not your approach? Suggest a different one. Does he name another publication that he thinks would provide a better home for your idea? Try it. Does he say "no" because he feels your idea wouldn't suit his readers, while you know it would be perfect for them? Convince him.

Sometimes the editor explains why she doesn't like your proposal, but encourages you to try her with something else. Use care in selecting another subject—either a similar one or one quite different, depending on what the letter said—and submit another query to that editor immediately. Keep good records of where and when you've queried on what, and don't accept a no as final. Often a new publication, a new editor at the same publication, or the same editor in a new mood, months or even years later, will transform a no into a yes.

Suppose you don't have any response to your query? How long should you wait to inquire? That depends on how urgent the time element is, but in general six or eight weeks. Then write a nice email letter of inquiry, attaching the original query, or, if you're on good terms with that editor, call or email to ask for a decision. Often the response will be something like, "I'm so glad you called. I was interested in your idea, but somehow your letter seems to have gotten buried in my email somewhere. Let's see what you can do with the article."

Dealing with the "Go-Ahead"

Not all answers to query letters are yes or no. A great many of them are maybe. That's what a go-ahead is—a maybe. That's what the editor is saying when he indicates, "We'd like to see it on speculation." This is not an assignment. It makes no guarantee. All it promises is a careful reading. When you do send your manuscript, addressed to the editor who gave you the go-ahead, it won't land at the bottom of the slush pile of unsolicited manuscripts but will be carefully read by someone who at least liked the idea in the first place.

A go-ahead does give you the advantage of being able to say to an information source, "XYZ Magazine is interested in having me write an article on Mount Rushmore. Can you help me with my research?" How long dare you wait to send your manuscript after the editor's expression of interest? That depends. It depends on the timeliness, both seasonal and topical, of the material. It depends, if you've queried before your trip, on how long you'll be away. It depends on the difficulty of the research. And it depends on the enthusiasm of the editor, which may or may not be related to a particular hole he has to fill, a special edition he plans, or the possibility of securing an accompanying advertisement.

What if the article is already written, having been rejected by somebody else? Should you send it as soon as you receive the go-ahead, thereby alerting the editor to his second-choice status? Or should you wait four or five weeks and pretend you're writing it just for him? A variety of circumstances will dictate your decision in this situation. Is the subject matter so timely it will soon be obsolete? Are there enough other possible markets for you to adopt a casual attitude toward rejection? Is the research so complex and time-consuming that this sale is all-important? There's no single "right" answer.

Always, though, reply to a go-ahead with a thank-you for the invitation to send your article. Indicate how long it will take you to complete the manuscript. In your estimate allow for all possible detours and distractions, and if in doubt, say, "I'll send it soon." Consider six months an outside limit, and aim for four to eight weeks.

Once your article is accepted, or even if it is rejected but the editor sends an encouraging note, follow up quickly with a new query for a different idea.

What Are Your Query's Chances?

How likely is the beginner to receive any kind of positive response to his query? The statistics on receiving a go-ahead are one in ten when you're just starting out. And then you may consider the article half-sold. That doesn't mean some other editor won't encourage your idea or buy your piece eventually—the statistics only mean it may take twenty queries to sell an article. More than twenty queries and no bites? Perhaps it wasn't such a good idea after all. Or perhaps your query isn't enticing enough, or your marketing itinerary was not astutely selected. Five go-aheads in a row—followed by prompt rejections? Either you haven't lived up to what you promised in the query or the five editors who gave you go-aheads have all died, retired, resigned, or been fired.

But don't be discouraged. As you learn to write better query letters, as you study markets and read between the lines of your rejections so that you're matching ideas and target markets more accurately, the statistics improve.

Add the skills of a salesman to your skills as a writer for an unbeatable combination. You'll sell your travel stories as fast as you write them when you learn to make your queries work for you.

CHAPTER 1 2

Going on with the Show

Writing, it is said, cannot be taught—it can only be learned. "But what about talent?" is a question potential travel writers frequently ask. "How can I tell if I have what it takes?" If you like to write and you like to travel, you can learn to write well enough to succeed. If you are writing for others rather than merely to please yourself, you'll want to follow the principles of effective travel writing, so let's pinpoint some of the fundamentals.

Slant Your Story

One basic precept we encounter again and again—and travel writers need to be reminded of it again and again—is that there's no such thing as "writing generally." Writing has to be *for* somebody—a particular publication, a particular reader.

Study your target markets carefully, as we've said before. Then slant accordingly. *Slant* is not a dirty word. Slant is a means of ensuring that your material is read by those for whom it is intended. If you're writing for the *New York Times*, slant it for *Times* readers. The well-written travel article is filled with general information and enough slanted specifics to appeal to a particular reader.

Online readers, too, generally read what's slanted for their individual concerns—in shorter versions. To capture and maintain their interest, the content needs to be directed to a global audience, average age thirty-two, mostly college educated, tech-oriented, with substantial income. And that content is usually presented in short chunks, with many subheads, sometimes bulleted, and often linked to other articles on related subjects.

Write a Capsule Sentence

Intrinsic to the travel article is the *message*. You must be able to express the idea behind your article—your message—in a single pithy capsule sentence. The capsule sentence should appear early on, and it should remain in your mind (and your reader's mind) from the first word to the final period.

What is your message? What are you trying to say?

- The Kona Coast is a beautiful place to vacation.
- Take your children on a Disney Cruise.
- New York in summer is very different from New York in winter.
- At Club Med the young at heart welcome new adventures.

Once you've settled on a clear-cut capsule sentence, tack it above your keyboard or write it on each page of first-draft paper as an ongoing reminder. Then everything in your article will relate to or confirm or amplify the message you've selected. Don't make that message too broad and general: "Wisconsin." "New York." And don't make it too narrow: "My little boy liked the endless buffet of desserts on the Disney Cruise" or "Take the Staten Island Ferry on July 14 at 2:00 p.m." Once you've decided what you want to convey in the completed article, it's easy to fit the pieces of information into the mosaic of the whole.

The length of your article can be controlled by manipulating the capsule sentence. If you need a longer article, broaden its scope: "Hawaii has many beautiful spots" or "Investigate the Club Med." If you need a shorter article, narrow the scope. Because computer screens are harder on the reader's eyes and articles often download slowly, the finished piece may need to be built around "The fishing's good at Donat" or "I learned to snorkel at Tahiti's Club Med." The length is especially important if your article is to be downloaded on a mobile device.

Unless all segments of your story relate to the capsule sentence, they form what editors call "a string of pearls"—a series of unrelated incidents.

No matter how interesting the individual anecdotes, unless they're skillfully slanted and connected to each other and to the capsule sentence, they will not hold the reader's interest. Until the writer can establish a capsule sentence that expresses the reason for writing about these particular experiences and ties each incident to that theme sentence, there is no story.

What Is Your Viewpoint?

Another fundamental is viewpoint: the identity from which you're telling the story. Every piece of writing is told from some point of view, so decide in the beginning which you will use. You have several choices. First person travel articles (I, or we, saw this and did that) of all types are becoming increasingly popular. And they are particularly popular in cyberspace, perhaps because the diary style seems to bring the writer and the reader closer to each other, whether the first person is a major or a minor character:

> My favorite experience in Japan was watching the cormorant fishing and seeing the merrymaking aboard adjacent boats.

Although most personal experience stories are written in *first person major character*, don't feel this is the only possible viewpoint for travel articles. *First person minor character*, while less common, sometimes works out best:

> On the boat next to ours they were setting off firecrackers. "Soon the cormorant fishermen will come," said the geisha girl. "I hope they never come!" I heard the man beside her say. "Or at least not for a long time. After the fishing boats have come and gone, then I'll have to go home."
>
> He spoke in English, which surprised me. . . .

Will Stanton frequently presents himself as the minor-character observer when he travels with his children. He tells the story through the major characters, the children, giving their reactions to New York or Disneyland.

Third person viewpoint, either major or minor, is used less often in travel articles since it lacks the warmth and on-the-scene feeling of the more personal "I" or "you." *Third person minor character* goes like this:

> Yoshi watched the geisha girl. She looked like she was getting tired, but she was still smiling. "The fishermen will be here soon," she said. He wondered if she . . .

Third person major character looks like this:

> The Japanese worker looks forward to cormorant season, not only for the spectacle itself but also for the fun aboard the chartered boat.

Sometimes a third-person travel article is unavoidable, as Louise discovered when she wrote about the travels of her daughter's Girl Scout troop. Since she did not accompany the girls on their trip, she tried to make up for the once-removed viewpoint with quotes from the girls, substantial amounts of dialogue, and liberal use of anecdotes that showed the Brownies and the Girl Scouts during the nine years they prepared for the trip as well as while they were traveling.

Second person viewpoint is popular in travel articles, usually used in combination with first person or third person:

I enjoyed the train trip.
You'll find the trains comfortable ...
Their room overlooked the river.
If you ask for a riverfront room ...

When second person articles are structured like recipes or how-to-do-its, commanding peremptorily, "Take the nine o'clock ferry" or "Buy the tickets in advance," it's still obvious that I, the writer, am telling you, the reader, what to do, even if neither the "I" nor the "you" is mentioned. For example:

In Japan be sure to take the excursion to see the cormorant fishing.

Another viewpoint without personal pronouns is the *implied*. Although the person telling the story is not identified, the reader is aware of someone providing the information. Through word pictures, active verbs, and strong emotional responses, the writer projects a "you are there" feeling. Implied viewpoint usually requires greater skill and more writing experience, so it often develops a stronger story.

Acting much like a Big Game busload of convivial old grads, a boatload
of Japanese co-workers makes merry while waiting for the cormorants.
Men and women, comfortable in kimonos, sing and dance as they cook
supper over hibachis, pass the sake bottle, and shoot off sky-brightening
fireworks.

The *objective* viewpoint appears only in such straightforward travel writing as the encyclopedia:

Cormorants can stay underwater a long time when they dive for fish.
They swim with their webbed feet.

The *omniscient* viewpoint, where the author enters the minds of all the characters—the Japanese worker, the geisha girl, the fisherman (and possibly the cormorant)—is presently eschewed by most writers since it produces a weak and wordy article.

Switching Viewpoints

Must the entire article remain in one viewpoint? Generally, yes. Since the reader identifies with the viewpoint, switching complicates the story and requires extra wordage to prevent confusion. However, many travel articles do switch viewpoints—the only popular feature articles to do so. The piece might begin in first person:

"Can it get much better than this?" A fellow passenger from St. Paul
leaned back in his deck chair and sipped from his champagne flute as
he asked the question. We were finishing our lunch of fresh salmon

157

mousse, accompanied by three kinds of wine, a sunny autumn day, and a languorous desire to watch the scenery glide by at four miles an hour as we floated through France's champagne country aboard the barge *Linquenda*.

Then the article continues in second person:

If you want to really see a country's hinterland, without the strain of driving, a week's barge trip on its waterways can be the most relaxing journey imaginable. You can stand at the rail and wave to the field hands harvesting the grapes or chat with the lock-keepers as they open or close the gates that move you from one water level to the next. Or you can ...

Next, an implied viewpoint:

The *Linquenda*, which carries a maximum of 14 passengers, has a pleasant sundeck, a lounge-dining room with books, cards, music, and a well-stocked bar that's open all the time.

Back to "you" again:

From the fresh-baked croissants in the morning to the chocolate on the pillow at night, you'll enjoy the five-star cuisine that includes ...

And back to "us":

We toured the cellars at several champagne houses, including Pomeroy and Moët & Chandon, and, of course, tasted as we went.

And implied:

This chalky, hilly countryside is ideal for the growing of champagne grapes, and it was here that Dom Perignon discovered ...

First person again:

An especially meaningful sightseeing tour to those of us who had heard our parents or grandparents talk about Château â Thierry and Belleau Woods, was the trip to ...

The transitions must be accomplished smoothly, and you have to make sure that every time you switch viewpoints, you gain more than you lose.

The Hook Must Catch Your Reader

Your narrator won't operate in a vacuum. A good travel piece has a beginning, a middle, and an end. Unlike the traditional inverted pyramid of a newspaper story, where the most important facts are told in the first paragraph, with decreasingly important facts spelled out in succeeding paragraphs to allow for hasty cutting from the end, the travel feature story is a unified entity, and can only be shortened through paragraph-by-paragraph or sentence-by-sentence or word-by-word deletions.

A travel article's beginning should be sparkling, exciting, compelling: a hook that induces the reader—and the editor—to *read on*. Considering you have only a few seconds to nab a busy editor, page-flipping reader, or online surfer and involve him in your story, the importance of your opening cannot be overemphasized. Some writers say they spend half their writing time on the hook. Yet it's hard to describe what makes a good hook, although many writing teachers have tried.

We recommend grouping travel article hooks into these three categories:

The *you* approach tells the reader why the information in this article will be especially valuable for him.

The *compare-and-contrast* hook builds tensions, arouses the reader's curiosity, and stimulates him to learn more.

The *scene-setting* hook hints, in an almost fictional manner, about a fascinating story to come.

The following "you" examples plunge right in and tell the reader how she will benefit from this article. Notice how many of the benefits concern money, such as:

> If you want a vacation spot where your dollars buy full measure of sunshine and sport, culture and cuisine, history and hospitality, head for southern Spain.

> or

> If you bemoan the fact that your travel dollars never seem to take you where you want to go, if you return from vacation feeling frustrated because you spent more money for less fun than anticipated, it's time to analyze exactly what you want your vacation dollars to buy.

Also notice how many "you" hooks are concerned with providing pleasure or alleviating discomfort, such as:

> For vacation activities to please every member of your family, try Buena Park in Southern California. There, you can ride an Old West Stagecoach, inspect a $250,000 Rolls-Royce, or pet a lion cub ...

> or

> If winter rains and post-holiday letdown are sending your thoughts toward a warm-weather vacation, remember it's summer in Lima and Buenos Aires.

In the compare-and-contrast type of hook, sometimes the tension that forces the reader to continue is provided by a surprise element.

Thanks to Prohibition, juvenile delinquency, a crippling accident, drunken brawlers, and Johnnie Holzwarth, Rocky Mountain National Park opened its first living-history exhibit.

This next hook compares and contrasts us and them:

Ask a Texan his nationality, and he'll tell you he's American. Ask a citizen of Germany's southernmost state the same question, and chances are he'll answer, "I'm a Bavarian."

Sometimes hooks compare and contrast now and then:

The fastest transportation available to man in the year 2000 B.C. was the camel caravan, which averaged approximately 3.5 miles an hour. Invention of the horse-drawn chariot raised the maximum speed for short distances to roughly 20 miles per hour. Little over a century ago this was still a record. It took 3,500 years to get man's travel speed up to 100 miles an hour. Yet in the past century it soared from the railroad's 100 miles to the now departed Concorde's designed speed of 1,350 miles per hour.

Some hooks compare and contrast here and there:

How does it feel to suddenly find yourself hospitalized six thousand miles from home in a strange land, worse yet in a country torn apart by riots demanding the resignation of the current dictator?

Comparing and contrasting seasons leads to a good hook:

It's summer. All the skis, toboggans, boots, sweaters, mittens, and snow shovels are gladly packed away. It's time to load up the kids and the dog, the golf clubs, tennis rackets, swimsuits, sunglasses, sunburn ointment, and picnic basket and head for the nearest ski resort.

That's right. Ski resorts are fast becoming the hottest summer vacation spots in New England.

A scene-setting hook lures the reader into the story. Conflict provides a big part of the enticement. All three kinds of conflict—man against nature, man against man, and man against himself—can be used to good advantage.

Man against nature:

He stands an instant, poised at the cliff's edge, then springs. His flying body plunges through the air, hurtling down more than 130 feet toward a narrow chasm of churning tidewater.

Man against man:

Anyone who has traveled abroad without knowing the local language has worried about being able to communicate. I thought I'd learned enough French in high school to get me from Paris to Marseilles, but a waiter in

Lyons taught me differently. He not only brought me cream of watercress soup instead of crème caramel, he overcharged me ten euros.

Man against himself:

After practicing six months in preparation for the canoe trip, I didn't believe the doctor when he said I wasn't strong enough to go. "I intend to go anyway," I told him. "Even if I have another heart attack, it's worth it."

Begin at the Mattering Moment

We can't help observing how many of these hooks don't begin at the beginning—just as Homer didn't start with the day Helen of Troy was born. Like Homer, learn to begin in the middle of the action, then occasionally flash back to those parts of the beginning the reader needs to know. Whether it's an adventure tale or a nuts-and-bolts travel article, begin at the "mattering moment." That's the moment immediately preceding the action.

Although the writer may flash back and tell us about his first heart attack and his canoe trip preparations, the moment he decides to defy the doctor is, for this story, the mattering moment. We may later learn about the Acapulco diver's training and practice and even something of the history of diving, but the story begins with the diver poised at the cliff's edge, about to start the action. Draw the reader into your story with something exciting, and then, later, give him the background he needs as briefly and unobtrusively as possible.

As far as tenses go, more e-zine stories use present tense than we find in print media. Perhaps this, too, is an effort to be close to the reader. W. Ruth Kozak's "Reaching for Heaven: Meteora, Greece," begins:

On a bright May afternoon I travel by train across the lush Thessaly Plain in central Greece, through the valley of the Pinios River.

Then come three paragraphs describing the landscape in an implied viewpoint.

Going back to first person, present tense, she says:

Here I find reasonable accommodation and set off to explore the hills behind the town, following a goat trail.

Salon's Mark Hunter writes this in "France's Hidden Treasure":

So when I walk across Mischa's acre, which hasn't been grazed in years and is now overrun by neck-high nettles, I look first and test the grass with a beech stick I cut in the woods.

Hunter, actually in the I/you viewpoint, keeps switching tense, too. Usually simple immediate past tense is easiest for both writer and reader.

Travel Stories Need Plots, Too

The travel article, like its cousin the short story, is plotted. Although you should never distort the facts to improve the story, you can, by careful selection and arrangement, through screening and emphasis, create a plot. Theodore Vogel begins at the mattering moment in his *Realities* story "Where It's Still Fair Whaling." While the subject matter is controversial, and the actions very graphic, it's a good piece for analyzing the use of flashbacks and flash-forwards.

> A harpooned sperm whale had turned and was coming back toward us with monstrous ease. Twenty-five tons of fat and muscle, and a tail four yards wide capable of disintegrating our frail boat with a single blow. . . .
>
> The gigantic snout rose slightly, then slipped below the boat.
>
> There are about thirty teeth in a sperm whale's mouth. A tooth can weigh ten pounds. No one had expected those teeth to surge from the water and clamp onto the *Claudina*'s rim—but there they were, just a yard away. . . .

Then Vogel flashes back two centuries:

> Azorians hunt whales the way it was done two hundred years ago, when American companies recruited oarsmen in the islands and introduced the whaler's ways. . . .

Back to the present:

> Today Azorians still hunt whales better than anyone else. . . .

A brief flashback:

> Four years ago the *Maria da Conceicdo* . . . harpooned an enormous sperm whale which turned and attacked the boat . . . the whale boat . . . smashed in three places . . . two men . . . dead.

He then flashes to his own pre-trip agreement to "'accept all the responsibilities that would result from my death.' I signed quickly, and handed it to the captain. . . ." He explains that lookouts in a whale-hunting village fire flares and radio the tugs when they see a white spout.

Then he takes us back to his own whale hunt:

> The sperm whales seemed monstrous to me in their surges and dives. . . . At a yard's distance, Almerindo flung his harpoon, hitting the whale just below the hump of its back. Everything happened so fast that I had trouble registering it.

Vogel discusses the danger and tells of whalers who have been hurt. Then he flashes to the present, where their boat is being towed by the whale. They move in for the kill, hunters and whale fighting, the water growing red.

An hour and a half and twelve spears later, the whale is finally dead. Vogel introduces philosophical remarks about the whaling industry, international protection of whales, and the future of whaling. Then back to the present:

It was 2:00 p.m. I felt as if years had passed.

A storm comes up, and the eight men huddle together in the stern, but they are in good spirits:

And for a moment, I really understood what it was ... that had sent men out to sea in ships, for centuries, to hunt.

Had Vogel begun with the history of whaling, mentioned his own adventure in the middle, where it comes chronologically, and then ended with the outlook for whaling in the future, the story would have lacked the drama, excitement, and emotional impact it imparts. When you write for others you soon learn to seduce your reader by presenting the most spectacular item in the beginning and adapting the chronology to your own plotting purposes.

The Anatomy of a Travel Story

Louise's article on the battleship *Wasa* in *Coronet* involved an additional problem, since the here-and-now aspects—the discovery and recovery of the ship—were already some ten to fifteen years in the past, too long ago for a news peg.

So she started with an earlier *mattering moment*, the day the *Wasa* sank:

As the seventeenth-century battleship *Wasa* raised sail to begin her maiden voyage, holiday crowds lining Stockholm's Royal Quay waved cheerfully and shouted good wishes. Sweden's naval pride moved majestically into midchannel. ...

And then the *Wasa*, sails billowing and flags flying, heeled over and vanished without making even the harbor exit.

Three centuries later the ship returned from her eighteen-fathom grave ... her figurehead still glittering with gilt and her captain's tankard still filled with schnapps.

Then the capsule sentence, appropriate for *Coronet's* general readership:

The story of the *Wasa's* downfall, her subsequent resistance to decay during three centuries of submersion, and her ultimate recovery is, indeed, stranger than fiction.

Next she tells about present efforts to preserve the *Wasa*, flashes back to events leading up to the mattering moment of the hook, and then explains subsequent attempts to raise the ship, extending over several hundred years.

Then:

> In a way, the teredo, or shipworm, led to eventual rediscovery of the
> *Wasa*, after three centuries.

Anders Franzen, as she explains, thought a ship sunk in the teredo-free waters of the Baltic would be well preserved. The flashback takes place in his mind:

> Surely, he reasoned, someone must have notified the king. After months
> of searching he found the message ... "Off Beckholmen."

Back to the immediate past, with divers discovering an old ship with two rows of gunports:

> ... Franzen was sure. It had to be the *Wasa*! But ... what does one do with
> 1400 tons of seventeenth-century warship anchored in mud, 110 feet
> beneath a busy harbor?

She continues with the salvaging and recovery of the ship and its contents. This leads to a discussion of seventeenth-century shipboard life. Then back to the present with a description of the museum where the *Wasa* and the finds are housed. Then more about seventeenth-century life aboard ship, tied in with the present museum exhibits. She next covers the steps being taken for the *Wasa's* preservation and her probable future. Then:

> Visitors can stand on the museum's catwalks and look down through the
> chemical fog to the heart of the ship. ...They can, with a little imagina-
> tion, see the *Wasa* as she looked on the day of her debut, sails billowing
> and flags flying ... sailed less than a mile in her lifetime ... reincarnated
> to live forever.

Ten years later, when Louise wrote a completely different *Wasa* story for *Off Duty*, she was able to tie the hook to the 350th anniversary observance of the ship's sailing (and sinking). Because *Off Duty's* European edition was published for U.S. servicemen who might go to Stockholm on leave, the capsule sentence of that story is:

> Today the *Wasa* occupies a museum, complete with skeleton sailors, sev-
> enteenth-century schnapps, and slightly rancid butter.

After mentioning the guns being fired with a false charge for the anniversary celebration, she goes back to the sailing day disaster, and then returns to what you can see today, interspersed with explanations of why everything is in such good condition. Then a chronological report of salvage efforts, the recovery of the *Wasa*, the building of the museum, and a forecast for the future, ending with:

... this ship now lives to carry tourists and scientists ... back into history.

A sidebar tells when the museum is open, how much admission costs, etc. It's easier to write a story like this when you have an anniversary peg to tie it to, but a heavily historical article written for a popular audience always requires many flashbacks and flash-forwards.

"Show, Don't Tell"

What else goes into your travel article? Ideally your content will sing with active verbs and precise nouns that appeal to the reader's five senses. Salt sparsely with adjectives and adverbs; avoid clichés, today's slang expressions, and anything that dates the piece or sounds cutesy. On the other hand, utilize all the tricks of the fiction writer's craft. Anecdotes, scenes, dialogue, characterization, and dramatic action belong in the travel story. Write with the breathless excitement of the best travel brochures—but only within the framework of truth and accuracy.

A *New York Times* travel editor summarizes the *Times'* formula for good travel writing:

> You must use all the devices of the writer's skill to keep readers
> interested—a hook beginning; a "billboard" to tell them what the article
> is about near the beginning; word pictures, which is what travel writing is
> all about; what it looks, smells, tastes like. Amateurs use adjectives instead
> of word pictures. They write, "It was a lovely scene," instead of telling us
> what kind of scene it was. Was the sun slanting in from the west? Was
> there ice on the ground? Were there leaves on the trees? What kind of
> scene was it? Show, don't tell.

When you hear a writer or an editor say "show, don't tell," it means you should sharpen it up by getting rid of all the nonworking words, all the dead weight, and, at the same time, flesh it out with details that count. For instance:

Telling: Many medieval people were convinced that the dust from the tomb of Saint John held extra-special curative powers, and many ailing pilgrims climbed up Ayasuluk Hill.

Showing: Medieval Christians on three continents whispered to each other that dust from Saint John's tomb held special curative qualities. Thousands of them plodded up Ayasuluk Hill carrying blind babies or lugging lame relatives on donkey-drawn stretchers.

or

Telling: One night during the cruise there is a passenger costume competition where everybody dresses up like a sheik or a dancing girl or

165

a mummy. Then passengers adjourn to the dining room for a spectacular Mideast buffet—from sculptured lamb to baklava and grape pudding.

Showing: When the pseudo-sheik with the bath towel turban beckoned to the black-veiled harem "girls," they thrust out their stomachs and belly danced around the passenger salon. ... They adjourned to the dining room. Earlier that day our guide had gathered us together and spelled out procedure. "Use your elbows and your shoulders," he advised. "This buffet is really something—and everyone rushes to be first in the dining room line. Don't stand back politely—push like everybody else!" Actually, there was plenty to eat, even for latecomers. But at first sight, that buffet table was worth a little elbowing. The artists of the galley had even sculptured the meat into the shape of a lamb, kneeling on a bed of rice that had been browned to simulate the desert. Roasted pheasants and game hens climbed an ornamental superstructure and a half dozen varieties of fresh fish surrounded the "desert." Purple half shells of savory eggplant alternated with stuffed green peppers and tomato-topped oriental salads. Dishes of black olives and plates of yellow cheeses adjoined the platters of grape leaves rolled into dolmas, which encircled a huge bowl of yogurt. Steam rose from the couscous and the kabobs. Melons, grapes, oranges, and a dozen unfamiliar but delicious fruits and a garden of miniature decorated cakes accompanied the baklava and grape pudding and were followed by demitasses of strong, sweet coffee.

Obviously, "showing" can take up a lot of space. It presents a challenge when writing for online markets or when your print editor is rigid about the number of words you're entitled to.

Good Writing Is Always Good Rewriting

When you feel your article is finished, put it away for at least a week and try not to think about it. You'll return to it with fresh insights and a renewed ability to recognize its faults and to set about correcting them. Many times you'll find ways to cut constructively. Practically all writing is improved by careful cutting. Consider:

> If you are a passenger on board a cruise ship, you will know whether or not to buy the ship's shore excursions. (22 words)

> Aboard ship, you'll know whether or not to buy the shore excursions. (12 words)

> Houseboat operators usually require a $50 to $100 deposit when you make your reservation. This becomes your damage deposit, which is refunded when you return the boat intact. (28 words)

> The $50 to $100 that accompanies your reservation becomes your damage deposit—refunded when you return the boat intact. (19 words)

You'll find the more times you go over your finished piece, the more words you'll discover you can cut. Don't skimp on rewriting time. In college Louise asked a favorite professor who had published many books and articles if he thought there was something wrong with her because it always took her five or six drafts to write an article. "If there is," he replied, "there must be something wrong with *me*, too, because it always takes me five or six drafts."

Read your article aloud when you're working on it. A word of caution, though: if you put enough vigor into your voice and your posture and your facial expression, anything sounds good; the editor, unable to see or hear your performance, will be limited to the words on the paper. So read it in a monotone, to recognize redundant words, "fat" that could be cut, inactive verbs that need active substitutes, abrupt transitions that should be smoothed, complex, dense, or convoluted sentences that need recasting.

Try to eliminate slang and jargon and any language that dates a piece you hope will live forever. Reach for unusual figures of speech as well as descriptive ones. Rolf Potts in Salon.com's "One Fateful Day in Istanbul" uses a number of figures of speech that pull the reader right into the scene:

> I fell over like a wind-up toy on a rumpled bedsheet ... [a] gypsy girl ... wore an oversized Metallica T-shirt ... from the lavish Ottoman halls of Topkapi Palace to the crowded dagger-and-houka pipe stands of the Grand Bazaar ...

A transition is like a road sign that points your reader toward the next paragraph. We're all familiar with the standard "ongoing" words and phrases, such as *and; furthermore; similarly;* and the "backup" transitions: *however, on the contrary; despite.* We know, too, the cause-and-effect relationships: *as a result; because; consequently.* These are often overworked, though, so look for additional types of transitions to guide your reader to the next phase of your story. Time is a good transition: *the next morning; the following year; by six o'clock.* More subtle time transitions might be: *my coffee grew cold; the daffodils were blooming; when our ship sailed in.* Repeating a word from the previous paragraph, repeating the rhythm of the last sentence, comparing and contrasting—all are good transitional devices. You'll find ways to smooth out your forward motion as you revise.

Leave Your Reader Satisfied
Your reader will consider your ending almost as important as your beginning. An article's ending should grow out of the article itself, to provide a finale that seems logical and inescapable, leaving the reader satisfied.

Many travel writers write the end at the same time as the hook. This not only brings you full circle, with beginning and ending written in the same mood, but defines the boundaries of where you're going. It's easier to stay on the track when you know where you will finish.

The ending should usually not be a summary of what you've said in the article, nor should it be what one professor called "a crashing conclusion"— an ending with more force than the story itself, an ending that "tells all" and then tells it again. Instead, it should be a convincing culmination that leaves your reader either smiling or frowning, but definitely thinking about what you have just said. Notice how these endings grow inevitably out of the article beginnings:

> **Beginning**: Sigiriya bursts upon you. As you round the bend of a jungle road in central Sri Lanka, the gigantic red rock "fortress in the sky" looms six hundred feet above its surrounding pleasure gardens. Visiting this preserve of a fifth-century royal murderer is a memorable experience. ...

> **Ending**: When you leave Sigiriya the red rock disappears as suddenly as it appeared. Then you see only the lime-green plain where Kassapa met Moggallana, and the ever-encroaching jungle.

> **Beginning**: The wonderful thing about oysters is that they taste the way the ocean looks and smells.

After describing a day's boating on Tomales Bay, which included fresh oysters for lunch, author Robertson Pease concludes:

> **Ending**: The wonderful thing about Tomales Bay is that it looks and smells just the way oysters taste.

Margaret Bennett's very good article "A Japanese Orientation to Travel" extols the excellence of the Japan Travel Bureau and the arrangements it made for her and her friend. She begins with a compare-and-contrast question.

> When is a tour more of a tour by being less of a tour? Although this question may seem to resemble one of those unanswerable Zen problems, like "What is the sound of one hand clapping?" It can be easily answered by anyone who has taken an "independent tour" of Japan arranged by JTB, the Japan Travel Bureau.

The story continues in first person, then switches to second in the last paragraph:

> So if you're considering a trip to Japan, you should also consider that considerate organization, JTB. If you do travel with them, when you get back home, although you still may not know the answer to the eternal Zen question "What is the sound of one hand clapping?" there will be no doubt in your mind as to the sound of two hands clapping— it will be you applauding the services and the personnel of the Japan Travel Bureau.

Oh, Yes, Your Story Needs a Title

You wonder perhaps how we've brought you to the end of this chapter without saying anything yet about titles. There are two reasons: First, the best titles often grow out of the article itself—sometimes we don't decide on the final title until we're putting the manuscript in the envelope—and second, the title should be influenced by the kind that your target market routinely uses. Are they usually mere labels ("The Alcan Highway") or questions ("Where Can You Find the Cheapest Airfare?") or direct orders ("See Europe This Winter!") or how-tos ("How to Travel with Teenagers") or cutesy ("Portuguese Climate, Customs, and Madeira, M'Dear")?

If a wonderful title occurs to you early on, of course you'll use it, regardless. If you can't think of a thing, try some of these possibilities: Everybody likes a title that talks about saving money or time; a title that promises improvement in health, creativity, or prestige; a title that hints of the newest, the latest, the most up to date; a title that tells you the article will tell you how to do something. *You*—either spelled out or implied—is a very important word. The title should be intriguing, startling, or thought provoking and usually no longer than six words. Its sales pitch becomes increasingly important in magazines that depend more on newsstand sales than mailed subscriptions. Today, more titles are used on the cover, to lure the potential buyer, and the titles themselves have more punch.

Even if the editor changes your title, and he often does, its value as a sales tool cannot be overestimated. Some of the best titles combine the familiar with the unfamiliar. "Lewis and Clark Were Name-Droppers" tells of their mapmaking activities; "Rooting Around in the Gambia" discusses the *Roots*-inspired desire of black Americans to find their own roots in Africa. Alliteration in the title is a plus: "Shannon is Super for Shoppers" or "Patriots in Petticoats." Hyphenation can be used to advantage: "Charm-ed, I'm Sure" (about travel charm bracelets) or "Turkish Delight-ful." Some of the best titles use reversal: "All Is Good in the Badlands" or "Wild Horses Could Drag You There" (about untamed stallions in Wyoming) or "Don't Come In Out of the Rain" (about taking travel photos in bad weather).

A play on words is always welcome: "How to Operate a Den of Antiquity" (about flea markets), "Virginia City's Silver Lining" (silver mining in the Old West), "They're Forever Blowing Bubbles" (a tour of champagne wineries), or "Last Resort" (Canada's northernmost fishing lodge) are all alluring. Another Canadian-inspired title about the Rockies in winter appeared in a February travel magazine—"Canada: To Brrr is Human."

Online titles are similar to print titles—just a bit briefer and more blatant. Would "I Fell in Love in a Korean Bathhouse" or "Scuba Mom's Gateway to Caribbean Dive and Vacation" tempt you to scroll in that direction?

Most cyberspace publications mention the destination's name in the title.

GoNOMAD, for instance, offers "Mama Mia Malindi! Kenya's Own Little Italy," "Chicago Charm and Chow Warm a Chilly Traveler," "Bicycle Touring in Europe: How to Choose the Right Tour Operator," "Saved by Beauty: Adventures of an American Romantic in Iran," and similar pointers to their travel articles.

The title should always, of course, give honest hints about what's in the story. Don't mislead your reader. Have you heard the legend of the old *Liberty* magazine's cover story from 1940, "My Sex Life" by Mahatma Gandhi? Well, the story begins, "In 1906 I took the vow of celibacy." And that's the end of the story. Don't try to fool your reader that way.

Do remember your reader as you're writing your travel article. Give that reader the best, most interesting copy you can write. Remember, a dull story from Istanbul or Bombay is just as boring as a dull story from Podunk.

CHAPTER 13

Small (and Large) Talk

The face-to-face interview is one of the travel writer's most important tools. Interviews translate abstract ideas into human terms, and they're indispensable for many types of stories. You, the interviewer, are not only asking questions you expect the subject to answer, you're acting as a sounding board, listening to the subject's message, and interpreting his stance.

Your purpose in interviewing may be to know more about an individual for a profile, but in travel writing it's more likely to be the topic that interests you. You're trying to draw out the person's expertise so you can write an authoritative story for your readers. It's very important to know your objectives. What are you searching for? Insights into personality, basic background, oral history, personal anecdotes, enriching secondary facts, pithy quotes—or do you have a variety of objectives?

You should, before you even arrange an interview, have in mind the *focus* of the piece you intend to write, or, in some cases, several different thrusts for several different pieces. Then you can successfully steer the interview toward the specific information you need.

Most People Like to Be Interviewed

Don't ever hesitate to ask for an interview. Most people *like* to be sought out. As a noted interviewer says, "No one objects to questions about the measure of his or her own accomplishment." You are not imposing or invading privacy. If face-to-face won't work, try email or voice to voice— preferably with instant messaging.

Even though original travel articles designed for online reading are usually shorter than those designed for print, the basic research of the interview remains just as necessary.

Sometimes beginning travel writers are timid about requesting interview time. "I don't represent anybody," one complained. "I'm a nobody, myself, and I can't even say I'm writing the article for a particular publication. How do I know if I can ever sell it?"

This is a problem. If you have an assignment, of course you'll mention it when you ask for the interview. But even if you have just a go-ahead answer to a query, you can say, "*Blank Blank* magazine has expressed an interest in this story." Or you can say, "I'm writing this for *Blank Blank* magazine," as long as you're careful not to imply an assignment that doesn't exist. Surely you'll have in mind the publication you'd *like* to be writing it for before you begin interviewing.

If you can, telephone, write, or email for an appointment, indicating the length of time you'll need—usually an hour—and whether or not you'll be photographing at the same time. If, however, an interview becomes important during your travels, and you've had no opportunity to plan it in advance, try to get it anyway. You'd be surprised how often such spur-of-the-moment attempts succeed.

When you have an assignment to write a cruise article, the chef is one of the principal characters. Other principal characters—such as the purser or the deck steward—may have something to say for your story, too.

When you need information, what do you do? You interview the people who can supply it. How many dozen eggs are whipped to froth in the ship's galley each day? What is the ratio of crew members to passengers? Do many people get seasick or need treatment for other ailments? How many hundreds of sheets, towels, etc., are washed in the ship's laundry every week? When celebrities sail aboard this ship do they sit on deck with the hoi polloi? Or do they relax in the solitary splendor of their veranda suites? What percentage turn out for the various shipboard activities?

If it's statistics you want, ask the head man, the purser. The deck steward is more likely to tell you an anecdote about the famous actress whose string of oriental pearls broke while she was swimming in the pool. He might even whisper the name of the aging politician whose tinted hair turned green in the sunlight. And don't forget the ship's doctor, the head housekeeper, and the cruise director.

Find Out What You Can in Advance

Do as much homework as you can before the interview. Search the Internet for general background about the person and the subject, and seek online information. If an opportunity presents itself while you're traveling, the Internet or perhaps the local library can provide clues, or the secretary or assistant to the person you're interviewing can give you some information before the interview itself.

If you can, ask in advance for printed materials, scrapbooks, excerpts from speeches or other interviews—anything to help you get acquainted beforehand and prevent you from wasting your time and the interviewee's with "Where did you go to school?" or "How long have you been with the company?" Already knowing the answers to questions like these saves time, and you get off to a good start when you can say, "How do you like it here in Texas? I understand you grew up in Wisconsin and went to college in Minnesota—this must seem quite different to you."

Some interviewers like to send the interviewee an advance list of possible questions or outline of areas they want to discuss. This gives the subject an opportunity to think about the focus before the interview and perhaps collect enriching information. These questions should be broad and open ended, not the kind that can be answered yes or no.

Aim for Specific Answers

You may not want to ask these specific questions when the time comes, but you'll want to at least jot down a few starter questions that will move the interviewee in the right direction. An interview should not be an exercise in "Q-and-A" but should give the subject an opportunity to speak freely about the topic, with the interviewer only occasionally inserting another question or deftly moving him back on track. Starter questions should be designed to encourage colorful, anecdotal, quotable answers.

Again you'll want to avoid questions that can be answered with yes or no or a date or statistic. The very broad question is fine for stirring up the interviewee ahead of time, but when you're actually talking to him, avoid this kind of question. Where there's no precise answer, sometimes the subject just talks on and on, without saying anything quotable. Try to get specific answers. From the specific you can generalize, but not the other way around.

The main thing to remember is: Put yourself in the place of your reader. What questions would *she* like answered? What part of your proposed article could be better explained through a quote from the interviewee? Often you, the travel writer, are merely the middleman interpreting your subject for your reader. Again the framing of the questions ensures the accuracy and completeness of that information.

Framing the Questions

Sometimes your editor, wanting the interview to follow a particular format, will suggest the questions.

Questions for people in the travel industry, such as those who work for hotels, restaurants, visitor bureaus, transportation, etc. could be: What changes have you experienced in the number of out-of-town visitors this year? Where do most of your clients come from? Are there changes in their budgets? Do they travel alone or in a group? What special service do you feel you have to offer? Are most of your customers realizing a lifelong dream or are they traveling because they think it's the thing to do? What changes do you think should be made in the travel industry?

Recording the Information

You must ask permission to use a recorder. This permission will usually be granted by people who are accustomed to being interviewed and who feel comfortable with mechanical devices. Sometimes they prefer it: They're sure of being quoted correctly. The recorder, of course, gives *you* a perfect record of the conversation, and on sensitive subjects that might provide a valuable reference for direct quotes. Try to use a recorder with a built-in microphone as small and inconspicuous as possible. Be sure it's working properly, has fresh batteries, and that the "record" button is depressed if necessary. Remember, also, that music or loud background noise of any kind, such as the clatter of dishes in a restaurant, may prevent clear reproduction.

Even if you use a recorder, take careful notes anyway. There are two reasons for this: first, the danger of mechanical failure. The second reason for taking notes is because it makes you focus on what the person is saying. Too often the interviewer relies on the recorder and doesn't listen attentively, thinking, "It's all there—I can replay it any time," thereby losing the essence of the interrelationship with the subject.

Getting it Down

"What do you use for taking notes?" is a question students frequently ask. Louise, like most interviewers, uses a stenographer's notebook—the kind issued to newspaper reporters. It's not only a good size—large enough to get lots of thoughts down, but small enough to handle comfortably—it also features easy-to-turn pages and a firm cover. It has an additional advantage, too: Many interviewees, accustomed to dictating to secretaries, are psychologically receptive to the steno pad. Today, most also are receptive to the interviewer's laptop or hand-held device, both of which become lighter, smaller, and less obtrusive every day.

Two note-taking rules every interviewer should commit to heart:

1. It *is* possible to take notes without looking down at them (thus losing eye contact with your subject). Practice. Keep your eyes on a person or a TV screen as you write what is being said.

2. Transcribe all notes before you go to bed that night. Regardless of what kind of personal shorthand you use, regardless of how well you think you'll remember every word that was said, "cold" notes lose about half their value in forty-eight hours and three-fourths of it within the week. A month later your notes, unless you've immediately clarified and amplified them, are practically worthless.

Some interviewers, of whom Truman Capote was perhaps the most notable example, spurn the recording, note-taking process, claiming total recall without memory aids. That may be. But if you don't take any notes, it makes the interviewee nervous.

Sometimes Your Memory Is All You Have

Sometimes, though, recorders of any type, computers, and even notebooks are prohibited, and the travel writer *must* rely entirely on memory. Such was the case in Cairo when Louise attended a briefing at the U.S. Embassy during a critical period in Middle East affairs. Although questions were permitted, writing and recording the answers was not, and the material discussed was to be used for background only.

While we're all familiar with movies where the cub reporter violates a confidence to scoop his competitor and everybody cheers his ingenuity, real life is different. The travel writer who accepts an invitation to a briefing at an embassy with the understanding that no direct or indirect quotes will result from it had better not violate that confidence—if he expects his sources to continue to help him.

A top reporter for the *Washington Post* feels it's very important to wear the same kind of clothes and behave in the same manner as your interview subject. "Create an atmosphere of sympathy. Don't scream, 'I am different from you!' as soon as you enter the room," she says. She relates it to method acting—actually becoming the person you're interviewing.

Ways to Warm Up Your Subject

Every interviewer has a special way of warming up the subject with preliminary small talk. Louise once heard Alice Phillips say, after doing hundreds of interviews, that she always asks a male subject who gave him his necktie, and this usually produces a good anecdote and leads into questions she wants to ask.

This is to get the subject into the habit of responding. Be sure to keep the focus on him. Do not permit him to turn the conversation to you for any length of time. If he asks how you became a travel writer, say something like, "I've always liked to write, and I've always liked to travel." Then turn it back to him with, "I know you've done a lot of traveling, too. What's your favorite part of the world?"

Keep in mind why you're there, and don't let the conversation ramble off in all directions. If the subject expounds on a technical matter in technical phrases, ask, "How shall I explain that to my readers in layman's language?" If she makes a controversial statement, don't pounce gleefully and hurry to scribble it down. Be casual. Ask another question while you're writing the controversial answer.

Don't bulldoze your way into the conversation: Use gentle tactics, beginning your controversial questions with "I imagine that ..." or "It appears that ..." If you can't seem to pin the interviewee down to specifics, give him a misquote, like, "Others are saying the airline is losing two million dollars a year." This encourages him to reply indignantly, "That's not true. It's less than a million! Only about $875,000!"

Some travel writers believe in interspersing the "hard" questions with the "easy" questions, while others favor an easy beginning, getting progressively harder and more controversial. With either method, make your last two questions soft and innocuous, to end the interview with pleasant feelings on both sides.

Keep 'Em Talking

If you want a reluctant subject to explain something, say, "Nobody seems to understand about this situation," implying that the interviewee is the only one who might be able to set your readers straight.

Silence is sometimes an excellent interview technique. Don't rush in to fill the void as soon as the conversation flags. Observe a moment of silence, and let the interviewee be the one to break it.

When you don't know anything about the topic under discussion, try to relate it to something you do know. When Louise was freelancing for her local newspaper, the city editor sent her, on ten minutes' notice, to interview a missionary visiting from her post in South Korea. Louise had never been to Korea and didn't know much about missionaries in general or her denomination in particular. But she soon discovered the missionary was an English teacher at a college. That she knew about—English and colleges. They progressed from discussing the architecture of the college to the architecture of the surrounding city of Seoul, from the teaching of English to Korean and Korea's place in the world today, from a woman's adventures teaching in a faraway land to the missionary's travel adventures and experiences in other places.

If your subject doesn't say what you want him to, sometimes you can persuade him by putting phrases in his mouth. Begin, "In other words . . ." and then frame the sentence you want, asking only for an affirmative nod.

Expert interviewer John Brady admits that you may not get results by saying to your subject, "Tell me an anecdote." He suggests using the phrase, "What can you tell me about your experiences in the field?" Sometimes, too, you can elicit an anecdote by telling a related one to the interviewee. If you tell him about the Greek Island jeweler who almost managed to get you arrested, he may respond with his story of a weekend in Guatemala under "house arrest" at his hotel. One mistaken identity story leads to another mistaken identity story. But don't get more involved in the telling than you do in the listening.

Physical Details Add an Extra Dimension

Give the reader the feeling he's met the person you're interviewing. Provide insight into character through selected details. Don't just note, "He's a big man," but be prepared to write, "He gingerly lowered his muscular six-foot frame." Don't be satisfied with, "He's fair," but fill your recorder or notes with details: "afternoon sunlight reveals sprinkling of freckles," "blond hair appears almost white."

When you see an office with a picture window, a rosewood desk, an oriental rug, you're seeing a man of substance. Observe how he sits at his desk—ramrod straight, leaning back with feet on the desk top, or simply relaxed? Is music playing? What kind of music? Is the desk cluttered or bare? What books are in evidence? Family photos? What is the subject wearing? A necktie? Desert boots? A gold bracelet? If you're interviewing a woman, did she have her hair styled for the occasion? Is she wearing jogging shoes? A diamond wristwatch? Are her fingernails short or long? Be a sponge. Absorb everything.

When Alex Haley was still traveling around collecting material for *Roots*, Louise heard him say at a writers' conference, "When you interview a man, if his wife is present, watch the expression on her face. It can tell you a lot." That evening, as Louise listened to another big-name writer present a rather boring speech, she glanced back a couple of rows to check out his wife. She was sound asleep.

"On" and "Off" the Record

Some interviewers have trouble with "off the record" and it's very important to clearly settle that matter at the start. Always set guidelines, such as: "Anything that is said will be on the record unless agreed to be off at the time it's said." This prevents the interviewee from remarking at the end of the interview, "Oh, you know, that whole bit I told you about the State Department investigation of the travel industry—that was off the record, of course." Whether or not to listen to off-the-record material depends on how badly you need it for background and whether or not you'll be able to get it on the record from somebody else. Once having promised it's "off," you must keep your promise. Then it's awkward if the same information comes to you on the record in another manner, so consider the overall situation and the various people involved before you decide yes or no.

When your subject says, "Not for attribution," you can use the content but must not name your informant. You must attribute the statement to some shadowy source, such as "a West Coast travel agent" or "an American traveling in Italy." While it's all right to use such quotes occasionally, too many of them destroy the writer's credibility. Be sure your article has fewer "blind" quotes than direct ones.

You may want to ask your subject's permission to refine the quotes since spoken language, full of extraneous sounds and words, often looks silly in print. It's usually all right, though, to go ahead and edit clumsy or unclear words if you're careful not to change the sense or the color of the statement.

At the interview, don't overstay your allotted time unless it's apparent that the subject wants you to. If you notice him glancing at a clock or an engagement calendar or if he says something like, "Well, I guess that's about all I have to say," it's time for you to leave. On the other hand, your interviewee will sometimes tell you more than you really care to know. One of the traits of a good interviewer is the ability to keep the subject on the desired track and not let the interview take up more time than is productive for the writer.

In any case, at the end of the interview be sure to say, "Is there anything I should have asked you about that I've overlooked?" Request permission to call back for any additions or clarifications you might need. Then listen carefully for the casual remark, the gem of an anecdote, the perfect quote that is nearly always uttered as you stand with your hand on the doorknob, glasses off, notebook put away.

Never Relinquish Editorial Control

Do be aware of libel laws and write your article accordingly. But never promise you'll submit the finished article for the interviewee's approval. You are under no obligation to do so. You may, as a favor to her and as an insurance policy for yourself, submit facts and figures or direct quotes to verify their accuracy. But under no circumstances permit the subject to delete something she told you "for the record" or to alter in any way the thrust of the article.

As the instructions to writers from the *St. Petersburg Times* say, "We like to think that editors are editors and writers are writers, and the subject of the interview cannot assume those responsibilities."

Do follow up the interview with a thank-you note via email or on your letterhead. This is not only common courtesy, but it also reminds the subject of where he can reach you should he think of any additions or corrections, and it paves the way for you to go back if you need to. If you promise to send a photograph, or copies of the published article, be sure to do so. Taking good care of your sources is future-story insurance.

The Telephone Interview

If a face-to-face interview is impossible, try for a telephone interview. For this, too, make an appointment and indicate how much time you'll need. You might want to suggest, "Call me collect Tuesday at two, or let me know if there's a more convenient time." Some writers find it best to conduct telephone interviews in the evening. The subject is more relaxed at home than at the office. Again you may want to presubmit a list of questions, giving the person a chance to prepare the answers before the interview. If the subject is willing, you might be able to record your telephone interview. Sometimes a telephone interview turns out to be more chatty and unstructured than a face-to-face situation; other times, it's more formal and punctilious.

The proliferation of cell phones frees the writer from the constraints of time and place. But don't let your interview fall apart because you and your cell phone have too many distractions.

Email Interviews

Email interviews can work out very well for the travel writer. You want to find an expert on how the current influx of cruise line port calls is affecting a tiny island in the Pacific. Through clever use of a search engine, up come the names and email addresses of members of the island's local government, a representative of the major retail establishment, a longtime island resident, two local pastors, and the public relations director of one of the cruise lines.

Sounds promising, doesn't it? It probably is. But be sure to verify any information you receive by email—including the physical addresses and telephone numbers of your informants. You may discover that both pastors left last month, the retail "representative" is only a "go-for," the cruise line fired that employee, and the longtime resident is a bum. Worse yet, the information you receive from the online sources may be partially or completely untrue. So, convenient as email is, it requires more checking.

Five Major Kinds of Interviews

What kind of interviews do you need? That depends on the story. A *here and now* story about a new tour being featured at San Simeon might materialize from the tour itself, some PR handouts, a few questions to the tour guide, and a phone call to the state official in charge of San Simeon tours.

A *definitive destination* piece would include interviews with a city official, with somebody from the chamber of commerce or tourist bureau, with a spokesman for each of several attractions, and probably with a hotel executive and several restaurant owners.

An *in-depth analysis* of a foreign country's new approach to tourism would probably require interviews with the director of tourism, someone in the public relations department of the country's chief airline, and the manager of the leading hotel. It should include scattered quotes from restaurateurs, on-the-spot tourists, spokesmen for car rental agencies, and other hotel managers. Several owners of sightseeing companies and tourist attractions, the mayors of principal cities, a museum director, and a representative of a wholesale tour that includes the country would make good additions.

When a travel story requires interviews with more than one person, it's especially important to remember your theme, and base all the interviews around it. That's what makes the piece hold together.

In covering an *event*, you'll usually have several people to interview: the fans, who are participating in the activity; the sponsors, who make the time and space available to enhance their public image; the experts, who excel at this particular talent; the public relations people, who are eager to catch your ear and often come laden with handout sheets; and the spokesman—usually the master of ceremonies or guest of honor.

Introduce yourself to the spokesman first, presenting your business card, of course. Ask about taking photographs. (See Chapter 14 for more on photography.) Discuss the problems involved in this particular field. Then, later, when you interview the expert, you'll impress him with your knowledge of his problems while, at the same time, you're getting information from his viewpoint.

A good example of roundup interviewing is "Living with Others in a Small Boat" by Patience B. Wales in *Sail.* Telling of a four-year world cruise she and her husband and another couple took in a forty-two-foot ketch, she says the number-one question people always asked was, "How did you all stand each other for so long in such close quarters?" That's probably what gave her the idea for this article, because she not only analyzes some of the factors that made this relationship possible but tells of other people she's interviewed whose relationships foundered in close quarters at sea. She did much of her interviewing in Tahiti, where, she says, "the waterfront seethes with the remains of friendships."

When Louise was researching *her* roundup story about what causes traveling couples to argue, many of those she interviewed protested at first that they had nothing to say. "We *never* argue when we're traveling," both Sally and John assured her. Then Sally remembered: "Of course, there was the time John got us lost looking for that old country inn in the Berkshires, and it got to be midnight and we hadn't had dinner and ..."

"*I* got us lost!" John interrupted. "*You* were the one that looked at the directions and told me to go north when you meant south!"

"What's there to argue about?" asked Tim and Ellen. "When we're on vacation we always have a great time."

"There's just one thing," Tim said hesitantly. "I wish Ellen wouldn't always take so long getting ready. When you're trying to make a plane—gee, I hate trying to get through security as they're calling our flight."

"*Tim!*" Ellen almost shouted. "How can you talk that way! You're the one who always leaves everything scattered all over the place. If you'd be neater, it wouldn't take me so long to get ready. And besides, if you'd ..."

The face-to-face interview can be revealing. It can also be amusing, informative, and controversial. It's one of the travel writer's most valuable tools, and using it with professional skill can make the difference between a good, publishable travel article and a batch of meaningless, indecipherable notations.

CHAPTER 14

Photos: Bringing 'Em Back Alive

The successful travel writer knows illustrations in print or online help sell his story, because they enhance and enrich his words, giving the editor—and subsequently the reader—the entire picture. He understands how more and more publications break up their blocks of type with photographs; and more and more editors prefer to receive manuscript and illustrations in one package, rather than having to make separate arrangements for photographs.

Even an inexperienced photographer can take pictures useful for recreating the travel experience, and a travel writer with modest shutter talents can illustrate his own stories. While it's impossible to "cover" photography in these few pages, we'll give you some practical advice. We'll also mention photo genres and photo mechanics, shooting on the move, selling what you have, sending pictures, avoiding legal problems, writing captions, and how to find illustrations if you don't have any.

Cameras

The digital camera has many advantages and has almost totally replaced film cameras. It is usually lighter and easier to handle than a 35mm camera. It whips through airport security, as experts believe its memory is not affected by X-rays. You can immediately see your shot in its LCD screen or viewfinder and quickly re-shoot if the picture doesn't quite suit your desire. You can transfer the picture to the computer, where you can crop, size, lighten, darken, adjust contrast, alter the background, and even ease an ex-spouse out of the photo of family festivity. You can print the picture at home or upload to one of several Websites for a printed version. Prints from a digital camera are less prone to fading or damage when displayed over a long period of time if higher quality paper and ink are used.

On the downside, the digital camera can gobble batteries like a hungry teenager gobbles food, so it's wise to use only longer-lasting lithium batteries or look for a camera with a rechargeable battery option, and don't forget to recharge them every night. Most of the chargers can be used in both 120 and 220 volts. Just make sure you have the proper electrical plug adapter for the countries you will be visiting.

The current technology makes sure that cameras deplete batteries more slowly than before. Still, a digital camera will consume more power than a film camera, because they have a lot of extra features.

Most digital cameras show a battery icon on their screen, which tells you that everything is okay when it's full and that you will run out of battery juice when it's almost empty. Always carry spare batteries in your day bag, as well, for when your battery is used up and the pope finally comes to the window.

Storing photos on the road is getting easier all the time. If you've got a fast connection on a public computer you can upload your photos to an online photo-sharing site, like Flickr. As long as your camera or your camera's memory card reader has a USB output cable, you should have little problem finding Internet café computers to plug into to offload your photos. You can then upload them to a photo-sharing site with just a few clicks. But if you've got a ton of photos or the file sizes are large, this can take a bit of time.

Another option is to keep the photos with you. Many Internet cafés all over the world do a brisk business burning CDs and now even DVDs full of photos for travelers passing through. You can get hundreds of photos on one CD. It's usually quite inexpensive, so you might consider getting a duplicate of each disc to store in a different place or even mail home. Some travelers bring re-writable CDs so they can keep adding photos to each disc until it is full.

If you are on a long trip or plan to take a huge amount of photos, you many want to consider bringing a small portable hard drive along with you. These are getting smaller and cheaper all the time, and many of them are made specifically for this purpose. Some of the more expensive models even have preview screens so you can sort easily. Make sure you have the right adapters before you leave home.

Digital cameras come in a great variety of makes, models, and features. Good sources for research are Imaging-Resource.com or bhphotovideo.com. You might also stop by your favorite local camera retail shop, ask for advice on what type of digital cameras they recommend, and get some instructions on how to use them.

Video cameras can provide both meaningful memories for amateur photographers and professional programs for the more experienced. While audiences are still interested in travel slide talks, the number of excellent professional travel videos increases daily, and both active and armchair travelers applaud them. A first-class script and excellent narration are important components of the travel video, as well as the travel audio, which sometimes accompanies photographic presentations. Although much of the information about still pictures applies also to images that move, your expertise with the video camera will evolve from reading the directions and practicing religiously.

Again and again we are reminded that the mechanical equipment is not the most important element of photography. What counts is the eye behind the camera and the brain that tells the eye what it all means.

What Photo Equipment Do You Really Need?

With over a dozen major manufacturers, each producing several camera types, the range of sizes, prices, advantages, and disadvantages is too great to discuss here. The main thing to remember is: If you're buying a new camera, get as much information as you can before deciding, and select a model that's best for the kind of work you'll be doing—action shots, portraits, heavy-duty work, wilderness photography, whatever. If you take a lot of action photos, be sure to check the speed of the camera between shots. Some digitals are notorious for being slow. Be sure to get a camera that feels comfortable in your hands and to your eyes. (To your glasses, too, if you wear them.)

If you're thinking of buying a camera or other equipment overseas, check out the exact model you want and jot down your hometown price, so you can see if you're really getting a bargain. We recommend that you do not buy a camera overseas or in a duty-free shop unless it's an emergency. Prices are always lower (about 30 percent) at U.S. big-box retailers such as Best Buy or Costco. But if you do, remember, you'll be losing your chance to try out the new equipment at home. If you buy a new camera *before* you leave home, be sure you're thoroughly familiar with it before you start on your trip. One of Jacqueline's friends bought a new digital camera right before leaving for an extended trip. Unfortunately, she didn't experiment with the camera before leaving home and discovered, much to her dismay, that the camera was so tiny that every time she clicked the shutter the camera would move. She wound up with a lot of out-of-focus photos of her round-the-world trip.

New camera or old, check all the batteries and replace them if there's any doubt about their lifespan. A pencil eraser cleans batteries and terminals, or you can clean the batteries and battery compartment with a cotton swab dampened with alcohol. Clean the other parts of the camera with lens tissue and a camel's-hair brush.

A time exposure requires a firm resting place for the camera—a table, a balcony rail, a windowsill. If no steady surface is available, you'll wish you'd brought your tripod. But large, sturdy tripods are a nuisance to carry, and small ones are often rickety and unreliable. There are several substitutes such as: a shirt-pocket-size platform with an elevating screw; a vise that threads into the camera and clamps to a firm surface; and a cloth bag filled with beans or Styrofoam that can be placed on a fence post or in a tree crotch, and the camera then placed on it.

Digital photography is so cheap, we recommend that you take a photo of a location's entrance sign, street sign, information kiosk, or other landmarks for reference later.

Keep careful records on whatever equipment and supplies you buy, and follow professional advice when it comes to deducting or depreciating it. Such photographic expenses as memory cards, supplies, reference books, photography-related phone calls, and materials for filing and sending pictures are probably deductible. More substantial equipment must usually be depreciated. For conventional expense deductions you need professional advice. Be sure to keep all records that show you're attempting to market photographs. (See Chapter 17 for more on tax deductions.)

Whatever photographic gear you decide on, don't pack it in a fancy camera bag. That advertises the fact that you're carrying expensive equipment. Since at some point it'll probably be left in a car trunk or hotel room, vulnerable to theft, most professional photographers choose something as unlike a camera bag as possible—an airline's bag or a shabby tote with several zipper pockets—anything that holds gear safely and blends inconspicuously. One worry is that if someone steals your digital camera and you have a stuffed memory card, they've got all your photos. That's why some journalists download their photos onto a tiny computer or a laptop each night, dump the ones they don't want, and hope they don't lose the computer. Don't forget to reformat your card after you've transferred the photos. Having multiple memory cards and changing them from your camera helps eliminate the worry about losing your camera with all your photos still in it.

Keep your day bag with your camera equipment firmly between your feet while sitting down. Draping the strap over the back of your chair is not an option because it allows a thief to easily slip the bag off the chair unnoticed. Nor is placing your camera on a table or a seat beside you, as a thief can grab it and run before you can stop him or her.

Your homeowner's insurance policy or your travel baggage insurance policy may or may not protect such items as electronic equipment and mobile devices. Check it out, and if necessary consider a floater policy.

Photo Mechanics for Travel Writers

The very first thing to consider is the subject: What is it and why are you taking a photo of it? Successful images have a point of interest, the key element around which the composition is based. It's probably the thing that caught your eye in the first place and should be able to draw and hold the viewer's attention.

It's important to consider the subject you are photographing, what it is and why it's important to your story. The most successful images are centered around points of interest, such as a street market, a vista, an old building, a child at play, etc. Capturing a scene, place, or thing should draw readers into the story and make them want to read it. Your first instinct when you see a beautiful scene or an interesting cluster of things will be to try and capture it all exactly as you're seeing it, but you need to understand that your camera will put a concrete frame around that scene which your eyes lack. This means that what you capture needs to fit comfortably within this frame.

There are a few simple rules you can follow to dramatically improve your composition.

Try to place the focal point of your picture in the middle of your frame if that object/person is close enough to fill most of the photo space. If that is not possible, position the subject on the side, and importantly, if it's facing or moving towards the left or the right, give it room in that direction, rather than making it point towards the photo edge and therefore unbalancing the composition. If the focal point or an interesting object in your picture is small enough, place it approximately in one of the frame's four corners. This technique is referred to as the photographic rule of thirds and with it, even seemingly uninteresting elements, like a lone tree in an empty field, can be shot in such a way as to make your picture beautiful.

You can also organize your shot using rules of symmetry. For example, if your subject is two people of similar size sitting back-to-back or facing each other, you can place them in the center of the shot to give it a pleasant symmetrical quality.

Be sure to take several photos of the same scene, using different settings. Most digital cameras have adjustments that can brighten or darken a photo. Read your camera's manual or ask for advice at the camera store.

Shoot both horizontals and verticals of each scene. You change the feeling of the picture when you turn the camera, and this gives the editor a choice. If you're hoping for a magazine cover, of course you'll shoot verticals, keeping in mind the need for an area for the publication's logo. A good composition will leave no doubt as to the subject of the photo.

Vary the distance shots and the close-ups. Get the overall scene and then the particulars. Be sure to make those close-ups close enough to capture the emotion and detail you need. The best photographers remember this rule: Move in until you think you're close enough—then step three feet closer. Try unusual angles on cliché scenes. Kneel down and shoot up or climb on something sturdy and shoot down. Framing your subject will help eliminate unwanted elements. It also helps overcome the mistake of making the subject too small. The point of interest should be the sharpest part of the photo.

Try not to date your picture by its background. Sometimes the people's clothing and hairstyles, cars, and advertisements for trendy items spell out the year the picture was taken. Clothing styles change less often for men, middle-aged women, and small children, so use them as models when possible. And perhaps you can block out parked cars and advertising. Make your picture usable for years to come.

If the person is the most important part of the picture, try to include a recognizable landmark. Centering the subject can create a static composition, so you may want to spend a few minutes thinking about where you want the point of interest to be. If you are taking a portrait, the person's face and eyes become the points of interest. In a landscape, you might find the point of interest could be a boat floating in a calm lake or a locomotive chugging up a hill.

A beach is a beach is a beach; but if Diamond Head is seen in the top corner, we know where we are. Titles and road signs are useful, too, when selected thoughtfully, so that they aren't distracting. Take pictures of the Continental Divide, the state line, the Mexican border, the highest point in the Sierras. If the sign says, "Elephants have the right-of-way" or "Golf balls in hippo footprints may be lifted without penalty," think about how to pose somebody looking at the sign.

Even if you don't have anybody to pose, you can take poignant pictures, as Tom Biema did for *Rider* magazine. His photographs of the Australian Outback include one of a road sign depicting a black wombat on a yellow background with the legend "Wombats Next 26 km." His riderless motorcycle stands beside it, a white helmet decorated with an American flag resting on the seat. Another picture shows the motorcycle in the foreground, the emptiness of the Outback stretching in front and on both sides, the mirrors reflecting the emptiness behind.

Sometimes, when you don't have any particular illustrations in mind, you'll want to take travel pictures as you come across them. Henri Cartier-Bresson, one of the most respected photographers of all time, tells us what to look for.

> To me, photography is the simultaneous recognition, in a fraction of a
> second, of the significance of an event as well as of a precise organization
> of forms, which give that event its proper expression.

187

Cartier-Bresson speaks often of the "decisive moment," that instant when something is about to happen: the hiker finding himself at the edge of the crevasse; the child about to begin dancing; the young man ready to take off on his motorbike; the tourist deciding which necklace she's going to buy. That "decisive moment" is the instant we try to capture.

The direction of the light is important. For example, a beautiful building with the sun behind it will be obscured by shade. The same thing can happen when taking a photo of a person. Always check on the direction of the natural light and avoid taking photos of subjects with bright light behind them. Backlighting, however, both natural and artificial, is what you need if you want to shoot an interesting silhouette. Pointing your camera towards a scene over which the sun is shining directly will result in dark objects and overexposed skies, so if there's a spot you particularly love and want to capture, try going during a time of day when the sun has shifted in the opposite direction. Heavily overcast skies also make for bad pictures, and in this case you just need to accept that there are times when you can't take great shots.

On bright, sunny days, avoid shooting light, white, or highly reflective objects or surfaces as your shots will turn out to be overexposed. Taking pictures in the evening as the sun is setting and at night is also problematic, with too little light making pictures grainy and the use of flash only resulting in yellow-tinged shots. Finally, when you're experimenting with low-light conditions, take plenty of pictures, as out of numerous grainy ones you might just get that one perfectly clear and sharp example.

Beating the Weather

Need we say it? *Always* keep your camera out of the sun and rain! When not in use, store it in your bag.

Avoid shooting in the middle of the day in warm climates. You'll get better pictures before ten or after three. However, digital cameras can compensate for this with their menu option for bright sunlight as well as low-light situations.

If you'll be a long time in the tropics, you'll need to take special precautions against moisture. Research advice online from your camera manufacturer on handling photography under extreme weather conditions. It's a good idea to keep camera and all electronics in zipper-lock baggies. Many insect repellents, such as DEET, on your fingers could melt your camera's case. A friend's shutter has her fingerprint permanently engraved on it.

In cold weather moisture is a worry, too. Keep the camera under your coat as much as possible, pamper it with sportsmen's hand warmers, and protect it inside a plastic zipper-locked bag. This way, whatever condensation forms after you bring the cold camera into a warm room will be on the outside of the bag, not the camera. Protect all your equipment from snow.

Rainy climates shouldn't deter you from picture taking. If you don't want to invest in an underwater camera or underwater housing for your camera, buy inexpensive special umbrellas and raincoats for the camera, as well as the photographer.

Sometimes the rainy-day, foggy-day, misty-day pictures are the best ones.

How to Send Your Pictures

How do you send your photographs to the editor?

While the many facets of electronic media represent an entirely new market, don't get carried away. We should remember the length of time it takes a photographic image to download to a not-very-fast computer. Web watchers and e-zine readers grow impatient if the picture is so elaborate that it takes extra time to download, and they are likely to surf on to something else.

With digital or print images, be sure to have your name, identifying number, and copyright notice on each frame. It is a good idea to ask the editor in what format they want the photos sent: jpeg, gif, etc. It is not a good idea to email a loose photo without checking with the editor first; their computers will probably reject it as spam and delete it.

Always keep copies of your photographs. Jacqueline heard a dreadful story of a photographer who lost thousands of slide images when the UPS truck that was delivering them crashed and burned. The photographer did not have backup copies of her work.

This is another reason to go digital. It is fast and easy to make backup CDs of your images.

Can You Shoot Both the Planned and the Unplanned?

In taking travel pictures, sometimes you plan in advance the pictures you want—for instance, something to illustrate a story already designed or already written. Other times the photography is spontaneous—you see something interesting and you shoot it.

To portray a geographic area so your reader can really know it, you'll want pictures of people of all ages and occupations in all types if situations, wildlife and domestic animals, landscapes and gardens. You'll also want food markets and restaurants, hotels and historical sites, clothing and costumes, handcrafts and souvenirs, art and architecture, signs and flags.

A common mistake that compact users make is to always take pictures at their own eye level, which often results in odd shots when the subject demands that you get yourself at its level. Here is a simple example: You spot a cat lounging on the pavement, and you simply point down at it and click. The resulting shot will probably look awkward and not particularly remarkable. It would be much better to get the camera down at the same level as the cat.

Then of course there are moments when you'll get your memorable shot by pointing downward (such as when on a terrace to capture the street life below) or upward (to give a feeling of the height and bulk of a particular object), or simply shooting from an unusual angle.

Perspective and angle are especially important when trying to take pictures of food you come across during your travels. It's not enough to simply point the camera downward at your plate.

What will you do with all of these pictures? Some you'll send along with the first article you write about the area. Send more than you think the editor will need—to give him a choice and perhaps to persuade him to use more photographs (and send you a larger check) than he had originally intended. Even in situations where the photos are part of the article "package," for which there's no extra payment, we've often found editors send a bonus for a large selection of good pictures. File your leftovers carefully, to use with future articles. Some of them might prove useful for roundup stories or roundup photo essays, where you have around-the-world variations on a single theme.

Just as some people collect rare gems or antique scimitars, Louise collects laundry lines. For years she's collected photographs of people washing, along with the lines of clothes they have washed. She also collects pictures of schools and colleges, uniformed schoolchildren, shoeshine boys, and several other universal themes. These make great international roundups—"Wash and Wear Around the World"; "School Days from Country to Country"—as well as illustrating individual aspects of a specific area. Jacqueline has a collection of photos of people leaning out of windows. A colleague collects photos of unusual toilets.

With the advent of digital photography, we no longer need to worry about taking pictures sparingly. Use this as an advantage and take plenty of pictures of the same scene from different perspectives, with different settings, and, when possible, at different times of the day. When you get home from your trip, don't simply upload every single photo you've taken, but make a selection of your very best and delete the rest. Jacqueline always saves her photos to a CD or a flash drive labeled with the date and location. Photos that are saved on her hard drive are filed with data from the stories she is working on.

How Will Your Pictures Be Used?

Certainly shoot whatever appeals to you. But if you're thinking primarily in terms of illustrations, it helps to think of how the photographs will be used. In a *picture story*, the photos do most of the telling and need little, if any, explanatory caption material. For instance, in Christchurch, New Zealand, where they have big red city buses with hooks on the front for carrying strollers and prams, Louise's husband shot a picture story from their hotel room on the main square. The big red bus is loading: a distraught mother, carrying a young baby in her arms and wheeling a toddler in a perambulator, looks around helplessly, obviously wondering how she will board the bus; a well-dressed businessman comes up to her and says a few words; she smiles; he lifts the toddler out of the perambulator and sets him on the bus step; then the man hooks the pram to the front of the bus; everyone climbs aboard and the bus roars off. All this with the very British-looking background of Christchurch Cathedral, vehicles moving to the left, and uniformed schoolboys in straw hats guiding their bicycles through the park.

A bridge overlooking Istanbul's Golden Horn harbor was the vantage point for another picture story. An old man in a rowboat that's tied to the bridge is frying fish over a charcoal brazier. As soon as the fish is browned, a blue-smocked helper puts it on a piece of bread and passes it to an eager bystander, who hands his money over the bridge rail, then moves on. The next customer pushes himself into position, the helper puts another fish on bread, and the old man continues to turn the browning fish in his pan.

Whenever you see action that's a story in itself, hasten to focus. Keep on the lookout for those picture stories—many publications use them. Some are always open to picture stories, while others consider only those that are outstanding in both interest and technical quality. There's usually no set number of pictures required—however many it takes to tell the story.

Photo Genres

A *sequence* uses several pictures, too. It can feature something occurring in stages, but is accompanied by explanatory copy; the pictures themselves do not have to carry the entire story. For instance: When you're packing for your trip, first you place the shoes and the toiletries bag in the suitcase; then you put in the underwear and nightclothes; on top you lay the dress clothes, spread out over the suitcase; then you fold them so they fit in; then you shut the lid and, *voila*, the next scene shows you carrying the case to the airport. Or a sequence might be an evening at a nightclub. First scene shows the headwaiter escorting your party to the table; next picture shows you ordering dinner; then comes the nightclub act; you and your friends applaud; then you lean back, smiling; then reach forward to toast with your brandy snifters.

If you witness something like the divers at La Quebrada in Acapulco, try to take the full sequence—the diver blessing himself at the shrine; descending the steps that have been cut into the cliff; mounting the starter platform; making the starter dive; scrambling up the steep cliff to the top of La Quebrada; and then the flaming torches illuminating his arc through the air; his sixty-mile-an-hour splashdown into the rock-girded cove; and finally his head emerging from the churning water, his arm upraised in a victory gesture.

A *juxtaposition* usually consists of two contrasting scenes. A picture of a Europe-bound Girl Scout troop as high school seniors and a picture of the same girls as second-grade Brownies beginning their plans for the trip would be juxtaposition. So would a photo showing a scene in San Francisco today placed next to one of the same area immediately after the 1906 earthquake.

For these juxtapositions you and your camera would have to have been present after the 1906 earthquake and when the Girl Scouts were in second grade, or know someplace to obtain a picture taken at the time.

To present a juxtaposition of a rural Finnish lake in summer and in winter, you'd have to make two trips there or work in tandem with a friend. Such a juxtaposition would be easy to do, though, illustrating some of the features of your home area. But the shot of the Acapulco diver standing on the cliff, juxtaposed with one of him in the water raising his arm in the victory salute, would *not* make a good twosome—the action in between, the *real* story, would be lacking. Captions for juxtapositions are especially important. Be sure to make the meaning of the two pictures clear to your reader.

The *stopper* is a one-shot situation. This picture is used to draw the reader's attention to the story, so it needs to be vivid and dramatic: the mountain fortress of Sigiriya rising from the plains; the parachute ride at Knott's Berry Farm; tourists viewing Montreal's Old Town from a horse-drawn carriage; the dramatic architecture of Funchal's casino on the island of Madeira, framed by mountains and sea; two canoeists exploring a river that's flecked with ice floes and bounded by snow-covered banks; a dramatic silhouette of Rio's seven-hundred-ton statue, Christ the Redeemer, atop Corcovado mountain—all are *stoppers*. But the parachute ride is photographed from an unusual angle, the canoe appears against an extraordinary background, the wheels of the horse-drawn carriage are distorted to emphasize a focal point of the picture—otherwise these situations would surely be clichés. Once the reader's attention has been captured, he'll learn from the writer's copy what the stopper is all about, so it doesn't have to tell a story all by itself—just hint strongly that an interesting story accompanies it. If you examine the pictures in print advertising, you'll find they're usually stoppers.

Drop-ins can consist of any number of shots, or possibly just one. They are what we often think of as illustrations—something strongly tied to the text, used by the editor to emphasize a certain aspect of the article, as well as to break up large blocks of type and create an attractive layout. Usually they are captioned with explanatory material.

Almost anything can be a drop-in. For instance, to accompany an article on Australia's Barrier Reef, Louise submitted six photographs: only two people in sight on the vast beach of Hayman Island, with the hotel and mountains in the background; adults and children beachcombing on the reef at low tide; the launch, with people aboard, leaving for the outer reef; the underwater observatory, with its huge viewing windows, on Hook Island; Hayman's gaily painted train that transports guests on this island where no cars are allowed; and the Hayman Island airport, with a helicopter about to land. The magazine used the beach scene as a stopper (at the top of the center-spread story) and the launch ride and underwater observatory pictures as drop-ins.

The most important thing to remember is: if the scene intrigues you, it will probably intrigue somebody else. Digital cameras make photo taking comparatively cheap, so if in doubt, shoot.

Can You Make It Look Real?

When you know ahead of time what you want, make a storyboard or a shooting script. Use an index card for each picture you intend to take, rough-sketching on it what you want the picture to show. For a "set piece," jot down all pertinent data: time of day, models, location, camera angle, clothes, props, etc.

Don't hesitate to use props that will enhance the meaning of your picture. Whether it's a parasol for a Japanese girl walking beneath the blossoming cherry trees or an ornamental lifebuoy chaperoning a shipboard buffet, if that's the prop that makes the picture, get it.

Can You Compose in the Viewfinder?

Although this chapter is not intended as a course in elementary photography, you'll find reminders of some basics you should keep in mind. Too many photographers don't really see what's in that viewfinder. Is your finger or camera strap in the way? Is a telephone pole growing out of somebody's head? Is your horizon line in the dead center of the picture, thereby ruining it? Are there a dozen distracting centers of interest? With your digital camera, of course, there is no excuse for such pitfalls since you can immediately check what you have just photographed.

Try framing your subject with a tree branch, an arch, a wall, to give it depth, keeping the frame at least five feet from the camera. Consciously look for a natural frame, such as the man playing bongo drums between the upraised arms of his fellow musicians, or the little girl's smiling face framed by the two dogs she's roughhousing with, or the woman walking between two tall buildings.

Learn to *see* what makes a picture. A natural line should lead into it—a pathway, a freeway cloverleaf, the movement of the waves, the placement of the objects. The viewer's eye moves, naturally, toward the center of interest, so any action shown should lead *into* the picture, not out of it. The repetition of forms gives unity; so learn to use the lines you see through your viewfinder to express your sense of significance. Look for rhythms—patterns of shape, length, angle, curve, direction, or interval that strengthen your composition and tie the elements together to present a unified picture for your reader. If what you see isn't exactly what you want to convey, move a few steps in one direction or another, shoot from lower down or higher up, adjust the scene until it is the one you want.

Use reflections whenever you can—the snow-capped mountain in the outside rearview mirror of the camper, your houseboat in the unrippled lake, the kids jumping into the puddle that reflects them.

Can You Shoot on the Move?

Yes, it is possible to shoot a usable picture from a moving vehicle. Louise sold and published a picture taken through a fast-moving car's dirty window of a boy on a fast-moving bicycle in the midst of heavy traffic just at dusk. Technically the picture leaves much to be desired. But the subject matter redeems it. (The boy had draped over his shoulder a live lamb he was taking home for his family's celebration of a Muslim holiday.) So don't think "Why bother?," just because there's motion or there's traffic or it's getting dark. If the subject matter is interesting, take the picture anyway, on the move or not.

Here's a tip for shooting out of a moving car or bus with digital—set the camera to work like a super Brownie. The distance should be fixed at the mountain icon, and the shutter speed at 1,000—the camera will pick the right aperture. What's then in focus is everything beyond about twenty feet if you are fast enough to avoid movement. This doesn't work if both you and the subject are moving, however.

Your best on-the-move photographs will result when you're sitting in the front seat taking pictures through the windshield of a car or bus, but you can shoot through the side window, too. Try to sit on the shady side of the car, bus, or plane to avoid reflections on the glass, and don't use a polarizing filter, which reacts poorly with Plexiglas windows and creates a bizarre effect. Take scenes in the middle distance, preferably those you're moving toward or away from, and pan to hold the object in position if necessary. Hold the camera close to the window, but make sure that neither it nor any part of your body is touching the vehicle frame—the vibration will blur your picture. On a heeling sailboat, however, you'll have to brace yourself.

Protect your equipment as much as possible to lengthen its trouble-free life and ensure high-quality pictures. To minimize the effects of vibration on your camera in a plane, train, or bus, put it on the seat, if possible, preferably secured with a seat belt. In a car, place it on the floor behind the front seat, on the side opposite from the exhaust. Avoid, as much as you can, the ravages of dust, sand, and sea spray.

Can You Picture the People?

Most good pictures are better pictures with people in them. Sometimes the people are mainly there to show scale—how infinitesimal is the human being looking up at the enormous statues of Ramses II at Abu Simbel, or the gigantic Daibutsu (each of Buddha's eyes is three feet long) in Kamakura.

When we say there should be people in the picture, we mean local people—not tourists. A photograph of the Plaka, with a dozen Athenians sipping ouzo at a tavern, is charming. A photograph of the Acropolis, with a dozen gaping American tourists, is not. If you want to shoot the Acropolis try to wait until the tourists leave.

How the people in your pictures look, how they're dressed and coiffed, can be very important in relation to the markets you're aiming for. Would you use the same models to illustrate an article for *Car and Driver* as you'd use for *Town and Country*? If the photo's okay for *Cosmopolitan*, does that mean it'll work for *Business Week*?

When a single human being is the focal point of the picture, ideally he or she will look at ease, will not be staring into the camera, and will be actively engaged in some pursuit typical of the locale and lifestyle.

Group shots are trickier. The more people there are, the more difficult it is to photograph everybody in an unselfconscious and flattering pose and retain the picture's interest.

Watch out for distractions in the background. Don't frame your picture with a "no smoking" sign. If a boy in a red jacket is flying a kite behind the statue you must shoot, wait until he leaves. Otherwise, nobody will look at your statue.

You may want to ask permission to take the picture. For a human close-up, that's only good manners. And people will usually welcome the photographer who wants to take home an image of them if you establish rapport, making them feel you're a friend who wants to share their activity rather than a foreigner who's ridiculing them.

Except at the farthest travel frontiers, people are accustomed to photographers and tolerate them, at least. We've always been amused by a friend who bought a miniature camera for his trip because he "didn't want to look like a tourist." This friend is six-feet-four, blond and blue-eyed, and the country he visited was Japan. In addition to the fact that he could hardly conceal his foreignness, no people in the world are more camera-happy than the Japanese. Everywhere you go in Japan, there are dozens of tourists *and* dozens of Japanese snapping away.

We've felt welcome as photographers in most countries. On many occasions we've taken a picture of a person or a landmark only to have other people rush up, begging to be photographed also.

Sometimes locals expect you to pay them for posing. It's rumored that the old man and woman in coolie outfits who position themselves at a popular tourist stop near Hong Kong's Chinese border have earned enough to send three sons through college in England. If the deal is made ahead of time, that's fine, but sometimes you'll snap the picture and *then* discover a row of outstretched palms. Jacqueline discovered that the colorful characters she encountered in Djemaa el Fna, the main square in Marrakech, were happy to pose for photos for a modest fee. You'll want to be prepared at least with small change, chewing gum, or other modest gifts. Sometimes, though, the gift for posing is refused. A group of us recently photographed some charming little Greek boys dressed in their national holiday costumes of the Evzone Guards. We had asked their mothers if we might take pictures, and then we asked their permission to give the children a few coins. They politely but firmly indicated "absolutely not."

Digital Enhancements

Photos can be easily enhanced or altered using a photo editing program on your computer, but just how much can you do? Marc Longwood, a successful travel photographer and journalist, advises that

> in photojournalism, where the news must always be truthful, you don't want to do anything more than you'd do in a traditional darkroom … crop, adjust exposure, dodge, burn, correcting distortion like perspective control, and color correct.

> For travel writing, and otherwise feature stories, it is acceptable to be a little more creative. Colored filters, creative cropping, remove some trash, etc. You can gloss it up a little bit to be creative, but always ask yourself, 'will this photo be misleading?' In other words, can someone

who visits someplace based on my recommendation see what I have shown them in my picture?

In photojournalism, you'd never move anything, or remove it. In travel, OK, but keep it real.

Lee Foster, an award-winning journalist/photographer, offers the opinion that

> if the travel photo is presented as news, purporting to show things as they are, then only very limited Photoshop changes are allowable. If the travel photo is presented as 'illustration,' then any number of imaginative changes are permissible.

> There is a common sense difference in the presentation that the average human person can detect. We are all interested in portrayals of the human condition. When we watch the evening news, we don't want any of the images doctored. When we go to an art museum opening, we are looking for some fresh perspective on life and our humanity.

The same applies to travel photos.

How to Avoid Legal Problems

Most of the legal problems surrounding photography can be solved with common sense. There seem to be two major areas involving the law. One is your pictures, the kind of rights you are selling and who is entitled to reproduce them. The other is the people in your pictures and their rights.

Most of the time you won't need a model release for a picture used for editorial purposes, but for some publications, both print and online, it's a good idea to try to get one anyway. If that picture is used for advertising, a release is imperative. And "advertising" may refer to more situations than you'd expect. For instance, a magazine's cover is considered to be advertising since it attempts to sell the publication. The entire magazine is advertising if it's a house organ or company publication since its purpose is to promote.

Sometimes you can take a picture in such a way that a person's identity is not apparent. Journalist Sherman Grant says he does this whenever possible, and when it is not, he insists on a release.

If, however, you have good travel pictures, with recognizable people in them for whom you have no releases, look for markets that don't require them. (Usually that information is included in the *Writer's Market* or *Photographer's Market* listing.) A Sunday supplement editor told Louise once that he never bothers with releases, except for the cover. "I've never had any trouble," he said. "Or at least only once." It seems he ran some freelance photographs of the Hell's Angels on the beach at Santa Cruz; one of them showed a Hell's Angel eating a popsicle. Monday morning the cyclist—and his attorney—were in the publisher's office, protesting that the picture destroyed his image, that the photographer had had no right to take it nor the editor to publish it.

The photographer did have the right to take the picture, and the editor did have the right to publish it because it was taken in a public place. The courts have held that it is not an invasion of privacy to take pictures in a public place since the photographer is a stand-in for the public—photographing something any member of the public could see if he happened to be there at the time. If, however, you go to somebody's house under false pretenses and with a hidden camera take pictures of him eating leopard's-paw soup with snail darter dumplings—that's an invasion of privacy. He'll probably sue you, and he'll probably win.

The courts have also ruled that the subject cannot recover damages from the photographer or the publication for taking and using his picture without permission if the picture was newsworthy and was published in the spirit of communicating the news, or if the person is a public personality, who has thus renounced the right to privacy.

Suppose, for instance, you're the survivor of a plane crash. You take pictures of the dead and injured, and a picture is published in the local newspaper and in a weekly news magazine. That's all right, but publishing that picture two years later, simply for its sensationalism, is all wrong, and the people pictured might have grounds for court action. Publishing the picture on the anniversary of the crash or as part of an air-safety campaign might be debatable. It would be wise to check with your attorney before submitting.

Surely you will want to restrict your photographs to those that don't violate privacy or good taste. But in case you want to protect yourself with a model release, here's an example of one:

> In consideration of value received, receipt whereof is acknowledged, I hereby give (*name of photographer or publication*) the absolute right and permission to copyright and/or publish, and/or resell photographic portraits or pictures of me, or in which I may be included, in whole or in part, for art, advertising, trade, or any other lawful purpose whatsoever.
>
> I hereby waive any right that I may have to inspect and/or approve the finished product or the advertising or editorial copy that may be used in therewith, or the use to which it may be applied.
>
> I hereby release, discharge, and agree to save (*name of photographer or publication*) from any liability by virtue of any distortion, alteration, optical illusion, or use in composite form, whether intentional or otherwise, that may occur or be produced in the taking of said pictures or in any processing tending toward the completion of the finished product.

Date	Model
Witness	Address

This is an example of the "ultimate" model release, and simpler wording might be equally satisfactory, and less intimidating, when you're trying to get a layman to sign. The main thing is to have the subject indicate he knows you're taking his picture and he's willing for you to use it any way you want without any (further) compensation to him. If the subject is a minor, be sure a parent signs the release.

Some countries prohibit the photographing of military installations, airports, harbors, or other strategic or sensitive areas, and it's not only good manners but also solid common sense to observe the restrictions they outline.

You Can Copyright Your Shots

Now let's talk about *your* rights, as a photographer. While we haven't room to discuss the subject of copyright, for either photography or writing, in any detail, keep in mind that the writer and the photographer do have rights and should protect them. For absolute protection of your photographic rights, register your pictures with the copyright office in Washington, DC. Since the per-picture fee soon adds up, either register a number of photos as a collection or group a number of them together and take a picture of the group, copyrighting that single photo. If your pictures are published in an uncopyrighted medium (e.g., most newspapers) before you register them with the copyright office, be sure the medium prints the copyright notice alongside the picture. Lee Foster advises

> that a work is automatically copyrighted the moment it is created by the travel writer or photographer. You own the copyright to your work unless you contractually give it to another, as in a work-for-hire contract.
>
> If someone infringes on your work, you can get fair use compensation for the use of the work.
>
> However, there is a higher level of protection, which is from "registering" your work with the Copyright Office. Details at copyright.gov/. This can now be done electronically for writing and for photography. A travel journalist needs to study the site, especially its FAQ, to get the proper forms, fill them out properly, and register the material.
>
> If your content is registered and then infringed, you might be entitled to greater compensation. You can claim for "statutory" damages as well as your fair use compensation. The damages can be quite high.

For up-to-date information on copyright law, visit the Library of Congress online. New material appears on a regular basis on the Library of

Congress Website. Check back often since many facets of copyright and payment for online photographs and online text change often.

Request special circulars relating to photography, as well as a copy of the revised statutes. Ask to be put on their email list—you'll receive a steady stream of material about every nuance of copyright.

Your Rights Are Valuable

Usually you'll sell "one-time rights," which means the publication is entitled to use the picture (and text) only once, and you may sell it again and again. Definitively state what you're offering: "One-time editorial use in one issue only." If you sell "all rights" or "exclusive rights," you should be paid several times the amount of "one-time rights" since you're relinquishing the picture's future value to you.

Whether you sell your photographs on assignment or on a freelance basis, be sure you and the buyer are in complete agreement, in advance, as to the rights offered, the price to be paid, the expenses covered, and any other possible sources of misunderstanding. Generally, we've found media people fair and decent, but it's always wise to have the terms spelled out.

Occasionally a photographer will complain that a newspaper has run a picture of his without paying him. Newspapers receive so many free publicity shots that you have to make it very clear that what you're sending is for sale, not a giveaway. In addition to indicating on the pictures and captions what rights you're offering, you might include a note that says something like, "I'll call you in a few days to see if you'll be using the pictures or will be returning them so I can submit them elsewhere."

Standard prices suggested for pictures used in various situations have been compiled by the American Society of Media Photographers (asmp.org). Check *Pricing Photography* by Michal Heron, *Writer's Market*, or *Photographer's Market* for current prices paid by individual photography buyers.

Selling Your Photographs

Often you'll sell the photographs you send as accompaniments to your article. But sometimes the pictures will be so outstanding you'll want to think first in terms of selling them separately, accompanied by subsidiary written material. Naturally you'll check *Writer's Market* and *Photographer's Market* for likely targets.

Many company publications, trade journals, inflights, newspapers, travel magazines, and so on sponsor photography contests, either regularly or sporadically. And many publications, from *AARP The Magazine* to *Diversion*, showcase their readers' photographs under a general theme, such as "Night Portraits" or "Pets from All Over."

As you become more and more expert, a new marketing possibility opens up. Practically every magazine occasionally runs some kind of feature on how to take good travel pictures. You can be the one to sell them that feature.

All About Captions

It is not enough to send a picture to an editor—that picture has to be carefully captioned. (You may sometimes hear it called a "legend" or a "cutline.")

What should the caption say about the picture? The first thing to do is study the captions in the publication you're dealing with. Do they use bare-bones identification, or is the caption a direct quotation from the text? Do they introduce subject matter that is not covered in the text, or do they use mere labels? Do they include lengthy chunks of information, or is the photograph integrated into the text in such a manner that it has no caption at all? In some cases you merely need to provide the reporter's who, what, when, where, why, and how to identify the picture.

Some publications, on the other hand, prefer rather literary captions with supplementary material. For such captions, don't say, "These are sheep." Instead, pick something that is not obvious to the observer and is not covered in the text. Something like:

> A flock of fat-tailed sheep, especially prized in the Middle East, graze on the slopes of Mount Atzmon, near the northern Israeli village of Tarshiha. The fat around the sheep's tails is used in baking special delicacies. The tail can weigh as much as thirty to thirty-five pounds; the shepherd must attach a special cart to the sheep's body to support the tail, which would otherwise impede the animal's mobility so severely that it couldn't graze.

It needn't be a literary masterpiece, but give the editor all the information she might possibly need. If you think of an especially charming line, send it along. But send the Five Ws information, too—in case the editor wants it.

Picture Sources for Non-Photographers

Photographs, of course, are not the only possible illustrations for either print or online articles. Maps, charts, and other types of graphics work well to break up the copy and create satisfaction for the reader. Artists usually travel with their sketchpads and return with drawings they can polish for publication.

But if photographs are needed to accompany your article, and you don't have any, don't give up—use somebody else's. There are hundreds of sources of travel photographs. Some sources will supply them free; others will impose a small charge. When the photograph is reproduced for an educational purpose, the reproduction fee is often reduced or waived. Promise the source that you'll ask for a photo credit, which is about all you can promise.

These few pages only touch the tip of the iceberg as far as photo sources go. They include suggestions, but you'll find additional listings in *Photographer's Market* and *Writer's Market*, published by Writer's Digest Books; *Literary Market Place*, published by R. R. Bowker; and on dozens of government and commercial lists. Most of these sources can be accessed online.

One writer, working on an article advising travelers not to forget their medical kits, garnered six outstanding photographs from six different pharmaceutical houses; another, writing about a visit to Stockholm when it rained every day, received a dozen sunny-day pictures from the Scandinavian Tourist Office; still another writer, preparing a nostalgic travel piece on passenger ships, was able to use three photos from the San Francisco Maritime Museum.

Contact the Superintendent of Documents, U.S. Government Printing Office (gpo.gov) for catalogs and information on pictures availability. The National Archives houses vast collections of pictures, with entries from Mathew Brady's Civil War coverage to the present, while the Geological Survey has photographs of earthquakes and volcanoes, historical mining operations, Lake Baikal in Siberia, Comanche Canyon Lands, and a lot of et ceteras. All government departments have photo libraries. These are just a few of the agencies housing usable pictures: the United States Armed Forces, the U.S. Forest Service, the National Parks Service, the U.S. Fish and Wildlife Service, the U.S. Children's Bureau, the Center for Atmospheric Research.

- **Foreign and domestic sources**. The United Nations and foreign government tourist bureaus have extensive files of photographs. Travel agencies, hotels, and sightseeing attractions, as well as airlines, cruise lines, and railroads, are glad to have you use their pictures.

  Tourist bureaus never charge for photographs—they want you to call attention to their attractions—so you're likely to get good results if you ask them for pictures.

- **State and city archives**. State historical archives, charitable organizations, public libraries, museums, zoos, and church headquarters often have fine collections of photographs. They'll sell you a print for a small sum. Local chambers of commerce are good sources, too.

  A random sampling includes the American Friends Service Committee, the Bancroft Library at the University of California, Chicago's Field Museum of Natural History, the National Recreation Association, the

Red Cross, the Southern California Visitors Bureau, and Philadelphia's Office of the City Representative.

- **Commercial archives.** The Bettmann Archive and Culver Pictures have huge photo collections, with subject indexes available. You can buy practically anything from them and surf the collections online.

- **News sources.** Sources for news pictures, both historical and current, include:

Associated Press Images

The New York Times

Keystone Press Agency

Fotos International

Also, check your local newspaper morgue, which may have pictures for sale.

- **Industry.** The Corning Museum of Glass, in Corning, New York, has the most comprehensive photo library in the world on the subject of glass. Most other industrial giants have photos available, too.

In New York City, AT&T lists, in a free catalog, pictures that show aspects of telephonic communication. Shell Oil can supply photographs of camping, fishing, vacations, and outdoor recreation. Westinghouse Electric in Pittsburgh has a photo library related to science and industry, and Wells Fargo Bank in San Francisco offers illustrations for many areas of the Pacific Coast.

If any of these sources are near you, it's best, of course, to visit in person and inspect the collection. Call first for an appointment. If you have to inquire by mail, allow plenty of time. Identify what you want as specifically as you can, and ask for a photocopy of the picture if in doubt.

Photo Sources Abound

Keep in mind several other sources of photographs, too. If your subject appears in a recent *Readers' Guide to Periodical Literature* or other magazine directory, in print or online, see if the listings say "il." indicating illustrations. If so, try either the magazine itself or the photographer for outtakes—pictures taken at the same time that weren't used. Newspapers and book publishers are often sources for outtakes, also.

Public relations agencies and PR representatives for practically all organizations are always ready to help you with pictures.

Be selective, though. Free or cheap isn't necessarily good. When choosing photographs to accompany your travel articles, apply the same standards of selection as you would to your own work.

Other possible sources of illustrations are picture-taking friends, if you can manage to neither sever the friendly relationship nor settle for artistic duds. But if you have a friend who takes good travel pictures, you may find exactly what you need—and start your friend off on a new career.

If the story is a local one, where the newspaper sends a photographer, see if you can arrange with him for extra prints. Consider, also, the possibility of having a high school or college photography student work with you on local stories. Clarify the financial arrangements in advance, and hand him or her a shooting script.

The most expensive way to find photographs, but still a satisfactory one in certain situations, is through photo agencies. Some agencies deal with clients (you) and photographers (maybe you some other time) on an assignment basis; you tell them what you want, and they find somebody to get it for you—at a price. Other agencies keep huge files of stock photos, paying the photographer when the picture is sold. Tell them what you want and they'll try to find the picture for you in their stock. Some of them have catalogs and Websites, and there are various "on approval" arrangements. There are hundreds of photo agencies, some specializing in black and white, some in color, some oriented to special subject matter or certain types of pictures, others more general. Study their listings in *Photographer's Market* if you think this might be the answer to your present needs.

The most satisfactory solution, of course, is to learn to take your own photographs—to learn to say with pictures, as well as with words, exactly what you have in mind. But if this isn't possible, don't give up—you can still accompany your article with photographs provided by others.

Photography is increasingly important to the travel writer, so don't forget the vitality of visualization. Explore the medium of photography. Experiment. Experience. Enrich your travels and your life.

CHAPTER 15

Find a Pattern, Make It Fit

Most popular travel articles follow one or another of twelve patterns. Falling into four general categories, the patterns interlock and overlap, and often more than one pattern is discernible in a published piece. Sometimes, on the other hand, it seems as though no definite pattern can be distinguished. But that doesn't mean the writer didn't have a pattern in mind—the bones of the structure may be camouflaged, but they provide a helpful framework. So it's a good idea to start with a popular pattern when you're planning or looking for a travel story.

Travel Articles from Your Own Experiences
These are the travel articles that only you can write. They are born of your own experiences, either mundane or unique, and they fall into three types: the *personal experience* article, the *advice* article, and the *humor* article.

The *Personal Experience* Travel Article
It seems, doesn't it, as though the easiest travel story to write would be your own? Isn't it always easy to write about your own experiences—the things that actually happened to you? And isn't that the best kind of story?

It is easy to write about your own experiences. But the very ease with which we write about the familiar causes us to lose our perspective, so it sometimes makes the good personal experience article especially hard to construct.

When we start a travel experience piece, it seems as though we could go on writing forever about our own adventures, with no time lost for research and no time spent searching for plot or focus. Sometimes that's part of the problem—we can't resist the temptation to tell all. Each of us, of course, feels that any happening we experience is spellbinding. So confident that the rest of the world will be fascinated, we tell the reader more than he cares to know:

> Today Maggie and I got up and brushed our teeth. We called room service for our breakfast. The waiter was late bringing it. He said he was sorry. The orange juice was in a tiny glass—only half the size of the glass we get at home.
>
> We went downstairs in the elevator and waited for Nick, our guide.

Yawn! Who would want to read this? The reader doesn't want a blow-by-blow account of your trip. What she wants is to see your trip through her eyes, enjoying the highlights and putting herself in the hero's role.

Far better than an hour-by-hour, day-by-day account of a trip is a highlighted account, showing some of the good, some of the bad, some of the commonplace, some of the unusual, in an order other than chronological. Charles and Renee Overholser begin somewhere past the middle of their "First Camping Trip" in *Family Circle*. After introducing us to their three children and discussing a fairly common experience, family travels by car, they describe one moment of the journey:

> The children had suffered six days of torture from poison oak. … The bait of Disneyland had been expended, and we still had 4,000 miles to go. We felt travel weary and glum. Then, a few hours later, in one of those switches so characteristic of a long trip like this, our mood changed! We stood on the rim of the Grand Canyon of the Colorado, breathless at the spectacular expanse that lay open before our eyes. Our spirits were suddenly refreshed and our enthusiasm rekindled.

After describing some of the most memorable sights of the trip, they go back to its original planning. Discussion of the mechanics of itinerary, food, campsites, etc., follows, interspersed with anecdotes about individual days, both good and bad, such as:

> … we nursed Charlie, temperature 102°, in the heat and dirt of a Cheyenne parking lot … while all around us, like a nightmare, swirled the noise and excitement of Frontier Days.

Or

> … the night near Yosemite when we counted 17 twinkling campfires strung along the shore of Tioga Lake like Christmas lights.

One of the differences between a publishable personal experience piece and a "Me and Joe," which all editors say they *don't* want, is in the choice of details. A publishable piece includes many details, but they are all relevant, all connected to the main theme, all interesting. A "Me and Joe" is a personal experience story in which the details are profuse but irrelevant and uninteresting to the reader.

The fiction writer creates plot through a combination of personal experience and applied imagination. The travel writer creates plot largely from personal experience; but the selection of material used, its *arrangement*, the *order* in which it is presented, and the *emphasis* accorded each facet—*that's* what makes the story.

While print media use a variety of article patterns, in cyberspace, stories written in the first person from personal experience predominate. Donald George, former travel editor of the *San Francisco Examiner*, has published many personal experience pieces. He says, "The best journeys illuminate not only pieces of the planet but also pieces of the person— and in so doing reaffirm the sacred connection between the traveler and the world."

In all successful personal experience stories, even when written in first person viewpoint, the main focus is not on the author but somewhere else. Among the most successful personal experience stories are those that tell the reader how he, too, can savor this experience. In these stories the "you" is strongly implied and the "I" small—so the writer is never the star.

Often it's this universality and familiarity that makes the personal experience worth writing. The experience was the author's, but it could be anybody's. The once-in-a-lifetime personal experience story, on the other hand, gives an enticing glimpse of faraway places and a taste of adventure that the armchair traveler can identify with in a roundabout way.

The unique experience—mountain climbing in Nepal, sailing solo across the Atlantic, even being at the critical place at the critical time as a war explodes into reality—doesn't necessarily invite the audience to participate by following the writer's example. But when deftly done, this most fiction-like personal experience technique draws the reader into the story and keeps him breathlessly awaiting development.

One of the masters of the once-in-a-lifetime personal experience story is Thor Heyerdahl, whose lifetime encompassed many. As Heyerdahl sailed across the Pacific on the raft *Kon-Tiki*, he wrote:

> Sometimes ... we went out in the rubber boat to look at ourselves by
> night. Coal-black seas towered up on all sides and a glittering myriad
> of tropical stars drew a faint reflection from plankton in the water. The
> world was simple—stars in the darkness. Whether the time was b.c. or
> a.d. suddenly became of no significance. We lived, and that we felt with
> alert intensity. ... Time and evolution somehow ceased to exist; all that
> was real and that mattered were the same today as they had always been
> and would always be.

And aboard the *Ra*:

> Once again the masts were jumping in their flat wooden shoes, while *Ra* writhed about in the wildest gymnastics to follow the chaotic dance of the waves. She was making a new, hoarse sound we had not heard before. It sounded like a mighty wind roaring to and fro as our ten thousand bundled reeds bent in the water.

Although Heyerdahl's experiences are unique, the emotions he depicts are universal. The strong, precise language puts the reader aboard the rubber boat or the pile of balsa logs or the ten thousand bundled reeds. When you read Heyerdahl, creating an exciting story from true personal experience seems compellingly possible, doesn't it? The plus value of his writing lies in his ability to show, so that one man's personal experience becomes an adventure for all of us.

Although the personal experience story is harder to write than it seems, it is an excellent article framework for describing travel experiences from the mundane to the unique.

The *Advice* Travel Article

Some of the most popular articles you can shape from personal experiences are those that offer advice. We have advised, both humorously and seriously, how to get the most mileage from your travel dollar and the most pleasure from your vacation, how to select a sightseeing program and a traveling companion, and many other travel-related "how-tos." Most of the themes have sprung from those notebook entries headed "Things I've Done Wrong."

At the Mount Kenya Safari Club, for instance, when Louise offered her husband a taste of her fish appetizer, he said, "Just cut me a tiny corner."

She started to cut the square in half.

"No," he said sharply. "I *told* you—only a small corner."

She pushed the plate toward him. "Here—take what you want."

He shoved it back. "Just cut me a corner!"

She burst into tears.

Did you ever hear of such a ridiculous quarrel? Back in their room, seething in silence, she began to write an article. She thought of other spats they'd had while traveling and of friends' arguments with spouses—in the Paris taxicab over who took too long in the bathroom and that's why we're late; in the New England rental car over who misread the map and that's why we're lost; in the Cairo airport over who wanted to buy that camel saddle in the first place and that's why we're paying all this overweight.

What is it that makes ordinarily congenial couples so touchy when they travel? Louise wondered. The article answers that question and suggests various ways couples can foresee friction and either avoid it or cope with it constructively. At the end, she explains about the eye infection, the jammed camera, the shortchanging, the springless safari bus, the lack of sleep, the paucity of game. It wasn't the fish appetizer—it was everything! Often an unpleasant travel experience turns out to be not so unpleasant after all, once enough time has passed so you can laugh about the experience—and convert it into helpful advice for others.

Evelyn Preston did just that after a disastrous auto trip to Yosemite. She warns that mountain vacationers are often so enthralled by woods and waterfalls that they forget the possibility of being stranded with "a volcanic radiator, stripped gears, or fading brakes." Her own experience with brakes giving out as she careened to a stop at the valley junction, smoke streaming from the front wheels, points up the importance of having your car thoroughly checked before you start off.

A "Things I've Done Wrong" notebook is an invaluable source of ideas for advice articles. Be sure to log all the information that you'll need to write your article.

"Things I've Done Right" can expand into advice articles, too, so jot down the details for future use.

When you think in terms of advice articles, be sure to select a relevant theme, and then show the reader how that theme applies to her.

Some themes are repeated again and again. Money—the saving of it or the spending of it—is always popular. Even articles with themes not explicitly connected to dollars and cents advise readers to consider in advance the amount of vacation money they'll have to spend, or remind them that car trouble at a resort can lead to expensive extended reservations or a rental car to transport them home.

Implicit in most money articles is the thought that the reader not only wants to save money while traveling, he wants to spend the money he has to buy the things that mean most to him. But when you're talking about money, know your readers; the words "expensive" and "inexpensive" are subject to a whole range of interpretation.

A travel advice article could take a hard look at the romantic prose of travel brochures or could deal with finding travel situations with the best of something—whether it's weather, food, accommodations, friendliness of the locals, nightclub acts, or ruins.

Comfort and Safety

On a more downbeat note, but still much needed and extremely useful, are the many advice articles that concentrate on the reader's comfort and safety:

the least tiring arrangements; the best ways to protect yourself from injury while traveling; the steps to take if you are injured or ill. Health advice runs the full gamut, from learning CPR to staying alert with in-car exercises to snacking on grow-as-you-go alfalfa sprouts.

You can help your readers prepare for their trips with wise advice such as getting a pre-trip tetanus shot or extra eyeglass prescriptions; a critical examination of the touring car and its insurance coverage; selection of luggage; guides to unraveling the mysteries of airfares; suggestions for the care of elderly relatives left behind. You can advise them on such post-trip matters as what to take off their income tax and how to present an interesting video show.

Travel advice can be general, or it can be directed to a special group: how retired couples can find quiet motel rooms; how to pack for a convention; how to stock a boat with a month's equipment and supplies; "Ideas for Easy Trailering"; "How to Care for Your Camera While Traveling"; "How to Protect Your Oil Pan in Baja."

Slant your article for your specific audience. The readers of *College Bound* won't look for the same advice as the readers of *AARP The Magazine*. "What to Do with the Children on the Rainiest Day of Your Vacation" won't appeal to the same audience that reads "Ordering Wine with Assurance at a Three-Star Restaurant."

Naturally, the travel advice article sometimes grades into the how-to-do-it or the self-help article, which is fine. What it should not become is a sermon. Take great care not to sound preachy to your readers. Be gentle and tactful; never make your reader feel foolish for not already knowing what you're telling him.

Present your information in a friendly, straightforward manner, and talk *with* the reader, not *at* him. Make sure he understands that you, too, are stupid sometimes and often share his shortcomings. On the other hand, don't make yourself seem like such a bungler that she loses confidence in your advice. A sort of "before and after" technique ("I used to do this wrong because I didn't know any better, but since I learned the right way, I want to share it with you") is best.

The responsibility of the advice-giver is tremendous. Remember, people are going to act on what you're telling them. That's why it's important to ask yourself whether your problem was a typical one or a fluke. Will what you're advising work in the demographic group you're advising it for? It's always good to incorporate the experiences of others with your own. Quoting others gives your advice substance and credibility. Some subjects, such as income tax or health care, *demand* quotes from an expert. And if you, as a result of personal experiences, are yourself an expert, be sure to make it clear to the reader why you are qualified to give this advice.

Update Your Information

The travel advice article can be tightly structured: "Ten Do's and Don'ts for Winter Travel"; "The Pros and Cons of the Organized Cruise." At other times it's more general or more subtle—the reader is being counseled, but gently.

The advice article may be in the first person, or it may be in the typical "how-to" pattern of the "I-you" viewpoint. Sometimes it's written in an implied viewpoint, without personal pronouns, that takes the reader on scene and into the story through active verbs and picture nouns, authoritative approach, and emotion-tinged information.

Although the theme of your travel advice article should be one that's of consuming interest to your readers, it need not be—it probably cannot be—a *new* theme. The same good ideas sell over and over again.

Some advice is timeless.

The *Humor* Travel Article

The travel humor piece is usually forged from your own experiences, also. It amusingly relates something you've done or seen or heard or felt.

Ask any editor what she wants, and she'll say more humor. Why then is humor so hard to sell? It's hard to sell because it's iffy—humorous *if* the editor thinks it's humorous. And often the editor doesn't know if what she thinks is humorous will be humorous to her readers. Because she doesn't trust her own judgment about what will make her readers laugh, she tends to decide conservatively.

Still, today's travel writer can sell amusing experiences if he takes the trouble to analyze the ingredients of a good travel humor piece. He may find himself writing the kind of humor that leaves the reader with a wry smile rather than a belly laugh.

That wry smile comes forth in response to tales of human foibles, where the reader can easily identify with the blundering traveler who's forever making wrong moves. Usually the joke's on you, the writer.

An inside look at the writer's ineptitudes makes the reader feel superior. However, hyperbole is often an element of humor. But, the exaggeration must be told within the bounds of logic. The reader should be able to say, even while he's laughing, "I know somebody like that," or "that sounds exactly like me." Gerald Nachman pokes fun at himself in "The Obsessive Sightseer":

> It doesn't seem enough, somehow, just to go someplace, or even take a
> snapshot of it. If you don't go all the way to the top (or, in certain cases,
> the bottom or the end or the edge) and collapse, you think you haven't
> properly "done" it.

There is the equally silly experience of going somewhere famous and not quite knowing what to do once you've arrived ... It took all day to get to Carthage and only about ten seconds to see it. ... I felt very dumb walking around the ruins looking for more ruins to look at and trying to think of more telling comments to make than, "Well, well, so this is Carthage, eh?"

Humorous Protest

While travel humor is often born of an unpleasant personal experience, it doesn't usually spring directly from raw, unleashed fury or righteous indignation. You have to wait until you've calmed down a little before you're capable of making it humorous social commentary.

Nobody who travels with a family ever runs out of humorous incidents to relate. Take care, though—before you set up members of your family as laughingstocks or embarrass them, be sure they'll perceive the experience in the same spirit as you do.

Excellent travel advice camouflaged by humor is often the best vehicle for reaching your readers. Gerald Nachman makes the reader wonder, "How does he know me!" His "Fear of Packing" begins:

After 25 years I still make the same mistakes in packing, only today I'm a lot faster at it. ... "You never know" are the three most lethal words in a traveler's lexicon. ... Maybe you'll spill shoe polish on your socks in Madrid and the stores will be shut for a big Spanish holiday. Suppose they don't sell Crest in Tokyo? ... What if you meet a wealthy couple in London who invite you back to their castle in Scotland for a fancy dress ball? Better bring that black bow tie and dark shoes after all.

And then he gives you the kernel that counts:

It is only in the quiet of your bedroom at home that all of these silly exotic notions occur. On the trip itself, it never matters what you have on.

Often it's best to select a small but universal subject, rather than write superficially about a vast one. As Richard Amour says, "In humor, part of the fun is seeing something inconsequential developed by the ingenuity and imagination of the author. The very overdeveloped may lead to the absurdity which, properly handled, is basic in a great deal of humor."

One "inconsequential" subject for travel humor is the universal misunderstanding of language. "English Spocken Here," for example, compiles signs from all over the world, like the one from the Cathedral in Seville, where "It is forbidden to enter a woman, even a foreigner if dressed as a man"; or the Hong Kong dentist's sign, "Teeth extracted by latest Methodist"; or this one on a ship's cabin door regarding the "Helpsavering

apparata in emergings behold many whistles! Associate the stringing apparata about the bosoms and meet behind, flee then to the indifferent life-
saveringshippen obediencing the instructs of the vessel." Why not become
a collector of such gems?

Other humorists translate from English to English, as in "How to Savvy
a Sign," which explains that

> A sign will inform you the next place down the road has a "Rustic
> Setting." This means the mosquitoes are terrific and the parking lot is a
> morass of mud. Or the sign might say "Leisurely Dining." This does not
> mean your leisure but rather that of the cook, who has a hot cribbage
> game going with a salesman.

It might seem like everything is stacked against the humorist from the
start because anybody feels free to object: "I don't think that's funny." Still,
with ingenuity and an indulgent attitude toward the frailties of human
nature, the travel writer can make important points while entertaining his
readers.

Travel Articles for Special Audiences

Travel articles for special audiences include the *who*, the *how*, and the
what. They are aimed at the reader who is interested in a particular kind
of traveler, a particular kind of travel, or a particular kind of activity at the
destination.

While it isn't absolutely necessary to be one of those people you're writing
about, you do need to identify with them as well as with the people you're
writing for.

Knowing just who your reader is is very important. It's a good idea to
write down a description of your reader, listing as many characteristics as
possible, including age, sex, income, marital status, education, job, where
they live, what they like to do with leisure time. Have they traveled? Where
to? Do they like to travel alone or with a friend/partner/husband/wife; how
much do they usually spend on vacations; how long are they traveling; what
type of accommodations do they like; what kind of food do they prefer; are
they early risers, or do they like to stay up late? Things like that. The more
you know about your readers, the easier it will be to target them when you
write your article or story.

The *Who* Travel Article

The *who* travel article is a people-oriented piece told in a straightforward
manner. You can tell a travel article is a *who* when the reason for the article's
existence is that it centers around parents with school-age children or mothers traveling with young babies; penny-pinching students or retirees with

more time than money; swinging singles or lonely widows; teenagers on initial solo trips or servicemen on leave; starry-eyed honeymooners or couples celebrating their golden anniversary.

Most readers have many identities—a man may be a golfer and also a father, a homeowner, a gardener, an employee, a stamp collector, an accountant, a Nebraskan, a son, a Methodist, a Rotarian, and a winner of the lottery. But if you're talking to him about the links at St. Andrew's, you're addressing him in his role as a golfer, and that becomes the organizing principle of your story.

When the people in your article share one of your reader's roles, that reader will care about their travels. So you have to ask yourself, "*Who* is doing the traveling?" and then, "*Who* is the interested reader?"

Bridal Guide and *Brides* magazines emphasize, predictably, honeymoon locales. Is Virginia what the newlywed couple has in mind?

> There is no better place to start a new life together than on a mountain. Looking down from your aerie over the landscape spread below, you can examine the life you've lived up to now, and the vastly different life you've just begun.
>
> There are no lovelier mountains for such beginnings than the Blue Ridge Mountains of Virginia.

While Virginia is a pleasant destination for non-honeymooners as well, and many aspects of trips there could be emphasized, this particular story is written about and for people who *are* going on a honeymoon.

Young Children

Chronologically speaking, the next traveler after the honeymooner may be the young parent, describing a trip with a young baby. While predominantly a *who*, because the *who* is the most important feature, an article on baby taking a trip could also be a personal experience or an advice article, with overtones of humor. If baby's going in a backpack, it's also a *how*. If you interview other parents on their best ideas for traveling with babies, your story could become a *roundup*; or you could relate it to a *here and now* or focus on a special *gimmick*.

But if we stick to the parents of the baby as the *who*, we'll find that such publications as *American Baby* and *Parents* magazine occasionally publish "Baby Takes a Trip" articles, especially in late spring. One successful story about seven-month-old Susan is a highly structured piece, with subheads pointing the way to "The Five Minute Preparation Bonanza," "The Right Kind of Car Bed," "Setting Up Happy Naptimes," "Keeping Baby Happy," "Quiet in a Restaurant," and other essential information. Remember, the *who* is not Susan but her parents.

"Camping with Your Toddler" is highly structured, too, with instructions for "Packing," "Meal Planning," and "Setting Up Camp."

Any parent should be able to write a *who*. Whether your travel experiences with children involve an hour's trip to the beach or a year's sabbatical around the world, whether you camped or cruised or visited relatives, your adventures with your children can be made into something other parents would like to read. Remember, though, to focus on only what will interest *others*.

A parenting story on teenage travel abroad describes in detail the various opportunities, but the article is not really addressed to teenagers—it's addressed to their parents, who will be selecting and paying for the arrangements.

You don't *have* to be a member of the *who* group you're writing for, but sometimes it helps. The seventy-four-year-old grandmother who writes in *Modern Maturity* about her "Adventure in the Galapagos" uses her kinship with *Modern Maturity*'s readers to good advantage in communicating her excitement to them. It's not just a trip to the Galapagos, it's one grandmother's dream come true by dint of moonlight jobs and help from her children.

Vocation or Avocation

Often the *who* is related to the reader's vocation, for vocation often influences vacation. A story about a jeweler studying the Crown Jewels at the Tower of London or a tennis player studying the prospective opposition from the stands at Wimbledon has vocation as the focal point. If you're an architect, like Bruce Beebe, you also might want to visit, as he did, Stonehenge; the Masjid-i-Jarm in Isfahan, Iran; Katsura Palace in Kyoto, Japan; Angkor Wat, Cambodia; and Chandigarh, India. What ties together these diverse destinations is the *who*—the architect who selected them as the world's most interesting architectural sites.

Trends naturally affect the *who* of travel—whether it's the promoter drumming up trade in China or the woman who wants to stay fit. Keeping abreast of trends is part of the travel writer's responsibility.

Sometimes it's the avocation that determines the *who*. When *Flower and Garden* published an article about Yorktown, Pennsylvania, it was, understandably, "Yorktown—a Gardener's View." This article appeals to anyone knowledgeable about gardens and/or about history; the way the two are woven together makes it doubly interesting.

Do you have a hobby that you travel with? Could you become the *who* and write about it? Or can you visualize a reader whose hobby makes him the *who* of your story?

Sometimes special circumstances determine the *who*'s identity. For example the *who* should be black in a story for *Ebony*, which publishes "achievement and human interest stories about, or of concern to, black readers."

Other special circumstances make the experiences of a particular *who* especially interesting to a particular reader. *Travel + Leisure's* article "The Bespectacled Voyager" was written by an optometrist. Using a question-and-answer format, he supplies information on such queries as "How can I make on-the-spot repairs?" and "Is it safe to have contacts duplicated in other countries?"

John Collins in *Arthritis Today* advises readers how to "Rent the Right Car," with a checklist of features to ask for. Other handicapped travelers often write their stories as personal experiences. While the *who* is the handicapped person, whose impairment makes special arrangements necessary, the story, if written well enough, will appeal to many readers.

You won't always travel under special circumstances, but you can find a *who* if you look for one.

The *How* Travel Article

In *how* stories, the method of transportation is the most important feature. The function of the story is to outline the conveyance's distinctive features and add helpful ancillary information. Whether it's water, wings, or wheels, you, the writer, must communicate to your readers the excitement of that particular means of "getting there." After all, as they used to say, that's half the fun. Water, the primal element, is enjoying a resurgence of popularity as a medium for getting from here to there, and travelers' choices of waterborne vehicles grow ever more varied.

A "Mini-Cruise Guide" in a trailer magazine begins:

> Nestled in the rolling Illinois farmland, less than an hour to the northwest of Chicago, lies the picturesque Chain o' Lakes. This chain, made up of ten interconnecting lakes, has the Fox River flowing right through it and offers boaters more than one hundred miles of boating pleasure.

The story continues:

> Launch facilities are far too numerous to list, so let's just say that no matter where you are on the Chain, a ramp is nearby.

> Fishing just below the dam is excellent, as it is at many spots along the way. Now and then a tiny riverfront bar pops into view, cradled softly in its picnic grove of oaks.

Canoe and Kayak Magazine assumes, not surprisingly, that its readers are already interested in getting wherever they're going in a canoe or kayak. Its articles tell of good rivers for paddling, good equipment to consider, good strokes for getting there. One of the best articles we've ever read is Marilyn Doan's "Kids 'n' Canoes," which gives the reader everything he ever wanted to know about safety measures, traveling with children, and "the acid test of any trip—the kind of memories brought home."

David and Lyn Hancock profiled an offbeat style of water travel for the readers of a boating magazine in "Adventure by Inflatable." *Adventure*, singular, may be the wrong term, since the Hancocks not only live for months at a time in a thirteen-foot inflatable dinghy "packed to the pontoon with all our requirements for living and working," but cruise in their rubber inflatable along the rugged Alaska–British Columbia shoreline. As David is a wildlife biologist, the Hancocks often carry as passengers a mountain lion, a seal, a raccoon, eagles, falcons, or sea birds. While much of the article deals with the Hancocks' adventures in camping with this arkful, the inflatable boat remains their constant (and often their only) link with the outside world, and its importance as a how-to-get-there figures prominently in the story.

If wings are your *how*, you'll find plenty of opportunities to tell readers all about it. We all know how many stories there are these days of new airline routes and old airline bankruptcies, of new kinds of service and old strategies that are changing. New fares, old fares, high fares, low fares—there's a *how* article in every one.

Wingless, but still airborne, and the epitome of adventure, is the ten-story-high hot-air balloon that takes you on an African safari, as described by Bert Keating. Lions, giraffes, warthogs, dik-diks, elephants, buffaloes, ostriches, rhinoceroses—"all the drama of an East African sunrise passed 500 feet below our feet."

Traveling on Wheels

Wheel stories abound. An airline inflight featured "Provence à la Cart," about gypsy carts and horses that can be rented to tour some of the most spectacular scenery in France, while "Covered Wagon Adventure" showed modern-day travelers, aged six to eighty-four, romping through Kansas in Stetsons and calico sunbonnets aboard authentic prairie schooners. A bike story can be even more ambitious in scope. In *Across Canada on Two Wheels* (now out of print), Mandy Joslin says each of her knees had to flex 4.25 million times to get her and her bicycle from Vancouver to Newfoundland on the Trans-Canada Highway. Her many adventures during her three-month journey are vividly rendered, with her *how* providing the focus.

Another wheeled adventure was undertaken by a fourteen-year-old boy, who navigated the Great Wall of China—by skateboard! In an interview with a reporter, he called it "a bumpy experience."

Riding the rails is a big *how*. A newspaper travel story about Scandinavian trains begins:

> Americans who remember train travel might agree that the clickety-click of the wheel on the rail is a pleasant inducement to sleep. But for passengers riding the rails in Denmark, Norway, or Sweden, each click is an invitation to see another distinctive view of fairytale villages, Arctic tundra, awesome fjords, towering mountains, great forests, glittering lakes.

The *how* is what's holding together the scenic diversity of the story.

For some travelers the only way to go is by animal-back. An article in *Aramco World* deals with Jordan's Camel Caravans, an organization that specializes in introducing Western visitors to a camel-back view of the desert. William Tracey, author of the article, describes the second day with the caravan:

> The next morning saw us "making friends with our camels," as the brochure explains it, a process that involves adjusting the foam rubber cushions beneath the woven saddle bags, stretching one leg across the kneeling camel's back, and hanging on frantically as the mount lurches to its feet grumbling and protesting. Once up, however, riding a walking camel is as easy as sitting in a rocking chair. Unfortunately the chair keeps rocking and rocking and rocking.

When you begin to think about "how to get there," dozens of ways present themselves. Some are exotic, some not so. But the best, most universal means of transportation, always available, always useful, is on your own two feet. "A Walking Tour of Honolulu," "A Walking Tour of Philadelphia," "A Walking Tour of Denver"—such articles appear with regular frequency. They're designed for the normally sedentary traveler who wants to explore the sights in a good-sized city. Current interest in fitness and ecology adds to the popularity of walking tours.

Perhaps, though, you'd like to write an article addressed to more serious hikers, describing wilderness areas that can only be reached afoot. Maybe you have in mind something like the *Sunset* article about Olympic National Park, titled "Walking—the Only Way to Go." Wonderful! Many readers would welcome your description of an off-the-beaten-track hike.

Whether it's on your own two feet or via pogo stick, cable car, or magic carpet, your transportation introduces your reader to a vital element of any trip—the *how*.

The *What* Travel Article

Active travelers are interested in *what* they'll be doing, and they like to read about the variety of activities at their destinations. Whatever type of travel activity you yourself prefer, you'll find readers interested in it.

Practically every traveler cares about the *what* of accommodations—eating and sleeping. Regular readers of such food-and-drink publications as *Bon Appétit* and *Food & Wine* naturally expect to have their taste buds titillated, whether or not they're planning to visit La Tour d'Argent in Paris or Masa's in San Francisco; but even "meat and potatoes" people are lured by references to sophisticated dining when the locale is on their itinerary.

Most regional and city magazines carry special restaurant sections covering their areas. A health magazine will review a restaurant that prepares its food "in the health tradition." Even the newspaper travel sections will sometimes run roundup restaurant reviews under such titles as "Dining Out in Milan." So if you think of eating as your reader's *what*, consider the target market first, before planning your story. But while you're on your trip be sure to jot down the details of memorable experiences.

Sleeping is a little different. Often the story deals with the ambience of a particular establishment, such as Frank Taylor's *Off Duty* article about the old Hotel del Coronado, which has been declared a national landmark. He not only describes the eight-foot chandelier and the brass elevator, but also reminds readers that it may have been here that Edward, Prince of Wales, first met Mrs. Simpson.

Sometimes sleeping and eating go together, as in a *House & Garden* travel feature on finding cozy places for bed and breakfast in the English countryside.

Camping can be the *what*, as well as the roof over the head, the dining site, and possibly the means of transportation. Camping-abroad stories proliferate—so much so that it's hard to sell one without a special angle. So create a special angle! Bill Thomas authored an article on "Theme Camping" that tells about camps with special facilities for farming, cow punching, exploring history, picking fruit, digging for artifacts, or panning for gold.

Often your readers will have a favorite activity they plan to pursue during their trips—the *what* they want to read about. Is it golf, tennis, skiing, fishing, or surfing? You can tell them where to find these activities and describe special festivities that may be connected.

For some travelers, the real *what* is in the shops. Information on what's available to buy is always popular, as is a recommendation of the best stores. Some notable shopping areas, such as the Virgin Islands, appear again and again in travel-oriented publications, with the writer telling the reader why the shopping is a bargain, what to look for, and what to do if you buy more than your customs quota. Even if your readers aren't shoppers, they'll be interested in features about offbeat purchasing such as at Madrid's El Rastro.

Madeline Dane Ross calls it "Madrid's Bargain Basement," and describes the setting:

> Sunday is the day for the pushcarts, canvas-covered stalls, and the largest display of wares of the whole week, placed right on the ground. ...
> You can find anything from camping equipment and plastic furniture to rosaries and even secondhand tombstones. Along with the vendors hawking, people arguing or laughing, and children yelling in their street games, you'll hear the guitars of gypsies and popular ... tunes from the secondhand records and players. On the breezes, too, you'll scent the sharp and tantalizing aromas of roasting chestnuts.

Enriching Activities

For some readers the *what* will involve animals—San Diego's Wild Animal Park, a dude ranch in Arizona, or the rodeo in Kissimmee, Florida. Perhaps they know about these attractions already and just seek specific details before planning a trip. Or they may be grateful to you for introducing them to a new vacation destination.

Part of the travel writer's function should be to introduce readers to enriching activities. For instance, Dorothy Loa McFadden says, "Nothing can hold your attention like watching something being made." She suggests that seeking out craftsmen—to watch, to photograph, to buy from—can lead to many happy traveling hours. "When you go to Europe," she says, "look for the places where you can see things made of native materials and with designs which have often been handed down for generations." She goes on to describe some of the craftwork that can be seen, telling her readers where to find it and how to arrange to watch the artisan at work.

Today many readers seek meaningful vacations. Would they be interested in your adventures tagging birds, counting coral, or digging into history as a contribution to the total body of human knowledge? Or are they seeking personal enrichment through learning to sail, scuba dive, photograph, or fly a helicopter? Do you have a *what* story to tell?

Perhaps you'll introduce your readers to a hobby like gravestone rubbing, which was the subject of an excellent article in a travel magazine. The article gives a little of the art, poetry, and history of gravestones, lists the equipment and supplies needed for rubbing, and explains the details of the technique.

If your readers have a long-treasured hobby, you can help them to enrich it through their travels.

> For those who are seeking solitude, unfortunately it is becoming almost impossible to find. Even our national parks, which once were havens of tranquility, are more popular—and more crowded—than ever before. Last year over 3 million visitors thronged Yosemite, elbowed for room around

Old Faithful, and bumped into fellow hikers on Glacier National Park's most remote backcountry trails.

But if you're planning a trip to a national park this year, take heart. Here is a list of serene, beautiful spots, many of which have not suffered exposure.

A bit off the beaten path but not inconvenient, these special places include homey motels that are clean and inexpensive, family restaurants that pack homemade muffins and preserves into your lunch bag, and trails that range from sandy tracks that take you to secluded coves to hiking paths with vistas so magnificent that you feel you can walk right into the sky.

Although the listing of the offbeat places might become a *roundup*, the article's search for solitude is so overwhelming that it becomes the basis for the *what*.

Look for the *what* when you're traveling. Think about which ones would interest which readers. Whether it's an old reliable, like playing ping pong, or a new skill, like racing down a bobsled run, do think about *what* your reader, the active traveler, will do at his destination. Once you've defined him and transported him, write about activities he's likely to enjoy.

Travel Articles That Take Readers on a Journey

So far we have talked of travel articles for the active traveler—the reader who is thinking of following in the footsteps you are delineating. But many readers are armchair travelers, and this group of articles appeals to the armchair as well as the active traveler. The *flavor* article, the *definitive destination* piece, and the *gimmick* story are for everybody.

The Travel *Flavor* Article

Whether your reader is looking forward to a trip or reminiscing about one traveled only in his daydreams, a *flavor* piece will take him on a journey. When done well, it makes him feel he's right there with you, experiencing the car-shattering sounds and shoulder-shoving crowds of the bazaar; or the quiet and tranquility of watching, just the two of you, the sun setting beyond the gentle breakers.

The flavor piece is really a literary exercise; to write a good one you must be a good writer. Also, you have to feel strongly about the travel experience and be prepared to recreate that experience for your reader through emotion-evoking details.

Can you make your reader see the flavorful details? Bill Thomas, in *Elks Magazine*, shows his readers the Suwannee River:

> The Suwannee runs slowly and meanders, its black water feeling its way between soft white sand banks and rocky shores, choosing an uncertain

path at times in the low cypress swamps that crowd close to each side.
And along its path are great blue-water springs that emerge from the forest to flow sweet, cold and fresh. ...The sandy bottoms of the springs,
some of them 40 feet deep, are carpeted with watercress and other edible
aquaplants. You can glide above them in water so crystal clear it's almost
like flying.

He reproduces the *sounds* of the river, too:

The rustle and swish of the lazy water is remindful of the pace of life here.
... Feel the earthshaking rumble of logs drifting down to the mills and
the chop and slap of the paddle wheel ghost boats. ...

John Updike's *New Yorker* article on Ethiopia takes us to the Addis Ababa
Hilton, where you can see the cruciform swimming pool and the long white
facade of the palace from upper-floor balconies. "In the other direction," says
Updike, "there are acres of tin shacks, and a church on a hill like the nipple
on a breast of dust."

He tells the reader what Ethiopia *feels* like, too:

Emerging from the pool, which feels like layers of rapidly tearing silk,
one shivers uncontrollably until dry, although the sun is brilliant and the
sky diamond-pure. The land is high, and the air is not humid. One dries
quickly.

And toward the end he tells us that the young American taking a picture
sees through his viewfinder a scene "exactly like the sepia illustrations in his
Sunday-school Bible."

Paul Theroux writes of a train trip in India:

At Sirpur, just over the border of Andhra Pradesh, the train ground to
a halt. Twenty minutes later we were still there. Sirpur is insignificant:
The platform is uncovered, the station has two rooms, and there are
cows on the veranda. Grass tufts grow out of the ledge of the booking
office window. It smelled of rain and wood smoke and cow dung; it
was little more than a hut, dignified with the usual railway signs, of
which the most hopeful was "Trains Running Late Are Likely To Make
Up Time." Passengers on the grand Trunk Express began to get out.
They promenaded, belching in little groups, grateful for the exercise.

Joan Didion imparts the flavor of Bogota to her readers. After viewing
a mine that produces enough salt for all of South America and a cathedral
carved into the mountain 450 feet below the surface, where ten thousand
people can hear Mass at the same time, she had lunch in a chilly dining room
on the side of the salt mountain.

There were heavy draperies that gave off a faint muskiness when touched.
There were white brocade tablecloths, carefully darned. For every stalk
of blanched asparagus served, there appeared another battery of silver-

plated flatware and platters and *vinaigrette* sauceboats, and also battery of "waiters"—little boys, 12 or 13 years old, dressed in tailcoats and white gloves and taught to serve as if this small inn on an Andean precipice were Vienna under the Hapsburgs.

I sat there for a long time. All around us the wind was sweeping the clouds off the Andes and across the savanna. Four hundred and fifty feet beneath us was the cathedral built of salt in the year 1954. One of the little boys in white gloves picked up an empty wine bottle from the table, fitted it precisely into a wine holder, and marched toward the kitchen holding it stiffly before him, glancing covertly at the maitre d'hotel for approval. It seemed to me later that I had never before seen and would perhaps never again see the residuum of European custom so movingly and pointlessly observed.

As we can see, each of these flavor articles introduces the reader not only to the geographic area but also to the personality of the place and of the writer.

The *Definitive Destination* Travel Article

The *definitive destination* article also takes your reader on a journey. For that kind of comprehensive article you have to know *everything*. You have to anticipate the questions your reader is likely to whisper and answer them before they occur. Some destinations are easier to define than others, and some destinations demand longer articles than others. In any case, the definitive destination article has to be information-packed and tightly structured, with sure transitions holding it together. And even though you're trying to tell everything, you'll still need to decide what to emphasize and what to skip over. You need a strong capsule sentence to define your message.

Trailer Life's article on Washington, DC, is a destination article. It begins:

If you're an American, no matter where you live—Dubuque, Dallas, Minneapolis, or Muleshoe—you have a second hometown. All of us do. That other repository for our loyalty and allegiance is our splendid national capital city, Washington, DC.

And it ends:

... only Washington is every American's second hometown, and every visit is a happy homecoming.

And everything in between is related to that framework. The article tells the history of the building of Washington and describes the sights in considerable detail. It goes into the geography of the city and the attractions on its outskirts, like Mount Vernon; discusses musical and theatrical events; and tells the reader how to see the government in action. But because of the readership of this publication, the article says nothing about hotels or restaurants. It does mention that there are no campgrounds or RV parks within the city limits but tells where they can be found outside the city.

Of course a destination piece for a different type of publication includes more on where to sleep and eat.

Bon Appétit's destination piece on Rio de Janeiro focuses, quite naturally, on food and drink.

> Brazilian wine is poor. If you must drink wine in Brazil ask for Chilean or Argentine, but here in the Alba-Mar and along the bay front nearly everyone drinks *chopp*.

Extensive research is needed to produce this kind of article. While some of it can be, and should be, started on the Internet, it's still vitally important to set up interviews with key people at the destination. Often a definitive destination piece results from an assignment, or at least a pre-trip discussion with the editor, and this opens the door to the key people. *National Geographic* stories often cover the destination completely. While the flavor piece is nearly always written in first person viewpoint, the definitive destination story can be in any viewpoint, and often shifts from one to another.

If it defines a large area, the definitive destination article is enhanced by subheads and sidebars—it's easier for the reader to get the whole picture if it's divided up into specific segments. The well-structured destination piece "Auckland," in *Pacific Travel News*, tells about the geography of the city, its population, surrounding areas, volcanoes, water on all sides, shopping areas, climate, and transportation. And then come the subheads— "Hotels & Dining," "The Overview," "Museums," "Sightseeing by Car and Boat," "Sports & Events," "Shopping," and where to send for more information. Still different, and more comprehensive in some ways, is Herbert Gold's definitive destination piece on Los Angeles. This is a type of piece that goes beyond mere detail in an attempt to actually grasp the *meaning* of a place. It expresses its theme by telling the reader the city's theme:

> Mobility is the theme of Los Angeles, not status, monuments, concern for the past. It is called a city: it is, in fact, an immense post-urban process, the tentative validation of a concept New York only hints at and neither Cleveland nor Des Moines dares to express. But L.A. is settled by refugees from New York, Cleveland, and Des Moines, from the Dust Bowl and the South, from Heartland America. They are here for this. It is the first American experimental space colony on earth.

And analyzing the ethnic components:

> That there are large black, Japanese, Chicano, Chinese, and Russian communities that guard their ethnic purity is well-known. There are also extended families of those faithful to UFOs and Scientology, and you

can listen to soft Scientological rock on an L. Ron Hubbard radio station. There are those who converse in tongues and those awaiting a call from mail-order prophets who bless cripples and change the tires on their wheelchairs.

Not exactly a travel piece perhaps, but definitely a destination piece. The author ends by urging the reader to laugh along with him at a city with signs such as this:

L.A. MINI SUPERETTE
Gas, Food, Tums
OPEN 24 HOURS A DAY
(Closed Midnight to 7 a.m.)

The *Gimmick* Travel Article

When you want to take your reader on a journey, consider the *gimmick*, too. The gimmick is a very narrow subject or a specific facet of a larger topic or a small topic treated in a special or unusual format. The gimmick is often a good travel story pattern and an easy one to write because it focuses so sharply. When you don't have enough space to tell everything, as in a definitive piece, or you don't have enough material to write an in-depth overview, or for some reason you can't or don't want to cover that much, write a gimmick.

The capsule sentence for the gimmick type of article usually falls into place easily. If you're taking your reader on a journey to the Kentucky Derby, the Grand Rapids Furniture Museum, or Seattle's Space Needle, your capsule sentence is limited by the objective of the story, so there are fewer choices and fewer bypaths down which the writer can accidentally wander. Individual sights and events often make good gimmicks when you're traveling, so learn to look for them, recognize them, and create them.

Very small segments of the traveler's world can be turned into profitable gimmicks. For example, "Our New Sign Language"—a description of the then-upcoming new highway symbols—appeared in *Motorland*; "Senet"—an ancient Egyptian game shown in the tomb paintings and billed as "King Tut's Favorite Game"—appeared in *Games*; and "Topkapi's Turkish Timepieces"—an outstanding collection of clocks and watches in Istanbul's Topkapi Palace—appeared in *Aramco World*. These are all fragments of a subject. They are definitely limited in scope.

Equally limited, although covering a bigger area, are subjects like "Wyatt Earp's Kind of Town" (the ghost town of Bodie); "Placer County's Big Tree Grove" (a special race of giant sequoias); "Day Outside Amsterdam" (getting out in the country to Vreeland); and "The Little Volcano that Couldn't" (a resort hotel in El Salvador that was built so guests would have a good view of the volcano erupting, which hasn't happened since the hotel was built and thus the hotel has had no guests).

"The New Face of Yellowstone Park" sticks to the changes that occurred in the park after the 1988 forest fires and explains why the park looks better—and worse—than visitors might expect.

Keep your eyes and ears open—and your field notebook handy—to record the significant fragments of your trip that will make good gimmick stories. Often the gimmick is a single event, perhaps taking up only a brief amount of time during the trip. Louise's sheep dog trial was like that. (Incidentally, by the time she completed all the research, the *New York Times* had a new travel editor who thought sheep dogs "not compelling enough.")

The most "gimmicky" kind of gimmick is the puzzle or quiz. You often see this sort of thing in inflight magazines. There's the crossword puzzle with gems like "What to eat in Honolulu, 26 across" and "What to call your friend's father in Spain, 39 down." Sometimes you'll see a map of a confusing area like the Caribbean, with all the islands numbered, and the reader is supposed to guess which islands the numbers indicate. Or there'll be a questionnaire with a heading such as "Are You a Graduate Globetrotter?" and questions like "Where would you be calculating coin-age if this is what you had in your pocket: yen, bolivar, or guilder?" or "Which country's airline would you be flying if you go: Aer Lingus, Swiss Air, Lufthansa, El-Al, or KLM?"

You've probably seen some gimmicky things like this, too—"Bermuda: From A to Z," with "A" for ale (they tell you which pubs to patronize) and "Z" for Zebra Crossing (the black-and-white-striped pedestrian crosswalk). If you're clever at making up games and puzzles of this sort, don't hesitate to work out a travel theme and send it off.

As you cultivate the habit of selecting travel gimmicks to write about, you'll wish the days had more than twenty-four hours.

Travel Articles with Easy Pegs
Stories with natural pegs are easy travel stories. You can train yourself to find them anywhere. The *roundup*, *history*, and *here-and-now* travel articles practically write themselves.

The *Roundup* Travel Article
The easiest peg to use, as well as the most familiar, is the *roundup*. You've seen these in many magazines, and the possibilities are endless. It's often easy to ask twenty celebrities, say, about their favorite vacations. You probably don't even need twenty: five or six might do. It's even easier to interview one

celebrity and ask him to name his favorite places for something or other, such as Lee Tyler did with Mike Roseto. She asked him to name his favorite golf courses, in terms of character, nearby accommodations, and surroundings, and a roundup of eight golfing areas resulted.

For a roundup the travel writer can take a group of whatever and convert it to a salable story—"The Covered Bridges of Indiana," "The Paradores of Spain," or "Burma Shave Signs I Have Loved."

Some publications seem to savor the roundup, even to seek it out. *Travel/Holiday* uses a roundup in nearly every issue, and the variety is astonishing. "Swiss Ski Resorts," "Britain's Stately Homes," and "Spain's Royal Palaces" may not seem so unusual, but how about "Aerospace Museums"—the many museums throughout the United States that document each step, from Kitty Hawk to the moon, during the past ninety-odd years; or "The World in Mosaics"—from the floor of Diocletian's Bath in Rome to the steps of a Jain temple in Calcutta.

Better Homes and Gardens runs frequent travel roundups, too. Is the reader interested in "America's Zingiest Zoos"—from Cincinnati to the Bronx, from St. Louis to San Diego? In "Indian Country Vacations" accommodations "from the super deluxe to the primitive" are mentioned, and the reader is told where to get additional information. Another issue features "'Foreign' Vacations in the U.S.A.," rambling from Little Tokyo in Los Angeles to Holland, Michigan's Tulip Time Festival and San Antonio's Paseo del Rio. Roundups of cruises, train trips, car rental agencies, and even articles about best buys in cell phones frequently appear online, as well as in print. Gorp.com recently ran a very good roundup of "Best Parks for Biking," including ten national parks.

Numbers lend themselves to roundups—"Five Great Places to Get Away from It All" in *Medical Economics*; "Three RV Tours That Are High Roads to Adventure" in *Minnesota Motorist*; and "Seven Great Tennis Vacations" in *Glamour*. Be sure you use the numbers instead of letting them use you. If there are only nine really outstanding nudist camps where your reader can reserve a holiday, don't round the number off to ten.

Roundups, like other travel articles, especially appeal to readers when they emphasize how to save money. Add the words "you" and "secret," and it's hard for the reader to resist looking to see what's offered. *Family Circle's* "Super Sunbelt Vacations Your Family Can Afford" is a case in point. Throughout this entire article, the themes of "super" and "sun" and "saving money" promised in the title are emphasized.

Roundups sometimes introduce the reader to things he can do himself. "Games Europeans Play" was a roundup of interesting keep-fit exercises; and *Gambling Times* tells "Where to Take a Gamble on Your Next Vacation," evaluating foreign casinos.

The items being rounded up don't have to be many—perhaps only two. A *Redbook* article on "Two Seductive Cities" links Santa Fe and San Francisco by more than their initials. If this is the year for your second honeymoon, says the author, you can find elegant hideaways, extraordinary scenery, and sumptuous but inexpensive dining in both of these cities, and there are so many things to do you may even want to take the children along.

Sometimes you can create a roundup from parts of several previous travel articles by finding a common peg to tie the information together. And sometimes, if you don't create the roundup, the editor does. When Louise sent an article on Buena Park to *Off Duty* without querying because she felt the article was perfect for the market, the editor informed her that another writer was already researching California's theme parks, but he had requested him to exclude Buena Park. When the article appeared in print, it included all that Louise had written plus material on Disneyland and other theme parks by Hal Schell. The editor ran it all together as a roundup and gave them a joint byline, although Schell and Louise had never met.

Practically any segment of the travel experience works well with this easy peg, and you'll find yourself using it again and again. Either first person or implied viewpoint suits the roundup.

The *Historical* Travel Article

When you're writing a *historical* travel article, it's your job to bring the reader right to the scene of the action, so you must make it read like fiction. Usually this is best done in an implied viewpoint, with many active verbs. You have to be sure, however, that your *facts* are not fictional but are absolutely accurate. Your target audience determines how many of these facts will be introduced and how scholarly your presentation will be.

Another factor, of course, is how much space you have. While a historical travel article on Peru in *Americas* would not be as scholarly or as finely tuned as one in *Archaeology*, if it's the lead article it must be significant and in-depth.

Let's examine a twenty-three-page, well-illustrated article on "Mexico: A Story of Three Cultures." It covers the geography and the cities and landscapes in considerable detail, dividing the country into northern, southern, and central sections. After explaining the constitution and government, the article moves on to culture and customs, folk arts, and literature. Under economic and social development it discusses labor, communities, housing, health, education, agriculture, gas, minerals, industry, electric power, banking and finance, foreign trade, communication, transportation, and tourism; thus the article becomes a comprehensive overview. Its major focus, though, is Mexico's history, from pre-Columbian times to the present. It discusses Mayan and Olmec civilizations, Zapata and Mixtec, Toltec and Aztec, and explains the present archaeological zones. Then it details the wars and revolutions, the backward steps, and the forward steps from Cortez to the present. Although factual and accurate, the article's style is readable:

> Father Miguel Hidalgo y Costilla issued the now famous *Grito de Dolores*: "Long live our lady of Guadalupe, down with bad government, death to the Spaniards!" His followers, an "army" of perhaps fifty thousand ill-clad men armed with bows and arrows, clubs, machetes, and a few guns, seized Guanajuato and nearby towns and marched on Mexico City.

As is often the case in historical articles, the writer assumes a certain knowledge on the part of the reader, as, for instance, when using the phrase "now famous." Online historical articles assume this knowledge, too, but perhaps in a different way since brevity is so important.

There are two frequent reasons for writing the historical travel article: to remind your reader and help her review the facts of history, and to shed new light on an old story. "The City That Died to Live," a *Reader's Digest* piece on Pompeii, does both. Although written long ago, its authors, Donald and Louise Peattie, did such an excellent job of bringing Pompeii to life, within the framework of historical accuracy, the article could serve as a model for all travel writers who try similar pieces. Notice the devices that bring the reader on-scene although more than 1,900 years elapsed between the time Mt. Vesuvius erupted so disastrously and the time the story was written:

> The city of Pompeii basked among its silvery olive groves and dark umbrella pines. The marble on suburban villas and on the temples in the heart of town glittered sumptuously as the sundial shadow crept toward the fated figure I *post meridiem*. The shopkeepers were closing their wooden shutters for the long Latin lunch hour. A baker shoved 81 loaves into his oven and closed the iron door. In a wineshop a customer laid his money on the counter. Suddenly an earthquake convulsed the city. The barmaid never picked up the money. The baker's loaves were burned to a crisp.
>
> Thousands fled at once. These were the wise—and the wisest kept on traveling all that afternoon and night. Nothing else could have put them outside the circle of death that Vesuvius was inscribing around itself.

Some publications lean especially toward historical travel articles, so we expect to see in *Ironworker* an article on the restoration of Colonial Williamsburg, in *Early American Life* an article about "Savannah, a City

Reclaimed," and in *National Motorist* an article about the copper mines of Jerome, Arizona. All of these stories combine history with the present, telling the reader what he can see if he goes there today and what it all means.

Instead of an entire community, sometimes the historical travel article deals with a more specific theme, such as the restoration of a nineteenth-century sugar plantation, in *Historic Preservation*, or the transporting of Cleopatra's Needle from Alexandria, Egypt, to New York City, in the *Saturday Evening Post*.

As with all kinds of writing, the easiest way to make history come alive is to tie it in with people who lived it. When Fanny-Maude Evans wrote "Take Along a Hero or Heroine" for *Redbook*, she emphasized to her readers the value of doing their homework before they traveled in order to know the people who made the places memorable. She tells about Harriet Tubman silently leading three hundred slaves to freedom along Maryland's Eastern Shore; Sybil Ludington, a "teen-aged Paul Revere," who summoned New Yorkers to rebel against the British; and Sam Houston, who hated violence yet "won one of the world's most decisive battles." She concludes:

> By reading about the men and women who helped to carve the nation's history, not only will you be giving your children inspiring models to follow but also you can make your travels more interesting.

Nostalgia, too, enters into the historical travel article. One writer who "first met Bill and Anna Wilkins at a flea market on Maryland's Eastern Shore when they had been dead for several years" took their scrapbook, stuffed with postcards and trip mementos, and followed in the footsteps of the trip to Florida they had taken forty-odd years before. He compares and contrasts the train ride, dinner in the diner, and the hotel. And then he flies home!

Whether you're introducing a bit of personal nostalgia or sticking to the strictly historical, you'll find that this pattern, with its easy peg, is often a good one to use.

The *Here-and-Now* Travel Article

In some ways the easiest travel article of all to write is the *here-and-now*. It takes advantage of the fact that a locale—or a topic—is already in the forefront of readers' and editors' attention for some reason. Sometimes you can hang a basic story on a here-and-now peg by merely adding a sentence or two at the beginning and another sentence or two at the end. For example, a magazine article about Evora in *Retired Officer Magazine* begins:

> Now that the political upsets in Portugal seem over, the country as a whole and the Algarve and Lisbon in particular are going to be prime tourist targets.

The article continues with the charms of Evora.

Other times, you'll be inspired by the event itself to write the here-and-now, so the peg will be integral. Look for news events, like improved relations with a foreign country such as Cuba or China; the opening of an entire new tourist area, such as Vietnam; or major political changes like the increased accessibility of Eastern Europe. A new kind of plane or ship being launched, wars, riots, strikes, adventurers taking off from or landing at a particular place—all these provide us with the nucleus of reader interest and the framework for a here-and-now story. But be sure to hurry when you're writing a story like this. A magazine's long lead time sometimes makes a newspaper travel section or an online zine a better market for a current event.

A major happening, such as the 9/11 disaster, spawns travel stories for a long time—what tours, cruises, and other trips have been cancelled, and which ones then reappear; what new security measures are being observed, and how difficult do they make transportation; how many people decided not to go to faraway places; and, most of all, reports from the people who did go—what was it like?

Before the Winter Olympics opened in Salt Lake City all media outlets searched for something new to say. In addition to stories about the upcoming games themselves, transportation to Utah, sleeping and eating upon arrival, and the landmarks of Salt Lake City, there were many articles about what to see in the surrounding area. There were even stories like "A Primer on Tippling in Utah," telling how and where to find alcoholic beverages in this anti-alcohol state.

Look for regional events to write about for local newspapers and regional publications: the county fair; the marble-shooting championship in the state capital; new attractions at the nearby theme park.

Can you make a here-and-now out of an anniversary? While the Pompeii story as history needed no other peg, a more recent *Reader's Digest* article was tied to the traveling exhibition, "Pompeii A.D. 79," which was drawing "record crowds" to view the three hundred artifacts recovered from the excavations. Both the exhibit and the article were tied to the anniversary of the Vesuvius eruption.

Anniversaries of cityhood, statehood, or nationhood and upcoming commemorations of other civic occasions give you more time to plan ahead if you're familiar with the place or going there. The Golden Gate Bridge, the Statue of Liberty, the Empire State Building, and dozens of other landmarks have important birthdays.

Many publications, both print and online, ran "before," "during," and "after" stories about London, and the British Isles in general, in recognition of Prince William and Catherine Middleton's wedding.

General trends, while not as mercurial as isolated news events, sometimes do change suddenly, so when you're writing about a trend, act quickly if you think a change is likely. Broad general trends are, however, likely to continue, such as younger teenagers traveling farther, "new" gold hunters becoming hobby prospectors, and people saving money by traveling close to home, which may give you a little more working time. Health and fitness will probably be with us forever.

As we've said, adventure travel these days is the province not only of the very young and unusually hardy; it is catching on with mainstream vacationers and senior citizens, tired of the three-day, four-night deal to Disney World with the complimentary rum swizzle; or the one-week Caribbean cruise on a ship that looks and acts more like a resort hotel. And the trend toward ecotourism, with care given to protect the environment, is even more all-encompassing.

Watch the Calendar

Learn to watch the calendar and allow enough time (usually six to nine months, but check the publication) to fit your story into seasons of the year and special holidays only salable to a certain periodical or online zine. Create "seasons" if you can, with phrases like, "Now that the kids are back in school" or "Now that the wildflowers are in bloom."

Be aware of annual events such as: the International Balloon Festival in Albuquerque each October; the Calgary Stampede in the late summer; Aloha Week; Tulip Time in Holland, Michigan; the New Orleans Jazz Festival; fall colors; whale watching; the Great Raft Race, which is the Labor Day blowout in Tulsa, Oklahoma; the Bay to Breakers foot race in San Francisco; and other repetitive occasions.

Seasons of the year make great travel stories. Spring brings "New Season Show in the Smokiest" and "Great Springtime Vacations Along the Gulf of Mexico." In the fall it's "Share the Excitement of a Football Saturday" and "A Rainbow of Fall Foliage Awaits the Camper Who Follows a Back Country Trail." In winter there's advice to "Go Winter RVing" and "Get Away for a Winter Weekend."

The holidays are a gift to the travel writer. *Travel Life* had a wonderful three-way Christmas travel piece—all personal experiences: a caravan Christmas in Mexico; "Head Home for Christmas"; and "Camp the Holy Land at Christmas." "Christmas in Europe" and "Christmas Around the World" are perennial favorites, supplemented by stories that tell how Christmas is celebrated in individual countries. If you have any new ideas on Christmas travel, editors will welcome them.

Washington's Birthday, Valentine's Day, and Halloween—all make good stories. Look for obscure holidays, too. Groundhog Day? Flag Day? Benjamin Franklin's birthday?

Another here-and-now can have what is termed a "this reader" peg. "This reader" will read your story because it's in a particular publication. Therefore, it's often a story with a limited market—only salable to a certain periodical. Usually, the story will concern travel connected to an association, an industry, a profession, a religious group, or an area of the world. Fishermen want to know where they're biting, and cyclists will read stories about the roads and trails. If you're writing for *Sea Kayaker* or *Trailer Life* or *Motorcycle Cruiser*, you have a built-in audience.

If you know of a Rotary International project, a shrine-hopping trip planned by a denominational organization, a "Sister City" or "Neighbors Abroad" event, your chances of selling an article escalate.

As we have said, many travel articles combine the elements of several of the dozen patterns described in this chapter, and the structure of the finished piece is sometimes blurred. But beginning with a definite framework will give you a head start, and you'll be able to decide on combinations of your own. You'll also find that you can apply several different patterns to the information gathered from a single trip, thus netting several different stories from your experiences and research.

CHAPTER 16

All You Don't Know
but Can Find Out

If you thought the personal computer revolution of the 1980s and the Internet revolution of the 1990s were big, well, they were. But a new revolution merging the best features of personal computing, instant anywhere-anytime communication, and carry-everywhere portability promises to dwarf them both.

Smartphones

The smartphone could be the technology that turns everyone into a radio reporter, causing many traditional journalists to ask, "Why do we carry these huge kits around?" And while news producers may be snobby about sound quality, consumers, generally, are not. One reporter says the quality of his field reports is 92 percent as good using his smartphone as when he used bulky broadcast equipment.

We heard about a journalist who arrived at an important interview only to find she had left her tote bag containing her recorder, microphone, etc., at home. However, she did have her iPhone with her and used it to record the interview. She was able to broadcast the session on her radio show the next morning with surprisingly good results.

According to John Jerney, travel writer and photographer,

> Smartphones, those amazing handheld devices that offer the Internet in your pocket, are the fastest growing segment in both computing and communications. With yearly unit sales in the hundreds of millions, and total worldwide sales estimated in the billions within a few years, these ubiquitous devices and associated applications and services are the hottest topic in the technology and publishing worlds.

234

Both iPhones and the Androids offer an amazing amount of options. Check all the available phones; talk to the salesperson in the store you visit. Ask about all the features and benefits of both formats. Most of them not only allow you to make phone calls but also connect with the Internet and your bank. You can download a huge library of books and a huge number (growing almost daily) of apps. You can access your email, send and receive text messages, and much more. Play with the models on display to come up with the smartphone that is right for you.

Mobile Apps

Mobile applications (or "apps") are fast replacing traditional travel guidebooks, and for good reason: They're lightweight, portable, interactive, inexpensive to publish, and quick and easy to update. That makes them appealing to publishers, authors, and travelers alike.

"Like guidebooks," states Laurie King, "travel apps require research, organization, and good writing. But they don't require technical skills; there are plenty of free and low-cost options for working with development companies or off-the-shelf software. Your biggest challenge may be choosing a topic."

If you've developed expertise in a particular geographic area or topic, start there. Lee Foster, for example, had already published a book called *The Photographer's Guide to San Francisco: Where to Find Perfect Shots and How to Take Them*. He had done the research, written and edited the copy, taken the photographs, and organized it all into a book, which he had published and sold successfully.

All Lee had to do was reformat his existing content for a mobile application. In fact, Lee's topic works even better as a mobile app, because it's now both portable and storable.

The app, viewable on mobile devices, helps users to create, collect, and enjoy their own postcard-perfect photos and memories of San Francisco. Lee presents his top one hundred views of the city, from vistas to iconic details, and shows the user how to duplicate them. The app has Lee's comments on how to make the photo and why the view is significant, even if you only want to enjoy the view and not photograph it. Interactive maps show what photos/views can be savored in a given neighborhood.

Apps are typically updated several times a year, and the industry standard is to provide free updates to everyone who has downloaded a particular app. That's both good news and bad news. It means you'll be tied to your topic for quite a while, so it's smart to write about an area you have easy access to. It also means you can keep your content current and push new information out to your readers, giving you an opportunity to communicate regularly.

Choose a topic travelers feel passionate about, and you can develop an ongoing relationship with them.

The market for paid apps is huge. The iTunes store reported that over ten billion app downloads had occurred by January 2011. Lee's San Francisco app, a best-seller, has been downloaded in forty-six foreign countries. By contrast, his parallel book on San Francisco will never sell outside North America. Paid travel apps are not the largest category of app sales (games are way ahead) and many apps are free, but there was already a robust market of about thirteen thousand paid travel apps as of January 2011.

Apps require a different style of writing and research than is used in a book. App writing needs to be quite truncated and brief, just a couple of paragraphs. Books encourage a more leisurely approach to the subject. Writing more concisely is an art. Also, one critical part of the research for an app is linking appropriate Websites for further information on a subject. You don't need to do that for a print book, but you might, of course, for an e-book.

Royalty rates for authors of apps are much higher than for authors of books, and for good reason. Lee gets 30 percent of the gross income from his $1.99 app sale, or 60 cents, which is roughly typical of the app world—30 percent each to the author, developer, and Apple store, with 10 percent going to administration. For his book, he has a 15-percent-of-net rate, which is good and possibly a little high. So, for selling two apps for $3.98, he gets $1.19. For a sale of a $14.95 book, his royalty is 15 percent net, and the book will typically be discounted 55 percent to sell on Amazon or through a distributor. Lee's royalty for that sale is $1.01. The app author and publisher have no printing press to buy, no paper or ink costs, no warehouse needed to store product, no distribution hassle, and no quantity manufacturing cost to achieve economies of scale, etc. A traditional publisher's strengths of capital and distribution do not apply. However, the app publisher needs software, and that is a substantial intellectual investment to create, license, or buy off the shelf, if and when such software is available.

The low price point of apps will build a new market. Lee set his price, so the price could be anything he wished. He chose $1.99 or $2.99. At these low prices, a purchase of his travel app product almost becomes an impulse buy. A huge number of buyers will enter the app market, compared to the small number who will pay for a book costing $14.95. For his first app, the San Francisco travel photo app, he had buyers in ten foreign countries in the first month. Apps can be sold worldwide in a rarified electronic ether. As mentioned, Lee's physical books will never sell outside the United States.

Apps have an interactive map capacity, far beyond the two-dimensional maps in books. The use of mapping capacity is one of the delights of a smartphone. You no longer need paper maps to get around Northern California. For Lee's San Francisco app, the map can show you where the photo locations are, with respect to where you are. A mobile device's maps can show you the cluster of photo opportunities in a neighborhood, such as Golden Gate Park. The mapping revolution can now be applied to travel products. Who would want to go back to paper maps?

A mobile device is small and compact, not large and heavy like a book. In the old days, one would need to carry around large guidebooks, possibly several. Or one would judiciously rip out sections of guidebooks, eliminating all the subjects irrelevant to the trip. Today, you need a phone anyway, so why not carry all your info, insights, and images on the phone, which is also your email device?

Apps represent a virtuous future in green publishing. Print materials will eventually become assessed as another cause of global warming. Climate change and resource depletion are already tied to the production of physical products, such as printed travel books and travel magazines, which will soon be rejected as luxurious. Why not convey all this info, insight, and photography in an electronic format at small environmental cost?

Apps, once created, require care and feeding if the author wants them to survive and flourish. There is an expectation of new releases, perhaps on a sixty-day cycle. There are always new entries to write, more photos to create, and an ever more energetic promotional effort needed to help your app stand out in an increasingly crowded field. Also, apps use evolving software that begs for new releases. For example, the latest software release from Sutro Media allows a user to email an entry to a friend. The iPhone and parallel mobile devices will have consequences as immense for all of us as the personal computer rollout in roughly 1980. The Apple iPad has emerged as another innovative, elegant app-reading device. The Google Android platform for mobile devices will be pursuing Apple's early lead.

Choosing a Publisher for Your Apps

The app publishing industry is changing so rapidly that we can't recommend a publisher, but we can provide guidelines for evaluating possibilities. Whether you work with do-it-yourself software or an established developer, consider the following issues:

- What's the financial arrangement? Is there an up-front cost, or does the publisher take a cut of your sales?
- What does the user interface look like? Will it be easy for you to work with, or will you end up spending an inordinate amount of time learning programming or dealing with technical issues?

- What features are included? Will your entries link to maps of the area? Can you include audio and/or video? Can users comment on your entries? How much interactive functionality is built in?
- Review the contract. Do you retain the copyright to your text and photos? Can you reuse the same content in a companion Website or a book?

Digital Cameras

Let's start out by reminding you to READ THE MANUAL that comes with your camera of choice. Take time when choosing a digital camera. Go over the features and benefits with a sales associate in the camera store or camera department.

The construction of digital cameras is usually as compact as possible. All component parts, including the flash, battery, memory card slot, and LCD display, are gathered in a body as small as possible. The camera body is made from light metal alloys or rugged plastic.

A digital camera uses no film rolls. All photos and videos are in digital format and are stored on memory cards right in your camera. They're great because you can see the result right away on the camera's screen and you can re-shoot the scene until you have what you want from the image. The use of a memory card is very useful for transferring photos and videos via USB to your computer.

Camera Phones

Camera phones are mobile phones with integrated mini digital photo cameras. These can take still images or mini video clips, which are stored in the phone's internal memory or on a detachable memory card.

Because of the relatively small sizes of mobile phones, these cameras are very small and have limited features and low image quality. They usually have a tiny fixed lens for capturing the image recorded by the tiny imaging sensor. A small number of camera phones incorporate optical zoom lenses. A mobile phone still must be light and slim for someone to buy it, so for construction reasons, the built-in lenses usually don't feature optical zoom.

The advantage of camera phones is obvious: Almost every person today has a mobile phone, and we take them everywhere. You can take pictures and clips in almost any circumstance, without being noticed. This is especially useful in public squares, street markets, and other crowded areas.

Long response times make phone cameras inadequate for use in action shots or shooting from a moving vehicle window. Some camera phones lack a flash and frequently many shots are blurred when hand-holding the camera indoors and in low-light conditions.

Because these cameras are integrated in the mobile phones that are in our pockets anywhere we go, many people use them instead of separate cameras. Camera phones are adequate for those who want to record memories on small trips, but to illustrate a travel story that you want to sell, you are better off using a digital camera.

There is more information about digital cameras in Chapter 14.

Self-Publishing

There are so many technological revolutions swirling around us. The pace of change is truly dizzying, and one substantial aspect of that change is occurring in the publishing of travel books. Fifteen years ago there would not have been an option to self-publish. It would have been very difficult to get distribution. Now, however, anyone can sell a book on Amazon. Today's authors frequently ask the obvious question: Should I publish my books independently, or should I go with a traditional publisher? With some effort, it is also possible to set up a bookstore distribution channel through a distributor like Baker & Taylor, which would allow every Barnes & Noble store to buy the book. So distribution is possible, even if difficult. Creating demand is another issue. If you can't create demand, there is no point in publishing a book either independently or with a traditional publisher.

Work-for-hire books is another model. Some publishers, such as Lonely Planet, do only work-for-hire. The writer is commissioned to write the book, receives a certain fee, and the project is done. The publisher takes full responsibility to market and sell the book.

E-books are becoming more and more important, and may at some point eclipse printed books. Print on demand books have become so high-quality at such a low price that this is now an option to consider, especially if a book does not have color photos. Similarly, they are a good option if you would be happy with color photos only in the e-book version suitable for the iPad and other tablets. There are several suppliers of print on demand services. Lightning Source and CreateSpace can guarantee that your book is listed in the Ingram catalog (the largest wholesale distributor of books in the world), making it a book every bookstore could order, if you can create demand through proper marketing.

CHAPTER 17

Minding Your Own Business

People think that, being travel writers, we are flown hither and yon, first class all the way, with all expenses paid by the client who will print our stories and photographs and pay us for our work. Sounds pretty wonderful, doesn't it? The reality in most cases is quite different.

The reality depends on circumstances that vary from trip to trip, from year to year, from day to day. Yes, being a travel writer generates some trip advantages and some tax advantages. No, it doesn't create a payless paradise of pure pleasure.

With freebies, it depends on *who* is offering and *what* and *why*, as well as *where* and *when*. And, most of all, it depends on how *obligated* you become.

As your name gets known in travel circles, offers of hospitality may come your way—from the Christmas cocktail party to the all-expenses world tour. We all know, though, that hospitality often carries at least an implied obligation. Since our opinion is not for sale, we never want to feel committed to praise something that might turn out to be unpraiseworthy.

We've spoken before of the travel writer's great responsibility—how readers count on finding a destination as you describe it. Sometimes readers pay out thousands of dollars and weeks of time to take a trip on your say-so. Sometimes it's the adventure of a lifetime for them—a honeymoon, a retirement, celebration, a return to the roots of their ancestors, or a place they've always longed to see. Are you going to advise Hotel A instead of Hotel B because you sincerely believe A is in a more convenient location, gives faster service, has more cheerful employees, and provides a better value for the money? Or are you going to advise A because the manager indebted you to spend a weekend as his guest? If the weekend was lovely, was it because your registration card was marked "VIP," or is Hotel A a regular provider of lovely weekends? It's your duty to find that out. And it's your duty to make it clear that you, as a person of integrity, will seek the truth to relay to your readers.

Travel Freebies

There are several kinds of freebies available to the bona fide travel writer, on a sometime basis. If, for instance, the country or the region invites you specifically to cover a recent change in government, an important anniversary, or a newly enthusiastic attitude toward tourism, it's likely the proverbial red carpet will be rolled out. You will be escorted to the airport, or at least met at the departure lounge, where you will be directed to a first-class seat aboard the country's chief air carrier. You will stay at the most luxurious hotels, eat and drink the most exotic offerings, and receive gifts that range from press kits and promotional gimmicks to flowers, fruit, champagne, and anything the public relations people think you might like. As for sightseeing—you'll be taken to see everything of possible interest. Your hosts will probably provide lists of story angles, research sources, and potential markets. You will be totally on your host's program and carted from one venue to the next like a puppy in a basket with no time to seek out things that are not on the prepared itinerary.

Hotel chains such as Hyatt, Westin, or Sheraton sometimes invite individuals or groups to tour several of their hotels that are new, remodeled, or especially newsworthy for some reason. They provide first-class transportation, meals, entertainment, sightseeing guides, and recreational opportunities.

Press Junkets

The press junket that includes representatives of various media from various parts of the United States—usually about ten to twenty participants—is often sponsored by hotels, transportation companies, or recreational attractions. Sometimes it's a special public relations event, like a Chinese banquet in San Francisco to promote travel to Hong Kong or a gathering at Hawaii's Mauna Lani Bay to watch chefs and winemakers prepare "Cuisines of the Sun."

Professional travel writers' organizations, such as the North American Travel Journalists Association, or the International Food, Wine & Travel Writers Association, often arrange special familiarization trips for their members—from the Arctic Ice Cap to the romantic Del Coronado. It's always a pleasure to "talk shop" with other travel writers, and that is a significant reward of such junkets. Networking is always valuable.

Freebies Have Advantages, Too

One of the most important pluses of the freebie is the opportunity to get behind the scenes and see and experience facets of travel that the ordinary traveler seldom knows about. Whether it's viewing an unreleased program at the Kennedy Space Center, riding in a balloon over the hidden vineyards of Provence, or walking through the alleys of San Francisco's Chinatown, you'll find the special angle for your story in the unusual and the memorable.

Sometimes your freebie is the result of an assignment. An editor will call and say, "XYZ Airline is opening a new route, and they invited me to cover the inaugural flight and be their guest for a few days, but I can't make it. Would you like to go?"

More often, the writer has to secure the assignment before the freebie becomes a reality. The public relations people handing out the hospitality want to be sure they're handing it, if at all possible, to "writers on assignment."

If the story that results from the hospitality is not an assignment, what will you do with it when you get it researched and written? Will it be acceptable to your target market? This whole business of freebies and how they might or might not influence the journalist's conclusions, and whether a periodical should publish the resultant stories, has been extensively debated among travel writers and editors.

Policies on Freebies

Several publications, of which the *New York Times* Travel section heads the list, feel that the travel writer cannot serve more than one master at the same time, and therefore they will not publish an article that grows out of a trip paid for by airlines, hotels, or any other organizations with an interest, direct or indirect, in the subject being written about. Other publications don't preclude the use of stories resulting from sponsored trips, but they want to know just how much hospitality the writer has accepted. Then they read the article with particular precision, searching for any possible bias.

Still other periodicals will not permit their staff or freelancers to accept freebies but are willing for them to travel at a deep, deep discount. Others pick up the travel tab themselves and pay the going rate for their writers to travel. Because travel, especially to faraway places, is such an expensive activity, it would be impossible for many travel writers to take the trips they write about without financial help of some kind.

Many jobs related to travel writing, such as teaching resort writing classes or editing a resort newspaper, are not exactly freebies, since you're expected to work in payment for your vacation, but they provide interesting interludes in a travel writer's life. Port lecturers, enrichment lecturers, or tour leaders work hard, but they sometimes find their jobs seem more like play than work. At home or abroad, there are more travel writing-related positions than you may think.

Freebies May Exact a Price

Sometimes we've regretted accepting hospitality because the thing our hosts wanted us to do was less interesting than what we had planned.

In one place, which Louise is purposely leaving vague, she was invited to tour a cultural center, watch the entertainment, then stay for dinner and the evening show. It was a three-hour drive from her hotel. Since the invitation said noon, she thought it began with lunch. Her mistake. But there was no mistake about it being noon. The midday sun fried her during the two hours she sat on bleachers in the open, watching some worse-than-mediocre folk dancing.

She then spent another two hours listening to the church that owns the cultural center patting itself on the back. Everyone assured her that the dinner would be lovely and the evening show outstanding, but she never stayed to find out. When she left at four, mumbling hurriedly invented excuses and handing back to the PR people the expensive, unused dinner and show tickets, she was hungry, thirsty, hot, tired, bored, and disgusted.

Mainly she was disgusted with herself for not finding out more about the program in advance. If the dinner and the evening show were the big thing, why didn't she spend the morning and early afternoon in beachfront research, departing for the cultural center around three? She didn't because her hosts insisted on showing her *everything*.

You soon learn to regard freebies in the same light as entertainment you're paying for. Ask yourself, "Is this going to be worth the time I'll have to spend on it?" Sometimes it isn't.

Freebie Philosophies

City guidebook writer Martin Fischhoff feels differently, however. He says bluntly that he lives on free meals. He defends this practice by assuming there's no way the restaurant can change its menu or do anything unusual to impress the guidebook or travel writer, even after he has identified himself. Therefore, according to Fischhoff, the reviewer's critical judgment cannot be impaired. He has found free meals easy to come by—except for one restaurant where the manager told him frankly that he had masqueraded as a guidebook writer for a year in New York to feed himself.

Some travel writers think that the writer's function is to encounter the travel experience exactly as a reader would, without preferential treatment of any kind. They feel that the acceptance of free meals makes a difference. It is an untypical, and therefore unreliable, experience.

Our own philosophy follows a line somewhere between these two. We feel it absolutely essential for the travel writer to keep in mind, "For whom am I working?" The freelance writer's obligation is to the reader. And while it is possible to do a terrific public relations job of glorifying a travel attraction, and also possible to perform an excellent journalism job of evaluating it from the reader's viewpoint, you can never do both jobs on the same story at the same time. Presumably, even your public relations job would be based on truth, but it would concentrate on presenting the most attractive side of your client's business. As a journalist, you compare this client against that client (mentally, at least) to give your reader the best possible advice. You are always representing *somebody*, and you must be clear yourself, and clarify for your readers, which *somebody* you represent on a particular story.

While the freelance travel writer has some responsibility to the attraction—to not, for instance, spew out a careless and undeserved witticism about a restaurant serving barbecued horsemeat or sautéed kitten that harms the restaurant's business—his real responsibility is to his reader.

One of our favorite types of hospitality occurs when somebody invites us to be a guest *after* we've written enthusiastically about a place we've paid to get to and simply loved. Then we already know what it's like, and we have an idea of the angles that might make good stories. The public relations people for the chamber of commerce, hotel, attraction, or whatever already know the way we write and apparently like it.

Freebie Ethics

Most national and international writers' organizations espouse specific rules and guidelines about freebies. For example, the Society of American Travel Writers feels that its purpose is to serve the traveling public by providing "complete, accurate, and interesting information on travel destinations, facilities, and services." The Society believes that "travel is a bridge between peoples," and its earnest desire is "to make and keep travel a quality experience for everyone."

Concerned with possible abuses, the Society "supports the limited and intelligent use of assistance from government travel departments, carriers, and others involved in the travel field. Reduced fares and trade discounts should be approved for bona fide travel writers to make such travel practical."

The Outdoor Writers Association of America is especially concerned about members accepting courtesy discounts on manufactured goods, and indicates that while discounts are common, ethical conduct precludes any stipulation that a favorable review be given in return.

The Travel Journalists Guild, the International Food, Wine & Travel Writers Association, the North American Travel Journalists Association, the American Society of Journalists and Authors, and other professional groups have similar guidelines.

As you become more professional in your writing and selling, you will probably want to join an appropriate writers' organization. Membership can be helpful, and you'll abide by the codes and guidelines of your organization.

Even more important, you'll want to abide by your own code of ethics. Surely you have enough common sense to know the difference between right and wrong, and enough gumption to proceed accordingly. Accept free hospitality? Perhaps—if you're positive your host isn't attaching any strings to it and you're convinced that you, yourself, would never be influenced to favor the most hospitable attractions in the travel industry.

Be Your Own Person

Usually when you're invited on some kind of press junket there's no mention of the story you might write when you return. And, of course, you may, for one reason or another, write nothing at all. Or you may write it but not sell it. Or you may sell it, but it falls through the cracks and never gets published. But even if there's no expressed expectation of publication, everybody knows what you're there for. Your hosts want you to have a good time, and they want you to report favorably on their facilities.

Be careful when writing unfavorably about a travel experience. Although it may be amusing and carefully written, it can discourage travel to that particular place. We are in the business of promoting travel and encouraging people to go. Doesn't it make more sense to tell your readers about places, things, foods, etc. that you enjoyed rather than the things you didn't? It could be the place you are negative about was just having a bad day. Why run the risk of ruining their reputation?

We absolutely must remember that the world does not revolve around our personal wants and needs. Just because we didn't enjoy the room right next to the pool, traveling families might prefer that room so they can keep an eye on their children. Say the elegant, sophisticated restaurant we were promised turned out to be a casual café with the food served family-style on long, oil-cloth covered tables. Sometimes these circumstances can lead to very good and amusing stories.

Some of Jacqueline's best, award-winning travel stories were about some of the particular insights and experiences that resulted from travel hospitality. A great many things were learned from hosted trips and press junkets, and she eagerly accepted the opportunities to see offbeat places and meet special people. She enjoys the hospitality but has learned to accept only if the arrangements fit in with her own writing plans and she is satisfied that the invitation is not a compromising one. She checks the proposed itinerary carefully before she agrees. If the program includes active sports like skiing, river rafting, hiking in the high mountains, biking long distances, etc., she knows the trip is not for her. If, on the other hand, the itinerary includes music, food, cultural events, history, sightseeing, etc., she happily accepts.

Tax Deductions

One business-book writer says she always keeps the receipts for anything possibly tax deductible because, she says, "Since you have to be in a position to provide the information, anyway, it's easier to keep the original receipt, and identify it carefully."

Our advice is to hold on to all records (receipts, canceled checks, IRS correspondence, etc.) connected with your tax return until the statute of limitations runs out for all applicable taxing agencies. State and local laws may differ from federal. Jacqueline files the receipts by month and then fills in an expense form that has a column for each month.

David Cartwright, senior tax consultant for his accounting firm, says that deductibility of travel and entertainment expenses, like all business expenses, requires that the expenditure be ordinary and necessary in the operation of the taxpayer's business and directly related to or associated with the business, as well as properly documented, and that it not be lavish. He explains that in order to satisfy the "directly related to" test, the taxpayer must expect to derive income or some other specific business benefit (other than goodwill) and demonstrate that active conduct of business was the primary purpose of the activity.

This talk of tax deductions may trigger other questions in your mind. Now perhaps you're wondering whether you can take a deduction for travel expenses only if *all* your income is derived from travel writing. Or *most of it*, at least. Can you show a tax *loss* from your travel writing business?

David explains that if an activity is not engaged in for a profit, no income tax deduction attributable to the activity will be allowed. "An activity is presumed to be entered into for a profit if profits result in three out of five years," he says. "If this requirement is not satisfied, then the activity may be considered a hobby. In that case, losses will only be deductible to the extent of the income."

In other words, if you make a million dollars in a real estate transaction, you can't reduce your tax liability by calling yourself a travel writer and deducting from the real estate profits your expenses from an around-the-world trip if the trip itself doesn't result in travel-writing profits. Or at least you probably can't do it unless your travel-writing business shows a profit three years out of five.

Again, the wise freelancer keeps good records. Louise was appalled to discover some of her students sending queries without retaining copies, and to discover some of them discarding rejection slips. They were astonished to learn that this negative correspondence might have value. Whether you paper your living room walls with them or keep them in a print or electronic file, evidence of queries and rejection letters may tip the scales in your favor when it comes to convincing the IRS that you're *trying* to make travel writing a business, not a hobby.

David reminds us, though, that the IRS will not necessarily refuse a bona fide deduction just because there was no net profit from travel writing.

If you use a room (or a portion of a room) exclusively as a home office you may be able to claim a proportional amount of your mortgage, insurance, rent, repairs, monthly utilities, HOA dues, etc. as a business expense. This is a particularly valuable deduction as it has the effect of turning personal expenses into business expenses that can reduce both your income and self-employment taxes. Any allowable deduction in excess of the writer's net income is deferred and can be used to offset future profits. The home office is claimed on Form 8829.

There are no easy answers to the questions of freebies and tax deductions. There are no foolproof guidelines, either. A tax expert can show you how you can, with honor, enjoy some of the fringe benefits of the travel writing profession.

Please see the appendix for a list of possible travel writer expense deductions.

CHAPTER 18

Good Writing Is Hard Work

Travel has always been at the top of the list of what to do with most people's leisure time, and you, the travel writer, will often help determine the choice of destinations. Will your readers rush to meet adventure, discovering the half-hidden peaks and uncharted beaches you told them existed? Will they hurry to experience the Penguin Parade in Antarctica, the running of the bulls in Spain, the Mardi Gras in New Orleans, the cog-railroad ride to the top of Mt. Rigi in Switzerland, the Danube River cruise from Budapest to Vienna, you promised would delight them? Will they follow in your footsteps to that wonderful little *taverna* in Athens, linger longer at the ancient amphitheater in Taormina, Sicily, to watch the sun set? Will they inspect the farthest picture gallery at the British Museum or wait patiently in the safari bus because you suggested they might find more to see? Will they dine at that wonderful little restaurant in Paris?

It's gratifying, isn't it, to enrich the lives of others as well as your own? It's frightening too. This power carries with it an awesome responsibility. Whether you're digging in the library stacks or surfing the Web or sharing a day in the life of a country veterinarian in the Highlands of Scotland, you'll be careful to interpret the facts with perceptiveness and integrity.

What Do People Want to Read?

Keep in mind who reads the publication you have in mind to publish a particular story or article. You'll be careful, too, to keep in close touch with what your audience wants to read.

A while back, a large cross-section of people were questioned as to what kind of travel articles they liked to read, in print or online. The group ranged in age from nineteen to ninety, male and female; varied in occupation, interest, educational level and financial circumstances; and included frequent travelers, infrequent travelers, eager travelers, reluctant travelers, former travelers, and future travelers. Two major threads seemed to emerge that are still relevant to today's travelers.

1. **People want advice, facts, and knowledge of how to do it.** "Guides for the green traveler like me," said one. "Realistic details and warnings about pitfalls," said another." How to save money"; "The basics: where to stay and eat, what to see"; "A knowledgeable traveler who tells the bad as well as the good—no babbling on about gorgeous scenery when the mosquitoes are big as bumblebees!"

2. **People want to hear about people.** "I like stories that humanize the traveler and the people he meets"; "I want to know the things that are unique about a place and its people, and also the things that are the same as at home"; "Tell me about the offbeat, inexpensive trips that pay off in opportunities to meet the locals." Others preferred "a story that gives tantalizing tastes of many areas and the people who live there"; "stories about the people in faraway places—I like to know about them, even if I never get to see them"; and "travel articles that make me feel as though I'm *there*."

The Quest for "Plus Value"

By now you know that the travel article with plus value doesn't begin with sitting down at the keyboard. It begins with the barest glimmer of an idea that you might someday be going to some particular place.

The preparations, we know, include seeking advance information from many sources and planning ahead for on-trip research, photography, sightseeing—knowing what to take along and whether to accept special privileges. Your pre-trip market study helps you plan itineraries for your stories. Ahead-of-travel query letters not only sell your article before you write it but also help you define what you want to achieve.

Keeping in mind "What will my reader want to know?" you'll observe, assimilate, and distill. You'll find that all aspects of your research reinforce one another. But don't worry if you want to write about a trip that you took before you'd read the suggestions in this book. These suggestions make it easier, but many are things you've probably done anyway. Though you've omitted some of the steps, you can still write a travel article. And you should. But before your next trip, you can begin at the beginning.

You'll discover that much of what we call "research" doesn't really *feel* like research. As you explore the ambiance of the place, traverse its hidden byways, and talk informally to local people, it may seem less like work than fun. But remember to note accurately the travel details, keep receipts, and record any possible income tax deductions. Jacqueline tapes an envelope inside the back cover of her travel notebook where she keeps receipts, business cards, etc. She dates each item and sometimes writes a short description of what she ate or what she saw, if she liked it or not, and the circumstances where she met the person who gave her the card. She clears it out daily and transfers the items to a large envelope in her suitcase.

You'll begin your quest for plus value by reading what others have written. Is there a writer in the world who doesn't love to read? Years ago Louise said she felt guilty every time she read for an hour—until she heard a very successful writer say, "If you have eight hours a day for writing, spend four hours reading, and if you can only spare two hours a day for writing, spend one of those hours reading." Read for information, for style, for marketing knowledge, for pleasure. Read enough to get different opinions so you'll be able to digest them, and then start off with a fresh approach of your own.

Even more important than reading is thinking. Discuss with yourself what insights you expect to bring home from the trip. Ask friends and colleagues for their thoughts and experiences of places you want to write about. Remember, your mission is more than counting cats in Zanzibar.

Change Is the Name of Travel

Prepare yourself for constant change. The travel writer soon finds that the most permanent aspect of travel is change. Prices soar, routes change, hotels open and close. A beautiful Victorian beachfront hotel in the South of France that Jacqueline loved and wanted to include in an article about unique places to stay along the Cote d'Azur was torn down to build an ugly bunch of very expensive apartments. The European Community has made travel in inner Europe much easier without Passport Control at border crossings. There are detours to accommodate the building of newer, straighter, wider roads, and military barriers to accommodate takeovers by new political forces. There'll be new restrictions and new restraints. Many places we've loved cannot be visited just now. But there's a happier side to this situation. Other areas previously off-limits are presently available. Perhaps one day worldwide travel will become as commonplace as a trip to the next town.

As technology breeds the kind of changes that may one day have us careening from New York to Los Angeles by underground commuter train in fifty-four minutes, the travel writer needs increasing amounts of discipline—*self*-discipline. As the world grows smaller, its attractions multiply. We're increasingly tempted by the cajoleries of travel: the lures of sun, sand, and surf; the enticements of music and dancing; the persuasions of the champagne-and-caviar circuit. How nice a travel writer's life could be—without the writing. As a journalism professor once said, "There aren't many people out there who like to write, but the world is full of people who would like to have written." Travel writers who succeed do so because they remember what they're there for and aren't distracted by beguilements. But that doesn't mean being a travel writer is all work and no play. "Oh gosh, [hand to forehead] I HAVE to try that new restaurant in Hong Kong; go to that street fair in Buenos Aires, Argentina; shop the farmer's market in Marrakech, Morocco; investigate the process of blowing glass in Murano, Italy; taste the wines of the Loire Valley in France; attend an opening night opera at La Scala in Milan, Italy." Nice work, eh?

Travel Writing Is Alive and Well

If you're moving toward realizing your potential as a travel writer, it's reassuring to know that great opportunity exists. Not only is travel an ever-growing industry, but so is writing. There are thousands of periodicals published in English worldwide, mostly non-fiction, and countless online opportunities, so your travel article has a very good chance of finding a home somewhere.

However, this is not a profession for the thin-skinned. Every time you address that query letter; every time you send off a disk or an email, you're putting yourself in the public eye. Is it good enough? Will they like it? Did I tell it the best way it could be told? All these thoughts buzz around in your head. Your mood may vary from inadequacy (they'll reject my story right away!) to belligerence (I'm a great writer, and they're sure to publish my story! If they don't they'll be cheating the world out of viewing my masterpiece!).

Writing is a public profession. You reveal so much of yourself. You may be writing about somebody quite different in a setting far away, but there's always a great deal of you in the story. Your secrets, your mistakes are there for the world to see. This is not a profession for one who takes each rejection slip as an indication of total failure or as a personal insult. And it's not for one who quakes at criticism or takes it out on others when the writing goes badly.

Nobody likes to read the email that begins, "Thank you for sending us your query, but . . ." However, even those experiences can give you a warm glow, as you learn to read between the lines that say, "Not quite good enough, maybe next time," or "Sorry, we have something similar on file. Try us again." There's always "again" and "next time," always the hope that if you keep plugging and do your best, sending it out to market after market on your list of possibilities, using your salesman's skills, your manuscript will eventually find a home.

Rejections, or as Jacqueline likes to call them, returns, have an additional value: they are positive proof that you are a travel writer, actively seeking outlets for your work. Take pride that you really and truly are a travel writer.

Keep on Stretching

To avoid postpartum depression, when you send something off, be sure you're already at work on your next travel story.

Remember, a travel writer has no neon sign, no skyscraper, no inventory. His capital assets are what he has seen and heard, smelled, tasted, touched, learned, loved, and disliked. And while they might not provide collateral, nobody can steal them, tax them, or appropriate them in any way.

If you feel that, even with strict attention to business, your work compares unfavorably with the professional travel articles you read, don't be discouraged. Everybody has to start someplace. Study and learn as much as you can, attend writing classes, find a capable mentor to help you, join one of the many travel journalists' organizations and listen carefully to professional criticisms and suggestions. There is only one thing that's required—that you do your very best each time.

Don't continually compare your efforts to someone else's (although that can have advantages in a valid learning situation), but measure yourself against yourself. Are you the best travel writer you can possibly be? Are you a better travel writer today than you were six months ago? Where will you be six months from now?

It feels wonderful to stretch. Stretch to the best that's in you. Reach for your best, and beyond. Reach for the opportunity to write for higher-quality markets and to write higher-quality material. Do your best—and then strive to do better. It is absolutely impossible to write beautifully if you have nothing whatever to say.

As a good travel writer you'll find gratification in creating something that didn't exist before. You'll find satisfaction in knowing you have written something others will read. You will find delight in your readers following the trail you laid out for them. You'll find pride in noticing the improvement in your own work and pleasure in the interesting ideas, interesting information, and interesting individuals you will encounter.

If you believe you can be a travel writer, you can be one. If you have a story you want to share and enthusiasms you want to convey, you can do it. Keep your reporter's notebook, recorder, camera, and mobile device handy. Put your Passport and business cards in the pocket of your travel day bag and when the next charter trip leaves for the moon, you'll be ready.

Glossary

Advance–Payment to the author in advance of actual sales, based upon royalty agreement.

App–An application, typically a small, specialized program downloaded onto a mobile device.

Blog–A continually updated Website or Webpage containing the writer's or group of writers' own experiences, observations, opinions, etc., and often having images and links to other Websites.

Byline–A line in an article/story that names the author and gives him/her credit for writing the article/story.

Clips–Copies of published stories/articles.

Contributors/writers guidelines–Instructions and rules for how to submit stories/articles to a particular publication.

Cyber café–A public place where people get Internet access with their own PC or by renting time on a computer owned by the café.

Cyber market–Generally refers to selling via the Web or email.

Digital camera–Digital cameras can do things film cameras cannot: display images on a screen immediately after they are recorded, store thousands of images on a single small memory device, and delete images to free up storage space. The majority can record moving video with sound as well as still photographs.

E-books–Electronic books to download to computers, hand-held book readers (e-readers), and mobile devices in digital form. You can store a whole library of e-books on your desktop computer, laptop, or hand-held device, keeping essential references right with you when traveling or working away from your studio/office.

Email–Electronic mail sent through the Internet.

E-zine–Abbreviation for the term electronic magazine. The term (also spelled ezine) applies to small magazines and newsletters distributed by any electronic method.

Facebook, Twitter, LinkedIn–Worldwide social networking Websites. Users may create personal profiles, add other users as friends, and exchange messages, including automatic notifications when they update their profiles.

Facebook is a social networking service and Website with more than 800 million active users.

Twitter is an online social networking and microblogging service that enables its users to send and read text-based posts of up to 140 characters, informally known as "tweets."

LinkedIn is a social networking site designed specifically for the business community. The goal of the site is to allow registered members to establish and document networks of people they know and trust professionally.

Freelance–Also, freelancer. A person such as a writer, designer, or performer who sells work or services by the hour, day, job, etc., rather than working on a regular salary basis for one employer.

Internet–A vast computer network linking smaller computer networks worldwide (usually preceded by *the*). The Internet includes commercial, educational, governmental, and other networks, all of which use the same set of communications protocols.

iPad and tablet–Mobile computers with flat touch screens rather than keyboards. These are a great way to utilize some of the functions of your computer without having to type a single key on a keyboard. Many electronic tablets come equipped with shortcut keys that allow you to easily access your software, change the medium in which you are writing or drawing, as well as access the Internet all with the touch of a single button.

Mobile devices–These include traditional cell phones, smartphones such as iPhone, BlackBerry, and Android phones, and PDAs (Personal Digital Assistants). Smartphones are not only phones, but also have basic Internet functionalities and high-end features such as email, mini-browsers, external

USB options, larger screens, GPS capability, and large memory capacity. Users can also choose to install hundreds of third-party applications, tools and programs to make their smartphones all-in-one devices.

Online–Connected by computer to one or more other computers or networks, through a commercial electronic information service or the Internet.

Query letter–The story pitch sent to an editor either via email or snail mail.

Sidebar–A block of information that runs adjacent to an article, often set off in a box or with a different color or typeface. These normally provide practical, factual information about how to get there, where to stay, eat, etc.

USB flash drive–Data storage devices often used for the same purposes for which floppy disks or CD-ROMs were once used. They are smaller, faster, have thousands of times more capacity, and are more durable and reliable because of their lack of moving parts. Until approximately 2005, most desktop and laptop computers were supplied with floppy disk drives, but these have been abandoned in favor of USB ports.

Website–A connected group of pages on the World Wide Web regarded as a single entity, usually maintained by one person or organization and devoted to a single topic or several closely related topics.

Appendix

Travel Writer's Expenses

Professional Fees & Dues
Association Dues
Professional Associations
Other

Continuing Education
College Courses
Course Registration
Materials & Supplies
Photocopy Expenses
Reference Material
Books Purchased for Research
Seminar Fees
Textbooks
Other

Telephone Expenses
Cellular, Land, Toll, Pay Calls
Paging Service
Fax Transmissions
Other

Auto Travel (in miles)
Between Jobs and Locations
Client & Publisher Meetings
Professional Society Meetings
Parking Fees & Tolls
Other

Supplies & Expenses
Suitcases, Totes
Business Cards
Business Meals
Computer Software
Computer Supplies
Customer Lists
Entertainment
Equipment Repair
Gifts & Greeting Cards
Online Charges
Legal & Professional Services
Office Expenses
Photocopy Expenses
Postage & Shipping
DVDs, Films, Videos
Stationery
Website Development
Website Hosting
Other

Equipment Purchases
Cellular Phone
Hand-held Devices
Computers & Printers
Modems & Computer
Peripherals
Other

Miscellaneous Expenses
Subscriptions
Donations
Home Office Deductions
Other

Travel (out of town)
Airfare
Car Rental
Ground Transportation
Parking & Tolls
Lodging
Meals
Laundry
Telephone
Gratuities
Other